More Praise for *Owning Our Future*

"I've been reading material in this genre for twenty-five years, and this book is one of the best I've ever read. It is visionary while including real stories that are actionable and practical. It's inspiring but grounded. It's radical and inviting. I don't get effusive easily, but this really is amazing."

—Sarah van Gelder, cofounder and Executive Editor, *Yes! Magazine*

"I am just awestruck by this book, moved nearly to tears. As a crusty old farmer and realist, I'm usually not so confessional, but this does indeed appear to be the central, organizing element we need—both for what's so wrong with the current design and for what unites the many alternatives in which we've all been engaged."

—Anthony Flaccavento, organic farmer and founder, Appalachian Sustainable Development

"With heart and grace, Marjorie Kelly decodes the imponderables of finance and business. Her storytelling gift enables us to see our power to create economies that serve life instead of drain it from us."

—Frances Moore Lappé, author of *Diet for a Small Planet* and *EcoMind*

"A guide to the cutting edge of hope on the frontier of the ownership movement—and a marvelous tour of the most inspiring democratic and ecologically serious enterprise forms."

—Gar Alperovitz, Lionel R. Bauman Professor of Political Economy and cofounder, The Democracy Collaborative, University of Maryland, and author of *America Beyond Capitalism*

"*Owning Our Future* is a highly readable single story of two entwined systems: the dying juggernaut of exploitive finance and the mostly unseen hothouse garden where new models of ownership are emerging. Many books about hopeful alternatives inspire cynicism; this one inspires a desire to take part."

—Art Kleiner, Editor-in-Chief, *strategy+business*, and author of *The Age of Heretics*

"Marjorie Kelly has done it again. This seminal book will be the guidebook for transforming the corporation, and it's hard to imagine anything more important now."

—James Gustave Speth, Professor of Law, Vermont Law School, and cofounder, Natural Resources Defense Council

"Marjorie zeros in on perhaps the single most highly leveraged design variable in the architecture of our social forms. She is bringing the *generative ownership* model to life in a way that makes it accessible and compelling to business leaders everywhere. A wonderfully profound and pragmatic contribution to the field of social architecture."

—Bill Veltrop, cofounder, Monterey Institute for Social Architecture, and former Exxon executive

"Of all the important elements lacking from progressive thought, ownership design is perhaps the most foundational. Kelly nails it in a way that can drive it home to everyone. This is the most thorough and properly nuanced treatment of the subject I've seen anywhere. Kelly is a brilliant writer."

—**David Korten, author of *The Great Turning* and *When Corporations Rule the World***

"This a must-read for anyone wondering whether there's hope for humanity. In this deeply thoughtful work, Kelly demolishes the myth that there are no alternatives to capitalism as we know it."

—**Peter Barnes, cofounder, Working Assets/Credo, and author of *Capitalism 3.0***

"This is essential reading for anyone interested in the future of business."

—**Lynn Stout, Distinguished Professor of Corporate and Business Law, Clarke Business Law Institute, Cornell Law School, and author of *The Shareholder Value Myth***

"Anyone who cares enough about capitalism to save it from its worst excesses should read this book. Marjorie Kelly demonstrates convincingly that ownership by employees, community residents, and mission-driven charities, rather than by absentee shareholders, is the key to world-class performance."

—**Michael Shuman, author of *Local Dollars, Local Sense* and *The Small-Mart Revolution***

"This book fills me with hope about our economic future. It takes a visionary like Marjorie Kelly to point the way to new ownership models that will one day be seen as the only reasonable way to organize an economy."

—**Jenny Kassan, Managing Director, Katovich & Kassan Law Group**

"Wow. It's so simple but profound: ownership is the unifying theory of the economy. As you take the journey with Kelly, you feel a little like Sir Isaac Newton getting hit on the head by not just one apple but apple after apple—until you, too, experience an epiphany."

—**Alex Bogusky, Founding Partner, Crispin Porter + Bogusky (retired)**

OWNING
OUR FUTURE

Also by Marjorie Kelly

The Divine Right of Capital

OWNING
OUR FUTURE

The Emerging Ownership Revolution

Marjorie Kelly

BK

Berrett–Koehler Publishers, Inc.
San Francisco
a BK Currents book

Berrett-Koehler Publishers, Inc.
235 Montgomery Street, Suite 650
San Francisco, CA 94104-2916
Tel: (415) 288-0260 Fax: (415) 362-2512 www.bkconnection.com

Ordering Information
Quantity sales. Special discounts are available on quantity purchases by corporations, associations, and others. For details, contact the "Special Sales Department" at the Berrett-Koehler address above.
Individual sales. Berrett-Koehler publications are available through most bookstores. They can also be ordered directly from Berrett-Koehler: Tel: (800) 929-2929; Fax: (802) 864-7626; www.bkconnection.com
Orders for college textbook/course adoption use. Please contact Berrett-Koehler: Tel: (800) 929-2929; Fax: (802) 864-7626.
Orders by U.S. trade bookstores and wholesalers. Please contact Ingram Publisher Services, Tel: (800) 509-4887; Fax: (800) 838-1149; E-mail: customer.service@ingram publisherservices.com; or visit www.ingrampublisherservices.com/Ordering for details about electronic ordering.

Berrett-Koehler and the BK logo are registered trademarks of Berrett-Koehler Publishers, Inc.

Printed in the United States of America

Berrett-Koehler books are printed on long-lasting acid-free paper. When it is available, we choose paper that has been manufactured by environmentally responsible processes. These may include using trees grown in sustainable forests, incorporating recycled paper, minimizing chlorine in bleaching, or recycling the energy produced at the paper mill.

Library of Congress Cataloging-in-Publication Data
Kelly, Marjorie, 1953–
Owning our future : the emerging ownership revolution : journeys to the generative economy / Marjorie Kelly. — 1st ed.
    p. cm.
Includes bibliographical references and index.
ISBN 978-1-60509-310-9 (pbk.)
1. Community development. 2. Cooperation. 3. Employee ownership.
4. Right of property. 5. Finance, Personal. I. Title.
HN49.C6K44 2012
307.1'4—dc23

                                        2012007065

First Edition
17 16 15 14 13 12   10 9 8 7 6 5 4 3 2 1

INTERIOR DESIGN/ART: Laura Lind Design
COVER/JACKET DESIGN: Susan Malikowski,
    DesignLeaf Studio
BOOK PRODUCER: Linda Jupiter Productions

COVER PHOTOGRAPHY: Yasonya, Veer
COPYEDIT: Elissa Rabellino
PROOFREAD: Henrietta Bensussen
INDEX: Kay Banning

For Shelley

CONTENTS

III Creating Living Companies

The Five Core Elements of Generative Ownership Design 147

FOREWORD

by David Korten

Of all the important elements lacking from much progressive thought and action, the issue of ownership design is perhaps the most foundational. Marjorie Kelly illuminates this crucial topic in a way that can drive it home to everyone. *Owning Our Future* offers the most thorough and properly nuanced treatment of the subject I've seen anywhere.

Most of the great political struggles of the past 5,000 years can be reduced to a simple question: who will own land, water, and the other essentials of living—and to what end? In the earliest human societies, ownership of the essentials of living was held in common by members of a tribe and included responsibilities of sacred stewardship. We might describe this as a form of shared ownership that confers shared responsibility.

As societies transitioned to centralized power structures, ownership of land, water, and other essential means of production was monopolized by the few. Even with the movement toward democracy, ownership of wealth has remained largely in the hands of an elite. Today, debilitating debt, bankruptcies, and foreclosures are a reminder of how little has changed and how many among us—including young people burdened by student loans—live under the power of those who control the issuance of credit.

Behind the workings of our economy lies an invisible issue that few of us focus on—the issue of ownership. During my years working in Africa, Asia, and Latin America, I came to realize that what we call "development" is in fact a process of transferring control over the basic resources essential to daily life from the people who depend on them to foreign corporations, whose primary interest is financial gain. Ownership of corporations is, in large part, in the hands of the wealthiest 10 percent.

Our well-being, indeed our future as a species, depends on restoring our relationships to one another and with the land, the water, the sky, and the other generative resources of nature that indigenous people traditionally considered it their obligation to hold and manage in sacred trust. The architecture of ownership is key.

The defining debates of the 20th century were crudely framed as a choice between two simplistically defined economic models: private ownership (capitalism) and public ownership (socialism/communism). Neither capitalism nor socialism ever achieved its ideal, but each came sufficiently close to reveal that both failed. Both support a concentration of the power of ownership in the hands of an oligarchy.

In *Owning Our Future*, Marjorie shows that a new model of ownership is arising and spreading in our time, which she calls *generative ownership*. It's most often private ownership, but with a purpose of serving the common good. Generative ownership models include cooperatives, employee-owned firms, community land trusts, community banks, credit unions, foundation-owned companies, and many other models that root control in the hands of people who have a natural interest in the health of their communities and local ecosystems. These are in contrast to the dominant ownership models of capitalism, which Marjorie calls *extractive*.

She offers a simple pattern language to describe what makes these two different models of ownership work. Extractive ownership features Absentee Membership and the rapid speculative trading of Casino Finance, built around the purpose of maximizing the extraction of financial wealth. This creates a disconnect between the common good and the global banks, corporations, and financial markets that control the means of living. Extractive ownership is at the root of most of the social and ecological ills we face today.

In Marjorie's prophetic words: "Ownership is the gravitational field that holds our economy in its orbit, locking us all into behaviors that lead to financial excess and ecological overshoot."

Generative ownership, by contrast, has the purpose of creating the conditions for the flourishing of life. It features Rooted Membership, in the living hands of employees, families, communities, and others connected to the real economy of jobs and homes and human life. It features Mission-Controlled Governance that keeps firms focused on social mission, Stakeholder Finance that allows capital to be a friend, and Ethical Networks that provide collective support for social and ecological norms. Most of these enterprises are profit making, but they're not profit maximizing.

Since her groundbreaking book *The Divine Right of Capital*, Marjorie has focused her attention as a writer on how to resolve the foundational issue of ownership, and in *Owning Our Future*, she shares the story of her personal journey of discovery. The book is written as a travelogue, with detailed accounts of her visits to each of the major initiatives she profiles. Marjorie combines the perspective of a tenacious reporter, the writing skills of an accomplished novelist, and the open and inquiring mind of a thoughtful and critical economic theorist. Her central theme is that the architecture of ownership defines the business purpose of the enterprise and largely determines whether it will operate in a generative or extractive mode. It is the design of ownership that creates the essential framework for the capitalist economy that is beginning to break down—and for a potentially new generative economy we can bring into being.

This is one of the most important books of our time. I found it so informative and inspiring that reading it literally brought tears of joy to my eyes. It gets my very highest recommendation.

THE

JOURNEY

AHEAD

We lost a couple of old trees in our yard a few years back, big orna-
mental pears brought down not by lightning or wind but by their
own structural weakness. These trees have a Y structure where two central branches push against one another, and over time the trees undermined themselves, eventually splitting apart. We mourned those trees
and wondered what to replace them with. But within a few months, the
little magnolia that had seemed so small beneath one of them shot up.
It's filled out that space magnificently now. Where the other tree once
stood, we can grow flowers in places we couldn't before. Sometimes when
you lose something you think you need, life surprises you. What comes
next turns out to be unexpectedly good. That may be the case with our
economy. There's a lot that's breaking down now, a lot of financial and
ecological upheaval—not because crises are coming out of nowhere and
hitting us but because the structure of industrial-age capitalism is causing them. It's a good time to open our minds to new things sprouting up.

Here's one. In Cleveland, Ohio, a city experiencing the bleakest form of
economic decay, a new model of worker-owned business is taking shape,
starting with the Evergreen Cooperative Laundry. At this green laundry—
supported by stable contracts with anchor institutions such as hospitals
and universities—employees buy into the company through payroll deduc-
tions and can build a $65,000 equity stake over eight or nine years. As work
supervisor Medrick Addison says, "Maybe through Evergreen things that
I always thought would be out of reach for me might become possible."

Other companies in the Cleveland project include Ohio Cooperative Solar, expected to employ 100, and Green City Growers, likely to become the largest urban food-producing greenhouse in the nation. Organizers envision a group of ten companies creating 500 jobs over five years—in a city where the poverty rate is above 30 percent. Efforts are underway to spread this model to other cities.[1]

It's hard to talk about hope in these troubled times, but hope is what we're called to. My sense is that a new kind of economy—one that serves the many rather than the few, one that's ecologically beneficial rather than harmful—is sprouting in little (and not so little) experiments here and there, in ways that weren't possible before. A lot of us don't see this, because we don't believe good things might come from the messes we're in. In the global capitalist economy, many of us are grim adherents of the TINA school of thought: There Is No Alternative.

My sense is that there is an alternative, and that the reality of it is farther along than we suppose. When we can't see this, it's because we've left no room for it in our imagination. If it's hard to talk about, it's because it doesn't yet have a name. I suggest we call it the *generative economy*. It's a corner of the economy (hopefully someday much more) that's not designed for the extraction of maximum financial wealth. Its purpose is to create the conditions for life. It does this through its normal functioning, because of the way it's designed, the way it's owned—like an employee-owned solar company.

Some may not believe this kind of economy is possible, except on the fringe. But in this book, I don't ask you to believe anything. Instead, I invite you to come along and see.

As I fly into Copenhagen Airport, the plane banking low over the harbor, I see seven wind turbines standing there in the waters offshore, their white blades gleaming in the sun, turning in syncopation. This is Lynneten Wind Farm, with an ownership architecture as innovative and hopeful as its physical architecture. Three of these turbines are owned by a local utility, four by a *wind guild*. Denmark's wind guilds were created by small investors who joined together to fund and own wind installations, with no corporate middleman. Denmark today generates one-fifth of its electric power from wind, more than any other nation. Many observers credit that success to the grassroots movement of the wind guilds.[2] It's an ecological success story made possible by the ownership designs behind it.

In late 2008, I awake one morning to news on the radio that global stock markets are in freefall, the heart-stopping 42 percent plunge that markets saw that year not yet at bottom. The funk that the international economy remains in today is descending like a black mood, like the tingly shock of opening a credit card bill after a spending spree. This is the day when I catch the bus to the Seaport World Trade Center in Boston to attend the annual meeting of the National Community Land Trust Network. *Community land trusts* (CLTs) are ownership designs in which individual families own their homes and a community nonprofit owns the land beneath a group of homes. This design reduces and stabilizes the price of homes while it prohibits speculative ownership. CLTs, I learn, have foreclosure rates *one-tenth* of those of traditionally owned homes.[3] As attorney David Abromowitz says at the meeting, "It's like a bomb went off and all the houses have been flattened, but there's one well-built house still standing." The metaphoric house still standing is the community land trust home. The reason is its ownership design.

On a brisk November day, I make the drive from Madison to nearby La Farge, Wisconsin, to visit the headquarters of Organic Valley and meet its ponytailed CEO, George Siemon. With more than $700 million in revenue, this organic dairy company was created to save the family farm. It's owned by close to 1,700 farm families. These include the Forgues family, which at one time struggled to make ends meet. Today their farm supports two families with relative ease because of the high, stable price that Organic Valley pays its farmers for milk, cheese, and eggs. While other companies aim to pay suppliers as little as possible, this company aims to pay its suppliers as much as possible. The reason is that farmers own this company.

When Leslie Christian tells me of her idea for a new kind of corporation—later to be called a *benefit corporation* (B Corporation)—it's on a long walk that we take together at the foot of the Rockies. A former

Wall Street bond trader, Leslie has taken a post as president of a socially responsible investing firm, Portfolio 21 Investments, in Portland, Oregon, hoping to use finance as a tool in building a more humane economy. As part of her work, she creates a subsidiary with a new purpose baked into its corporate charter and bylaws. The company's purpose is to serve many stakeholders—including employees, the community, the environment, and stockholders. Inspired by her, some young entrepreneurs start B Lab to promote aspects of the model. Within a few years, close to 500 companies become B Corporations, and a dozen states pass or are considering legislation to allow the formation of benefit corporations. Though the model is not without its critics, many business watchers talk about the benefit corporation as a potentially transformative new approach to ownership.[4]

In 2011, attorneys in every state of the United States begin filing lawsuits aiming to have the atmosphere declared a *public trust*—a commons, owned by all of us, deserving special protection. The suits are filed on behalf of young people, arguing that their future is threatened by climate change. If they achieve victory in even one case, it might create a ripple effect like that seen with gay marriage, where state after state follows. This could create leverage for legislation to rein in greenhouse gas emissions. It's a new approach to reclaiming our economy for the common good, using the power of ownership.[5]

These journeys have a common thread: ownership. In a way that many of us rarely notice, ownership is the underlying architecture of our economy. It's the foundation of our world. How ownership is framed is more basic to our daily lives than the shape of democracy. Economic relations define the tenor of our days: where we work for 40 hours (or more) each week or whether we work at all. How owners wield their power over companies determines whether we're empowered or belittled by our work, how much anxiety we suffer over our debts, whether we're able to own a home or be secure in retirement. Questions about who owns the wealth-producing infrastructure of an economy, who controls it, whose interests it serves, are among the largest issues any society can face. Issues of who owns the sky in terms of carbon emission rights, who owns water, who owns development rights, are planetary in scope.

The multiplying crises we face today are entwined at their root with the particular form of ownership that dominates our world—the publicly traded corporation, in which ownership shares trade in public stock markets. The revenue of the largest 1,000 of these corporations represents roughly 80 percent of global industrial output.[6] Stripped of regulatory overlay, the design of these corporations is the bare design of capitalism.

As a way of organizing an economy, this model made a certain amount of sense when the industrial age was unfolding. The modern age might not have come to be, without the emergence of corporations and capital markets. But as we make the painful turn into a new era—characterized by climate change, water shortages, species extinction, vast unemployment, stagnant wages, staggering differentials in wealth, and bloated debt loads—the industrial-age model of ownership is beginning to make less sense. Getting our arms around this large issue can seem difficult. Unable to even approach it, politicians instead fixate on how to jumpstart the economy and get growth moving again. But it's time to move beyond growth, to recognize that the economy as we once knew it will never return. Nor should it.

As the dominant form of ownership continues to spin off crisis after crisis in our time, alternative forms are at the same time emerging in largely unsung, disconnected experiments all over the world. We're at the beginning of an unseen ownership revolution. In this book, I visit places where this hopeful future is welling up like cold springs. It's a journey into the territory of the possible, a kind of advance scouting expedition for the collective journey of our global culture.

It's a book about deep change. It's about hope. It's about the real possibility that a fundamentally new kind of economy can be built, that this work is further along than we suppose, and that it goes deeper than we would dare to dream. It's about economic change that is fundamental and enduring: not greenwash or all the other false hopes flung in our faces for too long. The experiments I'm talking about are not silver bullets that will solve all our problems. They have flaws and limitations. But they nonetheless represent change that is fundamental and enduring because it involves ownership. That is to say, what's at work is not the legislative or presidential whims of a particular hour, but a permanent shift in the underlying architecture of economic power.

A PERSONAL ODYSSEY

As significant as different patterns of ownership are, they're hard to see, because they're deep structures lying beneath the surface of things. I learned about the importance of ownership from my father, and it was a lesson he delivered not in words but with the arc of his own life.

I grew up in a family of eight children, raised fairly comfortably on my father's single salary from the small business he owned in Columbia, Missouri. My maternal grandfather owned his own company, as did many of my uncles. When I was a child, no one in my extended family was rich. But we had what all families deserve and few today enjoy, which is economic security. The reason was that my parents owned things. They never saved much money, but they owned my father's business, our house, and a few other pieces of real estate. It was enough that when my father died at the young age of 62, my mother was able to live at ease for decades without working outside the home. There was no shortage of emotional dysfunction in our household (including a good bit of Irish Catholic drinking and stormy tempers). But the economic security we enjoyed helped my siblings and me to mature into stability. In a visceral way, I experienced financial security as a form of nurturance, as vital as food or shelter—something that sustained me and allowed me to thrive.

If I saw the positive side of ownership as a child, I saw its negative side at *Business Ethics*, a magazine I cofounded in 1987 and where I served as president for 20 years. In that time, I watched corporations rewrite the social contract. I saw mass layoffs shift from something companies did in a dire emergency to become ordinary practice. I watched companies I once admired hire union-busting consultants. In five short years, I saw the number of Washington lobbyists double.[7] I watched wages flatline and the proportion of taxes paid by corporations fall. When the scandals at Enron, WorldCom, Adelphia, Parmalat, and other companies broke out, it became clear that cooking the books had become disturbingly widespread.

At every turn, companies claimed to be acting in the interests of their owners, their shareholders. Ironically, the owners supposedly demanding those acts were us, all of us with investing portfolios holding stock in corporations, all of us who have children attending colleges with endowments, all of us who support churches, museums, and nonprofits that rely on donations paid for from financial holdings.

We're all tangled up in our system's ownership designs. And we're all tangled up in the messes they've left in the economy and the biosphere. Because we've yet to grasp how the crises we face are symptoms of deep structural problems, what lies ahead may be worse still.

Wanting to help in the search for alternatives, a number of years ago I sold *Business Ethics* and moved to the Tellus Institute in Boston. There, my colleague Allen White and I cofounded the initiative Corporation 20/20, bringing together hundreds of leaders from business, finance, law, government, labor, and civil society to explore alternatives to the dominant corporate form.[8] That work confirmed my growing conviction that ownership is the root issue. I remember a particular moment when it snapped into focus for the whole group.

It was 3 p.m. on a Friday and the energy in our group was flagging. Seated around the conference table were 30 of the most innovative thinkers I knew, all struggling to stay awake. If the topic we'd come together to explore, redesigning capitalism, was a worthy subject, by late on a Friday it was a boring one. We were in day three of our time together, in the third of these gatherings. It had begun to feel like we were half-crazed survivors dragging ourselves through one jungle of impenetrable concepts after another: stock options, Delaware law, fiduciary duty, and more. I looked around the table, thinking, we've got to get these people into a break. They need coffee, fast.

Then someone uttered a simple statement. I wish I could remember who said it. But I'll never forget what he said: "Ownership is the original system condition."

There was a pause, the nodding of many heads. Some chatter of agreement. Then the facilitator called for a break. Yet no one left the room. No one even touched the cookies wheeled in at the back. You would have thought the coffee had been delivered intravenously. The room was so alive with animated talk that it was as though we'd been huddled in a dark cellar, and someone had opened a door and thrown on the lights.

The energy in the group was back because we'd touched the root issue that defines corporations and capital markets today. It's ownership.

> *Ownership is the gravitational field that holds our economy in its orbit, locking us all into behaviors that lead to financial excess and ecological overshoot.*

During my work with Corporation 20/20, my premise was that the answers were about redesigning corporations. But then my Tellus work shifted to a new project with the Ford Foundation involving rural communities, and I began looking at forms of ownership that didn't involve corporations at all.[9] I studied shared ownership and governance of homes, farms, forests, wind farms, fishing rights, and more.

As I discovered more and more models, I realized that I'd found my way to the edge of a movement much larger than corporate redesign. Something is emerging that goes to the root issue, the institution with which civilized economic life began, back beyond the age of industry in the age of agriculture. That root issue is ownership. We are witnessing its spontaneous evolution.

HARBINGERS OF THE NEW

New models are emerging today, not from the head of some new Adam Smith or Karl Marx but from the longing in many hearts, the genius of many minds, the effort of many hands to build what we know instinctively that we need.

In both the United States and the United Kingdom, there's burgeoning interest in *social enterprises*, which serve a primary social mission while they function as businesses—like Greyston Bakery in Yonkers, New York, an $8 million profit-making business started by Zen monks with an aim of creating jobs for the homeless.[10] *Community development financial institutions* (CDFIs)—which in the United States provide financial services to underserved low-wealth communities—are growing by leaps and bounds. In little over a decade, assets have climbed from $5 billion to $42 billion, with new funds coming from depositors, investors, and government grants.[11]

Emerging experiments with *catch shares*, ownership rights in marine fisheries, have been found to halt or reverse catastrophic declines in fish stocks.[12] *Conservation easements* now cover tens of millions of acres, allowing land to be used and farmed even as it's protected from development, preserving it for future generations both human and wild.[13] There's a growing movement to protect the *commons*, honoring areas of our common life that need shielding from market forces. And there's the *viral world* of entities like Wikipedia, owned by no one and run collectively.

Revolutionary lawyers are busy crafting new models through law—like the *community interest corporation*, created in UK law.[14] And the *low-profit, limited liability company* (L3C) in the United States, intended to facilitate more social investments by foundations. In the space of only a few years, this model has been enacted or come under consideration by nearly 20 states.[15] And there's the notable success of the Bank of North Dakota, the only *state-owned bank* in the United States, which in the initial financial crisis enjoyed record profits even as private-sector banks lost billions. Its unexpected resilience has led some 14 states to begin considering legislation to create their own banks.[16] (State banks are not privately owned, but they do represent alternative ownership focused on the common good rather than on maximizing profits.)

In Quebec and Latin America, among other places, there's a growing movement for the *solidarity economy*—consisting of cooperatives and nonprofits—which in Quebec has gained formal recognition and government funding as a distinct sector of the economy.[17] And a surprising number of large corporations have adopted *mission-controlled designs*. Among these are the foundation-owned corporations common throughout northern Europe, such as Novo Nordisk, a Danish pharmaceutical company with $11 billion in revenue, as well as Ikea, Bertelsmann, and other large companies. Also included in mission-controlled designs are family-controlled companies with a strong social mission, such as S. C. Johnson and the *New York Times*.[18]

More exotic designs are also popping up, like Grameen Danone, a *social business* in which village women in Bangladesh sell yogurt through a joint venture between multinational yogurt maker Groupe Danone and Grameen Bank, the first microfinance lender. The enterprise is designed to improve the nutrition of the poor as it aims to pay investors a modest, 1 percent dividend.[19]

Two pioneers in the field of emerging economic architectures have received Nobel prizes—Muhammad Yunus, who founded Grameen Bank and helped create Grameen Danone, and Elinor Ostrom of Indiana University, who studies economic governance of the commons. She and her colleagues have found communities all over the world that have spontaneously devised effective ways to govern fish stocks, pastures, forests, lakes, and groundwater basins in ways that preserve rather than harm those ecosystems.[20]

Emerging ownership models are new members of an older family of designs that include *cooperatives, employee-owned firms,* and *government-sponsored enterprises.* In the UK, these include the John Lewis Partnership—the largest department store chain in the country—which is 100 percent owned by its employees and has an employee house of representatives in addition to a traditional board of directors.

As a class, these alternatives represent an emerging family of design. If industrial-age ownership is based on a monoculture model, emerging designs are as rich in biodiversity as a rainforest. Through studying these, grafting pieces of them together to create still more models, we just might create the greenhouse of design experimentation where the future of our economy could be grown.

These social architectures are harbingers of something profoundly new. They aren't yet fully formed, not yet ready to serve as the framework of a new social order. But their growing profusion is a signal. It tells us that we're entering one of the most creative periods of economic innovation since the Industrial Revolution. For what's at work isn't economic innovation as it's usually meant, which is about better and better ways to make more and more money. This innovation is almost unimaginably more profound. It is a reinvention at the level of organizational purpose and structure. It is about creating economic architectures that are self-organized around serving the needs of life.

GENERATIVE VS. EXTRACTIVE OWNERSHIP

These models embody a coherent school of design—a common form of organization that brings the living concerns of the human and ecological communities into the world of property rights and economic power. It's an emerging archetype yet to be recognized as a single phenomenon because it has yet to have a single name. Hannah Arendt observed that a stray dog has a better chance of surviving if it's given a name. We might try calling this a family of *generative ownership* designs. Together they form the foundation for a *generative economy*.

In their animating intent and living impact, these ownership designs are aimed at generating the conditions where all life can thrive. From the Greek *ge*, *generative* uses the same root form found in the term for Earth, Gaia, and in the words *genesis* and *genetics*. It connotes life. *Generative* means the carrying on of life, and generative design is about the institutional framework for doing so. The generative economy is one whose fundamental architecture tends to create beneficial rather than harmful outcomes. It's a living economy that has a built-in tendency to be socially fair and ecologically sustainable.[21]

Generative ownership designs are about generating and preserving real wealth, living wealth, rather than phantom wealth than can evaporate in the next quarter.[22] They're about helping families to enjoy secure homes. Creating jobs. Preserving a forest. Generating nourishment out of waste. Generating broad well-being.

These designs are in contrast to the dominant ownership design of today. To make the distinction clear, that design also needs a name. We might call it *extractive*, for its focus is maximum physical and financial extraction. Our industrial-age civilization has been powered by twin processes of extraction: extracting fossil fuels from the earth and extracting financial wealth from the economy. But these two processes are not parallel, for finance is the master force. Biophysical damage may often be the *effect* of the system's action, yet extracting financial wealth is its *aim*.

As we begin to build what economist E. F. Schumacher called an "economy of permanence" on our fragile planet, maximum financial growth will be ill-suited as a guiding purpose. In generative design, we see in practical detail how a different goal can be at the core of economic activity. Generative design shows us that a transformative shift has already begun and suggests how it might be amplified.

OWNERSHIP AS A REVOLUTIONARY FORCE

"There's a movement going on that doesn't know it's a movement," attorney Todd Johnson said to me (he's one of those revolutionary attorneys devising new designs). What's under way is an ownership revolution. It's about broadening economic power from the few to the many and about changing the mindset from social indifference to social benefit. We're schooled to fear this shift, to think there are only two choices for the design of an economy: capitalism and communism, private ownership and state ownership. But the alternatives being grown today defy those dusty 19th-century categories. They represent a new option of private ownership for the common good. This economic revolution is different from a political one. It's not about tearing down but about building up. It's about reconstructing the foundation of ownership on which the economy rests.

For centuries, moments of crisis have been times when people turned to alternative ownership designs for protection. The first modern cooperative, the Rochdale Society, was formed in England in the 1840s, when the Industrial Revolution was forcing many skilled workers into poverty. The Rochdale Pioneers were weavers and artisans who banded together to open the first consumer-owned cooperative, selling food to workers who otherwise couldn't afford it. The cooperative model they created has spread to more than 90 nations and now involves close to a billion members.[23]

During the Great Depression in the United States, the Federal Credit Union Act—ensuring that credit would be available to people of small means—was intended to help stabilize an imbalanced financial system. Today the assets of credit unions total more than $700 billion. Since the financial crisis of 2008, these customer-owned banks have added more than 1.5 million members. A key reason is that in the initial crisis, their loan delinquency rates were half those of traditional banks.[24] In Argentina in 2001, when a financial meltdown created thousands of bankruptcies and saw many business owners flee, workers kept showing up to work.

With government support, they took over more than 200 firms and ran these *empresas recuperadas* themselves.[25]

In our time, the need for alternative kinds of ownership is more critical than ever, for the path ahead forks. The path of business as usual points toward a fortress world, a place where the wealthy few retreat into enclaves of luxury and security while most struggle in fear and want. The path of transformation points toward a new economy, a potentially generative economy that yields prosperity both sustainable and shared.[26] Whichever world we choose, it will be ownership and financial architectures that give it its essential shape.

When I give talks about generative ownership design, people sometimes say, "It would be nice, but how can we get there?" The answer, I suspect, will be twofold. We'll need a pincer movement: one arm moving to rein in corporate abuse and reform corporate governance at existing corporations, the other arm moving to develop generative alternatives.[27] Both kinds of effort are necessary. But it's the second strategy—promoting alternatives—that today lacks coherence and momentum. It's difficult to unite and work for deep change when we lack a clear, shared vision of the kind of economy we truly want and a simple understanding of the designs that make it function.

The development of alternatives relies, initially, on *emergence*. As organizational change theorist Meg Wheatley has written, emergence is about connecting with people who share a common vision. This is how local actions spring up, connect through networks, and strengthen into communities of practice. With little warning, emergent phenomena can appear—like the rise of the organic and local food movements. Ultimately, a new system can emerge at greater scale: not magically, but through a combination of unplanned emergent activities and later more focused efforts.[28]

I explore emergence in chapter 8, "Bringing Forth a World," and offer more thoughts on change strategies throughout the book—particularly in the epilogue. But my aim isn't to create a roadmap of how to get from here to there. My focus is on *there*. My quest is for a vision and language, at once practical and profound, that might guide us in the tumultuous days ahead.

THE PATTERNS OF LIFE

If most of us understand the design of democratic power, we don't understand economic power. We don't understand the design of ownership. And we need to. What has yet to be done—and what I attempt here—is to devise a simple pattern language to describe the designs that underlie and unify seemingly disparate models. As architect Christopher Alexander has said, we need to discover how to talk about patterns in a way that can be shared. This means naming them. "We must make each pattern a thing so that the human mind can use it easily," he wrote in *The Timeless Way of Building*.[29] (I return to Alexander's work in part 3.)

I've found five essential patterns that work together to create different kinds of ownership: purpose, membership, governance, capital, and networks. These can be used in *extractive* ways—aimed at extracting maximum financial wealth in the short term. Or they can be used in *generative* ways—aimed at creating a world where all living beings can flourish for generations to come. If new models remain to be created, many of the underlying design patterns we need are already here and can be combined in novel ways.

Extractive ownership has a *Financial Purpose:* maximizing profits. Generative ownership has a *Living Purpose:* creating the conditions for life. While corporations today have *Absentee Membership*, with owners disconnected from the life of enterprise, generative ownership has *Rooted Membership*, with ownership held in human hands. While extractive ownership involves *Governance by Markets*, with control by capital markets on autopilot, generative designs have *Mission-Controlled Governance*, with control by those focused on social mission. While extractive investments involve *Casino Finance*, alternative approaches involve *Stakeholder Finance*, where capital becomes a friend rather than a master. Instead of *Commodity Networks*, where goods are traded based solely on price, generative economic relations are supported by *Ethical Networks*, which offer collective support for social and ecological norms. Not every ownership model has every one of these design patterns. But the more generative patterns are employed, the more effective the design.

In key ways, this book is a continuation of my previous one, *The Divine Right of Capital.* That book looked at the myths upholding the rights of capital, particularly the myth that wealth holders have needs that come before everyone else's needs. It also explored principles of economic democracy. In the decade since it was published, the ownership structures of our economy—the intertwined institutions of corporations and capital markets, and the perpetual growth and rising profits they require—have contributed to unprecedented new crises, such as climate change. It no longer seems sufficient to speak of economic democracy as the solution.

A more appropriate frame of reference may be the living system of the planet. The ultimate patterns that all systems must employ are *living patterns*—the patterns of organization that nature has evolved to support life. Systems thinking, which arose in physics and is spreading to other disciplines, offers a robust language for speaking about living patterns and processes. It's a language that applies equally to biological systems and social systems. Through systems thinking, we can see that the task of redesigning ownership is part of the larger task of bringing human civilization into harmony with the earth.

We know the next economy will require things like wind turbines, limits on carbon emissions, and sustainably managed forests. The questions that remain largely unanswered are about who will own these, who will control them, and who will flourish in the world they create. We need innovation not only in physical technologies but also in *social architectures.*[30] If physical technologies are about the *what* of the economy, social architectures are about the *who*: who will make economic decisions, and how, using what kinds of organizing structures? Social architectures are the blueprints of human relations, how we organize ourselves to do things. Will we continue to rely on economic architectures organized around growth and maximum income for the few? Or can we shift to new architectures organized around keeping this planet and all its inhabitants thriving? This book is a quest for answers.

MAPPING THE JOURNEY AHEAD

In part 1, I trace how extractive design in one industry, the mortgage industry, drove toward financial overshoot and collapse. I start with the foreclosed house that a friend of mine was trying to buy, for which he couldn't find any owner to whom he could make an offer. I follow this thread to the New York Stock Exchange, and into other worlds of financial engineering, to trace what went wrong in the social architecture of ownership. Ultimately, I set out to find the couple that the house once belonged to, to see how the subprime mortgage collapse impacted the life of one family.

In part 2, I look for the seeds of a new value system that might give rise to a new economy. I visit experiments in ownership of the commons: the Maine lobster industry, community forests, community wind, a cohousing community, and others. Embodied in these ownership models are values of sustainability, community, and sufficiency (the idea that after the pursuit of "more" comes the recognition of "enough"). These may be the values that one day replace the pursuit of limitless financial wealth, the focus on individualism, and the insistence on maximum growth, which remain embedded in today's ownership designs.

If part 1 is about the breakdown of ownership, and part 2 is about the ground of its evolution, part 3 looks at design patterns that are bringing generative ownership to life on a broad scale. Each chapter takes up one key pattern of generative design, looking at how these combine to keep social mission alive over time. I've seen many companies that once were generative lose their social mission when they grow large or when the founder departs. In part 3, I search for successful, substantial companies that have solved the "legacy problem"—keeping social legacy alive long after the founder is gone. I tour the employee-owned John Lewis Partnership in London. I visit foundation-owned Novo Nordisk in Denmark, a pharmaceutical with production based in Kalundborg, home to a famed example of "industrial symbiosis," where this company's waste becomes food for the ecosystem. Among other expeditions, I revisit finance, talking with a couple of investing advisers to see how I can use my own small investment portfolio to help in the transformation.

My hope is that these journeys will be of interest both to specialists and to the general, thoughtful reader. For those deeply immersed in ownership design, the simple design patterns I see at work might help bring coherence to what has been a disconnected field. For others, these journeys might help answer the questions that bedevil us: How did a civilization as advanced and fiercely intelligent as our own manage to get things so catastrophically wrong? How, in other words, did we get here? And where might we be heading in the most hopeful, if not the most likely, scenario? What kind of economy could we create if we turned the emerging ownership revolution into a concerted, organized social force?

If ownership talk feels unfamiliar, it did to me too when I began dreaming of launching *Business Ethics* a quarter century ago. I was in my early 30s then, and owning my own company felt so grown-up, so beyond me. It was something in the realm of the fathers, not in my realm as a young woman. I remember a dream I had one night of entering a building—a church, a bank, or in dream logic somehow both—where I saw men standing behind a railing, murmuring among themselves. A barrier separated me from them, like the communion railing separating the congregation from the priest, marking off a territory where only the banker-priests could enter. I stepped inside that rail. And to my surprise, no one minded. They acted as though I belonged. And I did. Moving more boldly, I began to dream of remodeling the space, throwing out a wall, widening the room, removing the barrier, allowing more to enter. I awoke exhilarated.

Having wandered around in the architecture of ownership a good long time now, I want to invite others in. Ownership is the ultimate realm of economic power. We all belong there—in the same way that we all belong in the halls of democracy. It's time for us to own this place we call an economy and stop leaving it to the banker-priests. When more and more of us become comfortable entering the seemingly forbidden space of ownership—daring to dream together of remaking it—that's when we will truly own our future.

THE DESIGN OF ECONOMIC POWER
The Architecture of Ownership

EXTRACTIVE OWNERSHIP	GENERATIVE OWNERSHIP
1. *Financial Purpose:* maximizing profits in short term	1. *Living Purpose:* creating the conditions for life over long term
2. *Absentee Membership:* ownership disconnected from life of enterprise	2. *Rooted Membership:* ownership in human hands
3. *Governance by Markets:* control by capital markets on autopilot	3. *Mission-Controlled Governance:* control by those dedicated to social mission
4. *Casino Finance:* capital as master	4. *Stakeholder Finance:* capital as friend
5. *Commodity Networks:* trading focused solely on price and profits	5. *Ethical Networks:* collective support for ecological and social norms

I

The Overbuilt House of Claims

Extractive Ownership as the Cause of Financial Collapse

The modern economy is built largely on the framework of a single kind of ownership: the publicly held company, with ownership shares trading in stock markets. It is an industrial-age model of ownership. Its purpose is manufacturing financial wealth in endlessly growing quantity. Because financial wealth is a claim against real wealth—a claim on future wages or housing values or company profits—this form of ownership works by extraction. We can call it extractive ownership. One sector where this model has been particularly pernicious is the mortgage and banking industry. A reasonable amount of wealth flowing to the financial industry is normal and healthy. Yet when too much wealth flows up into the financial sphere—the province of the big banks, hedge funds, and hyper-wealthy—this extraction weakens the vitality of the real economy of jobs, families, and communities. The system becomes overloaded with claims and prone to collapse. How this system impacts one family, one home lost to foreclosure, is the focus of the journeys of part 1.

ONE

DEBT, INC.

Extractive Design

As my friend Orion Kriegman and I climbed the pebbly cement staircase in the sidewalk that gave James Court a distinctive charm, he shared with me the story of his quest to buy the home we were on our way to see. It was a little two-unit at 56 James Court* in the Jamaica Plain neighborhood of Boston. After the family that lived there for 13 years lost it to the mortgage company, it stood empty for years. Orion had lined up bank financing to buy it. But when his real estate agent tried to make an offer, he couldn't find anyone on the other end to talk with. No owner. Or at least no owner that anyone could locate. Some entity somewhere in the chain of financing had gone bankrupt, and the company left in charge was in absentia. Orion tracked down that firm through the register of deeds, but when he called the company—not once, but over and over—he felt he'd entered that special circle of Dante's Inferno reserved for those on hold.

In his months-long effort to buy the home, he got as far as discovering that the "owner of record" was Ocwen Financial Services. But there the trail went cold. "Their phone service is a true nightmare," Orion said. "There's no category this fits in, so they transfer you to someplace where you can't leave a message." When he finally talked to someone, he figured he'd reached a call center in India, because the person spoke with an Indian

---

* The address of this home and names of its former owners have been changed to protect their privacy. The details presented are real.

accent and seemed to be working from a script with no provision for his particular problem.

"He gave me an 800 number, but I said an 800 number is not a direct line. 'Oh yes, it is, sir, I promise it is, sir,' he told me. So I tried it, and it took me back to the start." Consulting again with his agent, Orion got the name of the person at Ocwen in charge of foreclosed properties and phoned him. At one point, he even found a returned message on his answering machine. But after calling the fellow back three times, Orion was met with a final, enduring silence.

Odd. How does one lose ownership? Where did it *go*? This intrigued me. Somehow, the seemingly simple fact of ownership had been deconstructed beyond recognition and vaporized. That process had triggered economic crisis across many nations—something like the splitting of the atom triggering nuclear explosion. Because the owners who'd lost this home seemed close to ground zero for the whole thing, I thought the story of this one family might help unravel how things had gone so wrong.

THROUGH THE WEEDS

Orion finished telling his story as we reached the house, where we stood for a moment. "I don't even know if it has its plumbing anymore," he said. A lot of abandoned homes didn't. Scavengers had been known to strip out copper piping, rip sinks out of walls, and haul boilers out of basements. Since this home had plywood slabs covering its windows, we couldn't tell what shape the interior was in. We pushed through the weeds to the back-yard to try to see.

From beneath the side porch protruded the edge of a stained blue sleeping bag. "There's definitely someone living under there; I see him all the time," said a young man walking toward us (who didn't seem to have bathed that morning). He told us that he too dreamed of occupying the house, as a squatter. Like Orion, he said he'd visited the website for the register of deeds to follow the tale of the home's ownership. "It's like seeing people's life story in a handful of documents," he said. Peering past this home's boarded-up windows proved impossible that day. If I were ever able to see into the story of this home, I realized that I would have to be the third in our erstwhile trio to dig into the public documents posted by the register of deeds.

The tale began in 1992, when Helen Haroldson bought the 2,100-square-foot two-family house for $140,000, with a mortgage from Shawmut Mortgage Co. Five years later, she seemed to be getting a small business under way, because a Small Business Administration (SBA) loan was added in the amount of $23,500, secured by the value of the house. On SBA documents, the name of a husband, Michael, appeared for the first time—possibly indicating a recent marriage. With a home, a husband, and a business, Helen's life seemed to be coming together. For two more years, all seemed to go smoothly. Then in 1999 the couple took out an innocuously small loan, $16,000, from a local credit union. In less than two years, they'd fallen behind on payments, and the credit union gave them a few months to become current.

The growing equity in the home allowed that problem to disappear. The Haroldsons got a $233,200 mortgage from Aegis Mortgage Co., totaling $50,000 more than all previous loans combined. That likely meant they'd added some cash for themselves into the refinancing (as well as cash for the hefty fees no doubt charged by Aegis). It was easy to imagine their relief. Yet had it been a Shakespearean play, this would have been the moment when the plot turned. Aegis (a company organized in the state of Oklahoma, with a post office box in Louisiana and a street address in Texas) would appear again in the Haroldsons' life, as would a second corporation mentioned on this mortgage: MERS—Mortgage Electronic Registration Systems, Inc. MERS was a privately owned loan-tracking service created to facilitate the trading of mortgages. Its presence on the deed meant that this home's mortgage could be sold countless times, with few hints of those transactions showing in county land records. MERS was, you might say, the legal representative of the financial whirlwind.

Nine months later, the Haroldsons were back with another new mortgage, this one from Ameriquest Mortgage. I recognized the name, because when the meltdown came, it made headlines as the object of multiple state prosecutions for predatory practices—such as pressuring borrowers to refinance when it wasn't in their interest to do so. Perhaps in part because of lender fees and penalties, the mortgage was now $50,000 higher. It seems the Haroldsons had begun paying down old debt with new debt. From that point, it became painful to read on.

Six months later, another new mortgage—Aegis again. This one $71,000 higher. Another six months, another new mortgage, this one from a lender incongruously named Community First Bank, adding $44,000. Then an Instrument of Taking from the state Office of the Collector-Treasurer, threatening to seize the house for nonpayment of taxes. The notice arrived 12 days before Christmas. Five months later, the Haroldsons were back with another new mortgage—Aegis again (no longer organized in the state of Oklahoma, now reorganized in Delaware). This mortgage totaled a crushing $462,500. The Haroldsons hung on for another 18 months, and then MERS filed in court to foreclose.

Even in the dry prose of registered deeds, there was something raw about these transactions. The Haroldsons were clearly unsophisticated in the ways of finance, possibly lax, or, more charitably, desperate in their decision making. For whatever reason, they cycled through five mortgages in five years. Why did no bank counsel them? If reckless borrowing was clearly in evidence, the larger story—the enabling framework—had to do with reckless lending.

A TANGLED SKEIN OF OWNERSHIP

For years after the house was taken, the power of sale that MERS had claimed lay unexercised. Any ordinary bank would have wanted to see this home put on the market immediately. But this was no ordinary bank. MERS wasn't the owner but a processing agency acting on behalf of some unnamed other. I guessed that Aegis wasn't the owner, either, because companies like that often sold off mortgages within days. Aegis had also gone bankrupt, ceasing operations less than eight months after the Haroldsons' foreclosure.

I thought the most likely "owners"—and the word clearly needs quotation marks in this context—were the investors in mortgage-backed securities. What such investors generally invested in were not individual mortgages, or even pools of mortgages, but instead *characteristics* of pools of mortgages, packaged into collateralized debt obligations (CDOs). Many of these investing vehicles melted down in the housing crash, making them possible candidates for the missing owner. Because of MERS's presence, the whole thing remained opaque.

If the Haroldsons' house stood at one end of this tangle of financial arrangements, at the other end stood investors. These often weren't individuals but institutions—like the banks of Iceland, which were destroyed in the CDO meltdown, or the pension fund of King County, Seattle, which lost a bundle on structured investment vehicles. So it was that between, say, a Seattle policeman whose retirement depended on the performance of a mortgage loan and the mortgage payments made (or not made) by the Haroldsons, there stretched a complex of connections so densely woven as to be impossible to untangle when the need arose.

Holding the supposed responsibility for this snarled skein was Ocwen Financial Services. It was a story in itself. When I put its name into Google, I might as well have searched on the phrase "mortgage fraud," so numerous were the lawsuits and allegations of abuse. According to a Government Accountability Office (GAO) report, the firm had charged the Veterans Administration for home repairs never made, instead leaving houses in disrepair and covered in debris. The Better Business Bureau of Central Florida, where Ocwen was located, had given the company its lowest ranking, F, after receiving 520 complaints in three years. In a customer service survey, J. D. Power and Associates ranked Ocwen dead last, in large part because of what the *Palm Beach Post* called "its tortuous and unhelpful phone services." Orion's suspicions about the call center in India were well founded. I came upon an announcement that Ocwen had hired 5,000 new people for its operation centers in Bangalore and Mumbai.[1]

Ocwen's practices may not have been far from the industry standard. Abusive practices were in many ways the logical consequence of the incentives that financialized ownership creates. Mortgage servicers inhabited a cockeyed universe where fees increased as loans slipped toward trouble. The longer that loans remained in limbo, the greater the opportunity for junk fees. As mortgage servicers seized a property and prepared to resell it, they could funnel orders for title searches, appraisals, and legal filings to companies with which they were affiliated. Ocwen had established its own title company, Premium Title Services, in part to pocket more of that revenue. Because of these multiplying fees, mortgage servicers had little incentive to dispose of troubled properties quickly. They had little incentive to care what houses ultimately sold for, since the losses were not their own.[2]

Because Ocwen was a collection agency, interested in its own fees, it likely tended to see borrowers and their homes largely as production units: items in computerized databases with whom the firm had no enduring relationship. The players who had been part of a human relationship—those who arranged the loans—were gone. They'd sold the loans to financiers, who compiled the loans into products and sold them to investors.

If it was a mechanistic process, it was also a lucrative one. As a final note to the story of Ocwen, I pulled its stock performance chart. It looked like a fever chart climbing vertically. After a rocky period, the company found its footing in the post-crash environment and in a 52-week period saw its stock climb 140 percent. The reason was that Ocwen landed new contracts for managing troubled loans. Having likely played some role in the sub-prime mess as it unfolded, Ocwen was also making a bundle cleaning it up.[3]

When I thought back to the dilapidation of 56 James Court, the design logic that led there seemed clear. The breakdown in the physical architecture of the house traced directly (or rather, circuitously) to its ownership architecture. As ownership was deconstructed and repackaged, its atoms distributed hither and yon, the aim of the whole process wasn't to help people stay in their homes. When families like the Haroldsons could no longer be tapped for escalating fees, they were shunted aside like debris, and houses were left to deteriorate. As a home loan shifted from one financial institution to another, a single aim was at work: to extract as much financial wealth as possible and to avoid responsibility if things went wrong. Financial extraction by companies and physical extraction by vandals went hand in hand. But they were not parallel processes. Finance was the master force.

THE RULES OF EXTRACTIVE DESIGN

The simple rules at the core of this story began to resolve themselves in my mind like a photograph coming into focus. To the brokers who created mortgages, the financial institutions that repackaged them, and the processors like Ocwen who serviced them, their shared motivations amounted to a unified system dynamic. The rules were so widely understood that they rarely needed to be articulated:

> *Maximize financial gains and*
> *minimize financial risks.*

In their zeal to excel at this game, the players at certain points strayed across the line into fraud. Yet the problem wasn't so much that people had broken the rules as that they'd followed them.

> *To understand the behavior of an entire system,*
> *it's important to look beyond the players*
> *to the rules of the game.*

That point was emphasized by systems theorist Donella Meadows, the Dartmouth College professor best known as the lead author of the 1972 book *The Limits to Growth*, one of the first to make the case that growth cannot continue infinitely on a finite planet. She helped develop systems thinking, which describes the common functioning of all systems, whether bacteria, organisms, ecosystems, or economies.

In her final book, *Thinking in Systems: A Primer*, Meadows observed that beneath the detail and complexity of the world, simple rules are generally at work. When those rules are repeated over and over, they spin themselves out in intricate ways, creating complex system structures. She gave the example of how a snowflake can be generated from a simple set of organizing principles. "Imagine a triangle with three equal sides," she wrote. "Add to the middle of each side another equilateral triangle, one-third the size of the first one. Add to each of the new sides another triangle, one-third smaller. And so on. The result is called a Koch snowflake."[4]

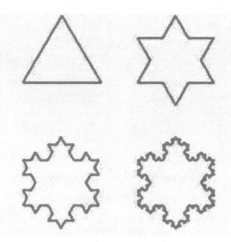

KOCH SNOWFLAKE

The way a single cell grows into a human being probably proceeds by some similar set of rules, Meadows said. "All of life, from viruses to redwood trees, from amoebas to elephants," she wrote, "is based on the basic organizing rules encapsulated in the chemistry of RNA, DNA, and protein molecules."[5]

Entire systems of organization can similarly grow from simple rules of self-organization—like the rules of maximizing financial gains and minimizing financial risks. These rules are based on deeper values, including individualism, the notion that the only relevant unit of concern is the individual self. What the rules say is to maximize gains for the *self* and avoid responsibility if *others* are harmed in the process. Harm to others is not something the system intends. It's something the system ignores. What the rules say is, take care of yourself; forget everybody else.

These are the rules at the heart of extractive design. This is the design at work in the myriad forms of conventional mortgage finance and in the behavior of most publicly traded companies. When common rules are at the core of structures, the structures tend to produce characteristic behaviors. These structures can be called *archetypes*. Archetypes are the deep, simple patterns of organization that lie beneath the complexity of everyday life.[6]

The rules of maximizing gains and minimizing risk originate in the human heart. But they become a collective force, shaping the behavior of countless individuals working in concert, when they are embedded in institutional design. Organizations are more than random collections of individuals doing what they feel like doing on a given day. Behind the complex behavior of an institution like a bank—behind its loan offerings, its policies, the behavior of its employees—is a system structure that binds it all together, giving that system coherence and momentum.

Social systems are organized around a *purpose* in the same way that natural systems are organized around a *function.* The function of an acorn is to become an oak. The function of a river is to flow. The difference between function and purpose is the element of human choice. The purpose of an institution is selected by those with the ability to make that choice, the company's owners. They express their purpose through the design of the organization.

Structure is purpose expressed through design.

This is the key lesson that systems thinking teaches us about the economic crisis: that the triggering events behind it were the result not simply of missteps by a few but of a larger system dynamic that encouraged those missteps. Financial Purpose was at the heart of it. The financial ruin of people like the Haroldsons wasn't anyone's aim. It was off the radar screen. Loans going bad didn't bother brokers or financiers as long as their own financial interests weren't at risk.

We're closing in here on the serious design flaws encoded deep in the social architecture of extractive ownership. What its individualistic rules fail to encompass are the larger realities of system behavior—like the fact that everyone in a system can be acting in seemingly rational ways, yet their actions can add up to a terrible outcome. Or the reality that a system can, without warning, leap into behavior it's never exhibited before.[7] To create a system design built for those kinds of unexpected outcomes—which seem to be showing up with greater frequency in the 21st century—a different set of operating principles will be needed.

TWO

THE COMMUNITY BANK

Generative Design

If I found the story of 56 James Court a depressing tale, it also left me pondering a hidden anomaly: Community First Bank.[1] In the five mortgages that the Haroldsons cycled through in five years, the bank that supposedly put "Community First" underwrote mortgage number four. It was a troublesome loan that lasted less than a year. It replaced a previous loan only six months old, and in the process it nearly *doubled* the family's debt load. Shouldn't a community bank have counseled the Haroldsons against signing their names to this loan? But instead, Community First Bank was the one inking the papers.

What was going on? In those boom years, had even community banks become little more than wolves in sheep's clothing? If this bank's name implied that it was a generative lender, why was it behaving like an extractive lender? Was my whole idea of generative ownership a crock? I decided I'd better dig in and find out.

Setting out to learn more about the ownership design of Community First Bank, I found the issue a slippery one. The first problem was its name. There was a Community First Bank in Butler, Missouri; another in New Iberia, Louisiana; still others in Harrison, Arkansas, and Kokomo, Indiana—to name a few. These were all separate legal entities, not branches of the same parent company. I finally tracked down the bank that the Haroldsons had done business with on the Federal Deposit Insurance Corporation (FDIC) website. It was headquartered in Baltimore County, Maryland.

There were other problems. This bank was apparently small and locally owned (didn't that mean it was one of the good guys?). And its legal structure didn't tell me much. It wasn't a publicly traded company, where ownership changed hands moment to moment. Instead, it was a privately held S Corporation—likely owned by a small handful of people, with key owners living in Baltimore or nearby. It also was a *limited liability company* (LLC). That meant its owners avoided liability for unpaid company debts or harms the company did. Yet for tax purposes, profits and losses flowed through to the owners. They got the gains and avoided the liabilities.

This legal structure was neutral. It was a shell inside of which lots of different things could be going on. I'd seen the LLC structure used by a southern Minnesota company called Minwind, which created wind farms designed on cooperative principles as a way to benefit farmers and keep wealth local. (I return to its story in chapter 12.) It was a great model, and because of the way tax incentives were written, it needed that tax pass-through. LLCs and S Corporation design patterns were practical, not sinister. To find the real purpose embedded in this bank's ownership design, I needed to look elsewhere.

Next, I found that this bank had a federal charter rather than a state charter. And in the post-crash environment following the 2008 meltdown, it had been "aggressively seeking to open new retail mortgage branches across the country," its website said. At that time, it had a dozen branches in a half-dozen states. I stumbled on a job listing for a franchise sales recruiter, who was to work full time on recruiting branch managers, each being promised "100% of the profits of the branch."

There was more. Paradoxically, this was a small bank—at that time with only $70 million in assets—yet it was cranking out a head-spinning volume of loans: $1.3 *billion* in the five years up to 2008. Compared with other banks named Community First Bank (more than a dozen in all), it was processing nearly *five times* as many mortgage applications as the next largest.[2] As far as I could tell, the others probably were banks aimed at serving their local communities. This bank was a mortgage machine. Because of its small asset size, it could not possibly be holding all the loans it created in its own portfolio. That meant it was selling them off, rapid-fire.

In sum, this was a bank standing on the head of a pin, churning out loans like so many widgets off a high-speed assembly line. And it was also selling mini-widget-making machines in the shape of bank franchises.[3]

This wasn't a bank likely to focus on whether the Haroldsons could afford a mortgage over the long term. Its "primary business objective," as its employee intranet site said, was "to originate mortgage loans through branch offices utilizing a web-based end-to-end paperless system." And if a loan were to go bad in less than a year, as the Haroldsons' had? Whoever bought that mortgage could seize the house and then sell it to extract the equity. Which is what happened with the Haroldsons' final mortgage.

ANY GOOD NEWS OUT THERE?

So, OK. It was pretty likely that this bank wasn't a generative lender. But I also hoped it was an anomaly. I began to wonder about other community banks. What about the banks that the Haroldsons *didn't* encounter—the banks genuinely rooted in community? Did they behave differently? In the months following the 2008 financial crisis, I searched the torrent of e-mails surging through my computer, trying to sift out bits of hope from the flow of bad news. I found some interesting morsels.

The first bit I caught in my mental net was Self-Help Credit Union in North Carolina, long a leader among the nation's 1,000 community development financial institutions (CDFIs).[4] As a CDFI, Self-Help was a banking enterprise with a special charter from the US Department of the Treasury to serve low-income communities not adequately served by conventional banks. It did business with the same low-income borrowers that subprime lenders dealt with. But Self-Help's mission was to serve these people, not to extract wealth from them. It meant taking care to place families in loans they could repay. The result—what a surprise—was that its loans, in those critical early months, held together as others were falling apart. As the *Durham News* reported in late 2008, "Prudent lender prevails amid crisis."[5]

A lot of folks might have said Self-Help was a responsible bank because it was "small and local." Yet it wasn't particularly small. Over a decade and a half, it processed close to $6 billion in mortgage loans. Nor was it entirely local. Beyond its headquarters in North Carolina, it had branches in California and an office in Washington, DC, and ran a program aimed at aiding borrowers in 48 states.[6]

What distinguished Self-Help was its ownership architecture: it was a member-owned credit union launched by a nonprofit. That design was shaped by the Living Purpose at its core, the mission of helping people underserved by traditional markets. Among those it sought to help were low-wealth families, women, people of color, and rural residents. It aimed to use the power of finance to make the lives of ordinary people better.

That included serving people like Brenda and Silvio Granados, first-time homebuyers of an affordable home restored by Self-Help in Charlotte, North Carolina, where the credit union purchased two dozen abandoned homes, hoping to reinvigorate a community devastated by foreclosures. Self-Help also helped Darnella Warthen launch A New Beginning child care center in Durham, North Carolina, where some of the center's kids had behavioral and mental challenges. Creating generative outcomes was at the core of why Self-Help existed. The fact that this organization had proved resilient in a crisis was welcome news. I soon found that it wasn't a unique tale.

UNSUNG STORIES OF RESILIENCE IN CRISIS

I uncovered a similar story about Clearinghouse CDFI, a lender in Orange County, California—home of the bankrupt mortgage lender Ameriquest, from whom the Haroldsons had received mortgage number three. Clearinghouse CDFI had never done business with the Haroldsons. But it made loans to other risky folk: primarily first-time homebuyers, about half of them minorities. Among the loans that Clearinghouse had outstanding in late 2008, fewer than 1 percent had been foreclosed.[7]

That was fairly typical of many CDFIs at that time. A study by the Opportunity Finance Network (a CDFI trade group) showed that through first quarter 2010, CDFI loan funds experienced loan losses *one-half* those seen by banks overall.[8] And this was despite the fact that CDFI loan funds dealt primarily with underprivileged borrowers.[9]

The story of resilience I was uncovering was very different from the narrative spun by business news anchor Neil Cavuto on Fox News. He said, "Loaning to minorities and risky folks is a disaster."[10] But that isn't true, apparently, if financial institutions aim to serve risky folks rather than prey upon them.

As the recession wore on, this story darkened as CDFIs began to feel the impact of operating in low- and moderate-income areas where housing values were dropping and people were losing jobs in growing numbers. "Even though they were mostly not involved in the sourcing of 'toxic waste' sub-prime loans," said the 2009 annual report of the National Community Investment Fund, CDFI banks were being hit hard by increases in delinquencies and loan-loss provisions.[11] As Saurabh Nairan of NCIF explained to me, CDFI banks were suffering because they worked in vulnerable markets hard-hit by other unscrupulous lenders. "So, even though they have not originated bad loans, they suffer because folks in these markets are suffering," he said.[12]

Looking beyond CDFIs, I dug into what was happening with the nation's 8,000 consumer-owned credit unions. I found that at a time when megabanks were receiving billions in bailouts, the vast majority of credit unions needed none. These customer-owned banks remained conservative lenders, generally holding on to loans rather than selling them off. That gave them incentives to care whether loans would be repaid. On the other hand, a small number of their larger brethren—"wholesale" credit unions, providing services to smaller retail credit unions—experienced billions in losses. They'd abandoned their community-based footing and dabbled in more exotic mortgage-backed securities.[13]

Turning to still another category of community-oriented lenders—the nation's 7,600 community banks—I found that most of these small, locally owned banks also seemed to be responsible lenders. A 2009 FDIC study found that in the post-crisis environment, banks with under $1 billion in assets remained the best capitalized, because their capital base hadn't been eroded by excessive risk. According to the Independent Community Bankers of America, small banks were the only part of the industry to show growth in loans in the early post-crash period.

Community banks weren't immune to failures, and there were some bailouts. But in general, they remained in good shape. By touting their strengths, some picked up market share. FirstBank of Colorado hired a single-engine plane to tow a sign over a Rockies game at Coors Field in Denver, reading, "This is the closest thing we have to a private jet." In Fort Worth, Worthington National Bank ran billboards urging people to "Just Say No to Bailout Banks." And in relatively short order, it found itself with $10 million in new deposits.[14]

The phenomenon I was tracking wasn't limited to the United States. In that stunned period as the US subprime mortgage meltdown morphed into an international banking crisis, the state-owned banks of India were widely seen as havens of safety because their ownership framework kept them on the straight and narrow. The State Bank of India—60 percent owned by the government, with a mission of uplifting the people of India—in the three months after the crash saw its deposit base swell 40 percent.[15] It wasn't privately owned, but it did have a Living Purpose. In the Netherlands, Triodos Bank—whose mission was to make loans only to sustainable businesses— also saw its deposits grow substantially after the crisis.

The UK yielded an intriguing twist on this narrative. It was a tale told by the New Economics Foundation (NEF) in a white paper, *The Ecology of Finance*. This story had to do with a set of alternative financial institutions in the UK known as *building societies*, which are member-owned banking organizations. Their purpose is not to maximize profits for investors but to serve their customers, who are their owners. From 1986 on, building societies joined a stampede to convert to traditional bank ownership, a process known as demutualizing—leaving behind mutual ownership to become investor owned. The result, NEF reported, was that *after the banking crisis, not a single one of these converted institutions was left standing as an independent bank.* They'd all been absorbed into larger banks, or gotten into trouble and had to be rescued.

The most spectacular example was Northern Rock, a massive lender so wounded that it had to be nationalized and kept afloat by tens of billions of dollars of public money. "Just a year before its fall," the NEF paper said, "the Rock testified to an all-party parliamentary group that 'mutual status does not encourage efficiency. ... [Our] success over eight years would not have been possible under the old mutual model.'" Yet in a crisis, the reverse proved true. The supposed efficiencies of the profit-maximizing model led Northern Rock to dash itself to pieces on the rocks of the financial downturn.[16]

SURFACING THE SUBMERGED

As I cast my net wider and wider, I found an increasingly coherent narrative of generative design. This story had been unfolding parallel to the tale of the Haroldsons and 56 James Court, but with a very different ending. It was the narrative of mortgage loans made to families by banks for whom lending remained a life-serving process: community banks, credit unions, CDFIs, and other lenders rooted in community. The loans of these institutions had, at a critical moment, been going bad in dramatically smaller numbers. Yet this was a story that wasn't widely understood.

The most remarkable tale of its invisibility was told by Jean-Louis Bancel, president of the International Co-operative Banking Association, an association of cooperative banks, which are member-owned financial institutions, found all over the globe, that are run democratically in the interests of their customers. In the crisis, Bancel said, the cooperative banking sector "showed its benefits as a factor of stability and financial security for millions of people."[17] In remarks made in 2010 to the Organization for Economic Development and Cooperation, he told of the surprising size of the cooperative banking sector, which in Europe holds 21 percent of all deposits. In the Netherlands, the enormous Rabobank holds 43 percent of all the country's deposits. Yet cooperative banks remain the "submerged part of the banking world," Bancel said.[18]

They meet with a "relative silence on the part of academics and regulators," he said. And he noted "a relatively widespread lack of knowledge" about this sector, even at institutions like the World Bank and the International Monetary Fund (IMF). In statistics kept by the IMF, he found no headings dedicated to cooperative banks. And as international regulators began crafting responses to the crisis, he continued, they proposed new capital requirements that would harm this sector. "Many cooperative banks may be compelled to abandon their cooperative status," he said, "at an abnormally high cost," to meet the proposed new requirements.[19]

Building societies, community banks, credit unions, CDFIs, state-owned banks, and cooperative banks each tell a story of success in crisis. Collectively, it is a tale of how generative design creates stability by avoiding excess.

> *The common outcomes generated by these models*
> *indicate that there are common rules at their core.*

A genuinely different archetype is at work. At a moment when the extractive archetype was generating chaos, this archetype was generating community well-being. Homeowners were staying in their homes. Investors were finding stable income. Neighborhoods were avoiding the devastation of foreclosure. These community-oriented models had been generating these beneficial outcomes for a long time. Yet it was at the moment of breakdown that the contrast became starkly visible.

A NEW ARCHETYPE TAKES SHAPE

This is generative design at work. Instead of being about ignoring harm to others, it is about being of service to others. Instead of being about maximizing financial gains, it is about being financially self-sustaining over the long term. It is a phenomenon that defies the old categories of for-profit versus nonprofit organizations. Yes, some of these institutions do occasionally receive grants. Some have tax advantages that traditional banks don't have. But for the most part, these are self-sustaining financial institutions.

> *They are profit making but not profit maximizing.*

This is an ownership model that isn't about extracting as much wealth as possible and then dispensing a few drops with a benevolent hand. Instead, these designs prevent wealth from concentrating in a few hands in the first place. They keep economic activity rooted in its original purpose of meeting human needs. Living Purpose is at the core of this archetype, in the sense of helping people to buy homes, start businesses, run day-care centers. This archetype is about generating the conditions for life to flourish.

This is the "true economics" that economist Herman Daly and theologian John Cobb Jr. describe in their book, *For the Common Good.* It is an economics that "concerns itself with the long-term welfare of the whole community." It doesn't center on *homo economicus*, that lone individual out to maximize his or her own income. Instead, what's at work is a new kind of economic person, which they term *person in community*. It is about seeing one's own well-being as integrally related to the well-being of others.[20]

If person-in-community is a new conception of the economic individual, generative ownership design is its logical counterpart: a new conception of the economic organization. It embodies a new set of rules. Instead of *maximize financial gains and minimize financial risk*, the new formula goes something like this:

Serve the community as a way to feed the self.

Come to think of it, this isn't new at all. It's what economies have been about since time immemorial. It's what the butcher, the baker, and the candlestick maker have always done—serve the community as a way to make a living. The profit-maximizing corporation is the real detour, and a recent one at that, historically.

If the large, publicly traded, profit-maximizing corporation today is the single dominant model, generative design involves a variety of models. Member-owned credit unions are different from federally chartered CDFIs, which are different from the state-owned banks of India or the privately owned community banks in the United States. What makes them a single genotype are the common outcomes they generate and the common purposes at their core.

The different behaviors I saw at these institutions seemed unlikely to be the result solely of good people clustering at one set of organizations and bad people clustering at another set of organizations. There may have been a good deal of that. But somehow, one set of institutions made bad behavior *more likely*, while another set of institutions made good behavior more likely. How?

THE BANKER DOWN THE STREET

To trace the answer, I decide to look into the community bank where I've done my own banking for years, Beverly Cooperative Bank. It's truly rooted in one community, for I could reach all four of its branches in a single afternoon on my bike. At the branch a few blocks from my home—the two-story brick building on New Derby Street in Salem, Massachusetts—I ask CEO Bill Howard to meet with me one day.

With his gray suit and square jaw, Bill is central casting's ideal of the no-nonsense banker. Yet there's an unmistakable kindliness beneath his reserve. He's been at the bank more than a dozen years, he tells me, and in that time has seen fewer than ten foreclosures. "We've had no foreclosures this year and none the last year, and we have 1,000 loans," he says. "If you look at other community banks, you'll see similar stuff. They understand the community and have good underwriting standards."[21]

As a small bank with $300 million in assets, Beverly Cooperative Bank wasn't spared in the downturn. Some of its borrowers lost their jobs, and the bank worked with them as they struggled to repay loans. "We may go interest-only on their mortgage for a period of time," Bill says. If people needed to talk, they could find him with relative ease, he says, adding, "Good luck finding anyone at Bank of America or Citibank."

For 120 years, this bank has been chartered as a "mutual bank."[22] Unique to New England and the Midwest, mutual banks are classic hometown banks, the most famous of which is Jimmy Stewart's fictional Bailey Building and Loan in the movie *It's a Wonderful Life*. Mutual banks are state-chartered banks that have no outside investors and are run in the interests of depositors. Historically managed in conservative ways, these banks stayed on a relatively even keel through the Great Depression and the recent recession. But mutual banks are becoming a rarity. In the decade and a half leading up to the downturn, more than 300 abandoned depositor ownership to sell shares on public stock markets—in a process similar to UK building societies. I found that in the United States, fewer than 800 mutual banks remained.[23]

I ask Bill if he would consider going public. "My preference would be not to," he tells me. "When you're public, you have a different constituency," he says, because stock analysts pressure publicly traded companies to grow their profits and create higher returns for stockholders. "The culture of a bank is different if it's a mutual," he continues. With no stockholders demanding higher returns, he doesn't have to worry as much about short-term earnings. He can focus on his mission of serving the community.

If Beverly Cooperative Bank played little part in the mortgage meltdown, it's nonetheless struggling in the aftermath—in part because the FDIC is levying higher assessments to cover the missteps of other banks. A few years earlier, the bank paid the FDIC fees of $26,000. Howard says he expects the fees to soon hit $600,000. "That's 30 percent of our bottom line," he says. Also creating hardship is an increase in auditing, which adds to expenses. "We're audited to death," Bill says. "We have an internal auditor. We have an external auditor. We have a commercial lending auditor. We have an IT [information technology] auditor. The state and the FDIC audit us. It's rare we don't have an auditor in here, and it increases every year. How can small banks do all this and survive?"

While many other bank presidents led their institutions to demutualize, Bill avoided that path. Yet what drove him didn't seem to be benevolence or self-sacrifice, but some deep-rooted sense of how his own well-being was tied up with that of his community. The bank's ownership design encourages that sense. Yes, leadership is also critical. Yet the largest element in Beverly Cooperative's behavior seems to be *its own design*. This is a self-organizing system, with its own innate idea of what constitutes appropriate behavior.

FEEDBACK LOOPS:
THE GOVERNING STRUCTURE

The bank's behavior has to do with what systems thinking calls *structure*. Its structure shapes its behavior in the same way, as Donella Meadows put it, that the structure of a Slinky shapes how it bounces down the stairs. Beverly Cooperative Bank is a system self-organized around its own purposes. Self-organization is what makes an enterprise a system rather than a random collection of people. Meadows emphasized this in her definition of a system: "A system is a set of things—people, cells, molecules, or whatever—interconnected in such a way that they produce their own pattern of behavior over time."

This is more profound than it seems. In eight simple words, Meadows articulated a truth that it took me 20 years to see at *Business Ethics*:

System structure is the source of system behavior.

All the auditing requirements placed upon Beverly Cooperative Bank suggest a different assumption: that the source of system behavior is the external rules fencing it in. This small bank has an internal auditor, an external auditor, a commercial lending auditor, an IT auditor, a state auditor, and an FDIC auditor because the regulatory apparatus assumes—as an unspoken premise—that banks can be controlled only by external watchdogs. That is why regulators reacted to the banking crisis by adding rules, which threatened to crush the small community banks and cooperative banks that for the most part didn't contribute to the crisis.

Often left unseen is the issue of design: the notion that *systems do what they are designed to do*. Beverly Cooperative Bank aims to serve its community, rather than prey upon it, because that purpose is designed into its structure. Just as cows eat grass because their stomachs are structured to digest grass, and earthworms burrow in the dirt because their bodies are designed for burrowing, Beverly Cooperative Bank makes good loans because it's structured to serve its community.[24]

Community First Bank of Maryland behaved differently because it was structured differently. But its structure couldn't be reduced to its legal form. Its legal status as an LLC and an S Corporation didn't govern that system.

> *The real structure is found in the rules of the game*
> *by which the system operates.*

If the rules of the game originate with purpose, they become embodied in an organization through the *feedback loops that govern behavior*. In systems thinking, feedback is a loop where information is fed back into a system to direct its behavior. *Reinforcing feedback* loops amplify behavior. *Stabilizing feedback* loops moderate behavior. A system run only by reinforcing feedback will race out of control. Stabilizing feedback—like the thermostat on a furnace—maintains the equilibrium that living systems require.[25]

The design patterns that controlled Community First Bank's behavior—plans for aggressive expansion, a national charter that facilitated this, and compensation that rewarded aggressiveness—came together to create a reinforcing feedback loop. Regardless of the bank's name, and regardless of the fact that it was small and locally owned, this feedback loop governed its behavior.

> *Purpose and governance created*
> *the reinforcing feedback loop that made this bank*
> *behave like an extractive lender.*

Beverly Cooperative Bank, on the other hand, had stabilizing influences that moderated its behavior. This wasn't a bank focused on maximizing profits. It defined success as serving the community. It wasn't led by someone out to maximize his own income, for if Bill Howard had been intent on that, he would have taken the bank public. Its mutual bank charter, its definition of success, and its humane leadership worked together to create a balancing feedback loop, making this bank a generative lender. This feedback loop was inseparably bound up with the bank's purpose and governance.

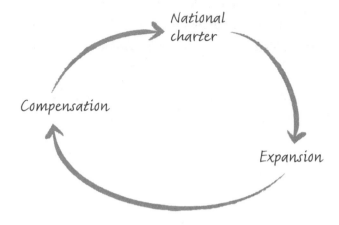

REINFORCING FEEDBACK LOOP

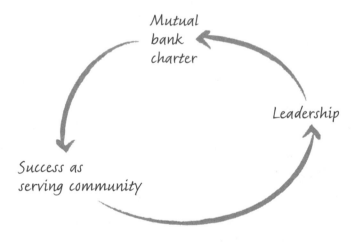

BALANCING FEEDBACK LOOP

Had lawmakers recognized the role of ownership design, they might have treated generative banks as part of the solution to the crisis. Regulators might have used bailout money not to prop up failing megabanks but to shift mortgage assets to community banks, CDFIs, and credit unions. In doing so, they might have enlisted the help of caring bankers in reworking troubled loans, possibly helping millions to stay in their homes (which Self-Help did, apparently with success).[26] Along the way, our culture could have used the crisis as an opportunity to grow the generative economy.

If regulators didn't take this path, citizens have begun to, with initiatives like the Move Your Money project, which encourages people to shift their assets to local lenders, helping them to find the most reliable ones.[27] When the next financial crisis hits, perhaps we'll make better use of the opportunity to shift assets from Wall Street to Main Street.

But thus far, the differing character of economic institutions is not something we as a culture think about very effectively. We don't see that institutional character might be as simple as this: that generative lenders like Self-Help Credit Union and Beverly Cooperative Bank consider it their purpose to serve the community. And through local ties, balanced leadership, a definition of success focused on community service, and responsible compensation schemes, they remain tied to and accountable to a living place. Another group of institutions, including Aegis and Ocwen and that aggressively expanding Baltimore bank, considered it their purpose to maximize profits, which led them to focus much less on community impact. The abandoned 56 James Court stood as an emblem of where that extractive design led.

Still, the design of individual enterprise isn't the whole story. These financial institutions are feeders into something larger than themselves. Bill Howard at Beverly Cooperative Bank hinted at what it was. There was little risk for mortgage lenders making abusive loans, he told me, "because the ink wasn't dry before they were sold; if there had been no market for those loans, they wouldn't have gotten done." It was the purchasers of the loans—the megabanks located primarily in Manhattan's financial district, the ones that sliced and diced and repackaged mortgage loans for further sale—who called the tune to which smaller lenders danced. To follow the thread of this story through, I needed to take a trip to Wall Street.

THREE

WALL STREET

Capital Markets on Autopilot

It was a trip I'd been meaning to take for a long time. For over two decades, my brother had worked on Wall Street, first at Salomon Brothers and later as a specialist on the floor of the New York Stock Exchange. There he'd been one of the auctioneers in the open outcry system through which, in the prehistoric days of the 1980s and 1990s, some 80 percent of stock trades had flowed. I'd intended many times to go watch Michael doing his job, and many times I'd put it off. Today Michael's retired. The position of specialist has virtually dissolved. The Exchange visitors' gallery is closed. When I asked him not long ago if he could arrange a tour of the Exchange for me, he called around and the message came back—in sum, no.

Well. I still wasn't giving up. So one gray morning on a business trip to New York, I took the subway to the Broadway-Nassau stop and walked the four blocks south to the corner of Wall and Broad, pulling my laptop computer in a rolling bag behind me—planning to at least visit the Exchange from the outside. This was months before the Occupy Wall Street protests that later dominated the scene there. But even then, as I neared the Exchange, I could detect apprehension in the air, a sense of a place feeling itself under siege.

Street barricades for blocks around made the vicinity off-limits to all but pedestrian traffic. At the Exchange building itself, a more elaborate security apparatus came into view. The building's main entrances—seven of them, each elegantly arched, with the regal mien of bank vault doors—

were no longer in use. Instead, there was a single narrow passageway on the side, marked awkwardly by concrete barricades, where people were being shunted into the building under the gaze of security guards. Another clutch of guards scanned the sparse pedestrian traffic ambling by, as though the building were a soccer stadium where violence might break out, rather than the "financial crossroads of the world," as street lamp banners proclaimed. A team of German shepherds stood leashed and ready.

Standing before the Exchange itself, I stopped and gazed at this Parthenon in lower Manhattan. Its neoclassical façade, marked by six Corinthian columns, gave it the presence of a Greco-Roman temple, a kind of hybrid between a house of worship and a house of government. It had the feeling of a public space—the market open to buyers and sellers that economic theory posited. And at one point, it actually had been a semi-public institution, because it was chartered as a not-for-profit. Yet as a small sign on the building told me, the Exchange was owned by Euronext.[1] It had been sold to a publicly traded company. In a conundrum of the sort that artist M. C. Escher might have depicted, the exchange where stock traded had itself been turned into shares of stock that traded inside that exchange.

The air that the place exuded, there at the corner of Wall and Broad, was of an empire past its zenith. As I stood there wondering how I might render such thoughts on the page, I felt the gaze of a security guard on me and then on the laptop bag at my feet, which suddenly felt to me over-large and sinister. My visit to the Exchange, I realized, was at an end.

Thinking it best to saunter off, I strolled across the street to 23 Wall, the J. P. Morgan Building —"luxurious but unmarked, like a prestigious private club," the plaque informed me. Down the road, I found the site where the City of New Amsterdam had in 1653 erected a plank wall—running from the Hudson River to the East River—to protect white inhabitants from Indian attack (the Indians perhaps angered after the "purchase" from them of Manhattan Island by the United West India Company). Eventually that wall had been torn down. But the dirt lane in front retained the name: Wall Street. It was along that lane that merchants and traders met to buy and sell the stocks of America's emerging companies. When the current Exchange building opened there in 1903, it featured a sculpture I could still see, gracing the triangular pediment atop the six Corinthian columns. Its central figure is a caped female presence, standing with arms outstretched over other toiling figures. She wears the winged hat of Mercury, god of commerce.[2]

THE INVISIBLE LIFE OF CAPITAL

From this street emanates a magnetic force that is central to the system logic I am tracing. Things happen here that completely transform the nature of ownership. That change begins with capital formation.

The process of capital formation has been most charmingly described in an odd little book, *The Mystery of Capital*, by Peruvian writer Hernando de Soto. When Helen Haroldson took out that first mortgage for $140,000, her home, in de Soto's words, came to "lead an invisible, parallel life" alongside its material existence. It assumed a second identity as a financial asset. Through this alchemical transformation, the value of property was drawn out and transformed into capital. Money appeared seemingly out of thin air—though in reality, it was the liquefied value of a tangible asset, the house on James Court.

We're all "surrounded by assets that invisibly harbor capital," de Soto wrote. "But only the West has the conversion process required to transform the invisible to the visible." In many nations, he found, the poor have houses built on land where ownership is unclear, or they operate businesses that are unincorporated, and this lack of clearly defined ownership prevents them from turning their assets into capital. "In the West, by contrast," de Soto wrote, "every parcel of land, every building, every piece of equipment or store of inventories is represented in a property document."[3]

It is ownership that makes wealth creation possible.

Ownership is the original system condition. The act of legal registration of property—an act that the Haroldsons and their lenders performed with the Suffolk County Register of Deeds—initiated the process allowing the house at 56 James Court to generate capital. This documentation meant that property could be used as collateral for credit. Through the lending of money, property is made liquid and releases capital. In the logic of ownership design, property ownership undergoes cell division: it comes to have both a *real* identity ("real estate") and a *financial* identity (a mortgage).

In the development of civilization, the harnessing of this alchemical process enabled the emergence of the industrial age as surely as did the harnessing of fossil fuels. If ownership was the foundational social architecture beginning in the agricultural age—allowing for the first time the settled life of farming—it was only with the development of capital formation processes that the latent power of ownership was fully unleashed. As the railroad barons and kings of capital harnessed the coevolving powers of capital formation and fossil fuels, it was as though Prometheus discovered fire a second time. Capitalism was born. The modern age came into being.

Today we're encountering the hidden dangers of limitlessly burning fossil fuels and are similarly witnessing the dangers in limitlessly creating capital. But if the first danger has found a simple label in the phrase *global warming*, the second danger has yet to be clearly recognized. For want of a better term, we can call it *excess financial extraction*. More commonly, it goes by the enticing name of *wealth creation*, a process that society sees as ideally limitless. Therein lies the problem.

Capital formation begins innocently enough, when the ownership rights attached to a house are divided. As every first-year law student learns, ownership is not a single concept but a bundle of rights. We can think of those rights as a bundle of twigs that can be separated, with different twigs given to different parties. Thus when a homeowner obtains a mortgage, one twig is given to the lender, and it passes to whomever subsequently purchases the loan. The real owner—inhabiting the "real" estate—becomes a contingent owner, liable to lose her estate if she fails to pay. A new partial owner, the bank, obtains a claim on the house. A homeowner like Helen Haroldson still holds the majority of twigs from the ownership bundle, including the right of use, the obligation to maintain the home, and the right to pocket the home's increasing value.

Yet the lender also obtains a significant right. For the twig that the lender holds can become a wedge in the door of property ownership—a way for that lender to potentially one day enter and take over the home. As our culture describes this event, *foreclosure*, it happens when the borrower "defaults." The word itself implies that it's the borrower's "fault." But in recent years, the nature of this arrangement has changed. That twig in the door has been turned into a Trojan horse: a way for the lender to insinuate itself into the borrower's financial affairs in the form of hidden closing costs, balloon payments, high interest charges, and prepayment penalties.

As time showed, it mattered whom the Haroldsons invited to share their home. When lenders are generative—like authentic community banks, credit unions, and CDFIs—home loans can enhance homeowners' well-being. But when lenders are extractive, homeowners can end up with the twig they've handed over being wielded against them like a two-by-four.

The ownership design of the lender makes much of the difference. In a world where most of us can't make much sense of the six-inch stack of documents we sign at a closing, we fall back on trust. We don't expect those documents on that walnut desktop to contain hidden time bombs, set to go off at some future date and destroy our lives.

The purpose and structure of lenders has a lot to do with why some conduct lending as an act of war while others conduct it as a neighborly relationship. Yet who lenders are connected to also matters. The *networks of trading and investing* that surround lenders have an enabling effect. Generative enterprise is supported by Ethical Networks, the rating systems and legal charters and groups of ethical investors that serve as a collective force, holding in place social and ecological norms. Extractive enterprise, on the other hand, is wrapped up in Commodity Networks, willing to trade or invest in anything—even destructive loans like those made to the Haroldsons—as long as there's profit to be made.

Trading in the Commodity Networks of finance is vital to how money is made on Wall Street. After the initial act of capital creation, after wealth is drawn out of a house like 56 James Court, other conjuring acts of wealth creation occur that are unimaginably ingenious. Here in Manhattan, over and over again, formulas have been devised that create wealth—in mystically growing quantities—out of thin air.

ACTS OF FINANCIAL ALCHEMY

If I or the protesters who later gathered here had managed to get past the guards and crash through one of the sealed entrances of the New York Stock Exchange, it wouldn't have mattered much. There's no one in this seat of government to sit down and negotiate with. No one's in charge. The essential action of the place is mathematical. That's why its magic remains impenetrable to most people. People working on the floor of the Exchange, like my brother once did, don't run the place or even need to fully understand how it runs—in the same way that people don't need to understand how their home heating system runs, yet still they manage to stay warm. The genius of it all is built into the architecture. It's designed into the logic of the system.

It's hard for us to grasp this. So in the wake of financial crises, the inevitable hunt for villains has gone on, and quite a few, not surprisingly, have been found. But the heart of the matter is more subtle—more ordinary and more mystical, both. The action of finance is mercurial: not theft but ingenious sleight of hand.

The god known in Roman mythology as Mercury is in Greek mythology known as Hermes. He is the god of commerce invoked in Homeric hymn as a shape-shifter, "blandly cunning … a cattle driver, a bringer of dreams, a watcher by night."[4] Hermes is the patron of boundaries and of the travelers who cross them—the god of exchange and commerce. Hermes is a deified trickster.[5]

He's an apt symbol for the magnetic force that pulled the housing and financial systems out of their customary orbit and into the path of crisis. In the process of exchange, or trading—in the issuance and sale of mortgages, and in the issuance and sale of ownership shares in banks—alchemy happens.

Financial wealth not only is released from property.
It grows.

In the mercurial process of trading, the liberated molecules of owner-ship are spun and spun again into a larger body of wealth.

THE MAGIC OF THE MULTIPLE

At the heart of the design of the publicly traded company is a bit of alchemy called the *magic of the multiple*. It's a capital formation process similar to the issuance of a mortgage. In the same way that value is drawn out of a house, it can also be drawn out of a company, like a bank. Its value is lique-fied and released into the world through issuing *equity*.

The company comes to lead an invisible, parallel life alongside its material existence—assuming a second identity as a financial asset. This time, the asset is embodied in shares of stock sold to investors. This is the process that mutual banks in the United States and building societies in the UK went through when they demutualized and became publicly traded. They liberated the inert financial value of their institutions (along the way, allowing executives to pocket some of that liberated wealth for themselves).

Yet this wealth doesn't just go into capital markets and circulate there, unchanged. It grows with the growth of profits, also called *earnings*. Here's how.

For the sake of mathematical simplicity, let's imagine JPMorgan Chase has $100 million in revenue and makes 20 percent profit. (Its revenues are in fact much higher, but its profits, in the years before the initial downturn, were pretty close to 20 percent.)[6] How much will shareholders pay to own a machine that can churn out $20 million a year in earnings? That deter-mines the value (market capitalization) of a place like JPMorgan Chase.

Let's say that we as investors decide to pay ten times earnings, for a total of $200 million. This means that as owners of the machine, we can in ten years' time earn back our entire investment. And our machine will then hypothetically go on churning out $20 million in profits every year. This company has a price-to-earnings ratio of ten (that is, the company's stock price is equivalent to ten times its earnings—roughly what JPMorgan Chase's P/E ratio was in 2007).[7]

But let's say the machine is revving up. Everyone expects it to churn out $22 million in profits next year and $25 million the year after. Now what will investors pay? We might pay 15 times earnings. But let's say lots of people are eager to buy this machine and there's an auction. The price begins to climb. Now we might pay 20 times earnings. The P/E ratio rises to 20, which is where it stood for JPMorgan Chase in early 2010.

Let's unpack what happened. At a P/E ratio of 10, this company is worth $200 million. But with the P/E ratio climbing to 20, *the same earnings stream is suddenly worth not $200 million but $400 million.* The perceived value of the company doubles. Money appears out of thin air. It's due in part to auction psychology, and also to speculation. When speculators jump in en masse and chase shares, those shares can inflate beyond their underlying value. The trading process unleashes the *magic of the multiple.*

This is why publicly traded companies often have higher valuations than privately owned firms. The difference is something that economist Paul Samuelson tried to calculate in the bull market of the 1990s. He estimated that a company was worth about three times the value of its annual gross output if it was privately held and *five times* the value if it was publicly traded.[8]

Say you and I own a company with $5 million in gross output, or revenue. By Samuelson's calculation, if we sell that company in a private sale, it'll fetch three times output, or $15 million. But if we take that same company public, it'll fetch five times output, or $25 million. The trading of ownership shares "creates" $10 million out of thin air.

Don't worry if you don't entirely get the math. It boils down to this: Taking a company public is like getting a license to mint money. Most of the time, people act as though this wealth is free, as though it just falls out of the sky. But it comes with a hidden cost. Watch how that cost is paid over time, and by whom.

Imagine that Bill Howard changes his mind and decides to demutualize Beverly Cooperative Bank, turning it into a publicly traded company. He liberates the wealth locked up in that company and sets it trading in capital markets. Now he is no longer the president of a mutually owned bank, designed to serve its community; he's the CEO of a bank with an ownership structure aimed at maximizing profits. Instead of being controlled by a stabilizing feedback loop, the bank's behavior is now controlled by a reinforcing feedback loop. Profit is supposed to increase as fast as possible, forever. One design pattern keeping this loop turning is stock options. Whenever the bank's stock price goes up, Bill is rewarded handsomely.

The community he is serving now is Wall Street, which exerts an enormous and continual pressure to keep earnings (profits) growing. Let's say the bank's stock has a P/E ratio of 20.[9] That means that *every dollar of profit the CEO can squeeze out is transformed into $20.*

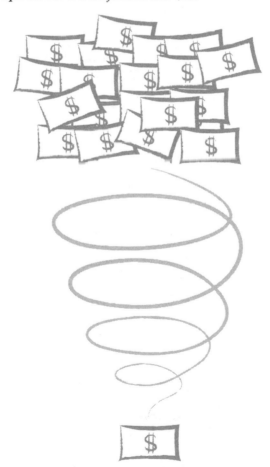

THE MAGIC OF THE MULTIPLE

For every additional $100 of profit he can squeeze out of the bank, he will create—Eureka!—$2,000 in shareholder value. The alchemy of stock trading multiplies that $100 in earnings by 20. If this magic works wonders for investors, it can have a less benevolent impact on others—like employees, the community, and customers. If Bill can somehow extract $100 more in junk fees out of a borrower, he will create $2,000 in shareholder wealth. If he can charge $100 more in fees to checking account holders, shareholders will get another $2,000. If he can shave $100 off employee wages, shareholders again pocket $2,000. If he can reduce employee benefits by $100, another $2,000 shows up for shareholders.

If the magic of the multiple is indeed a form of modern alchemy, it also represents a kind of sleight of hand. Every dollar it can surreptitiously

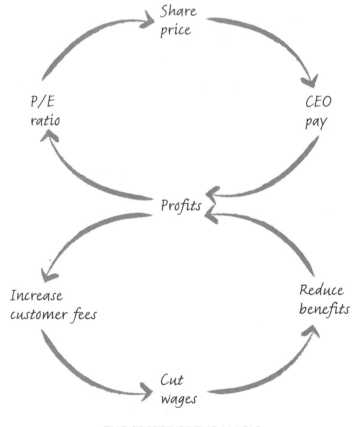

THE SECRET OF THE MAGIC

slip out of one pocket appears magically as $20 in the pocket of another. Consider that the revenues of publicly traded companies represent more than three-quarters of global GDP, and you begin to get a sense of the machinery behind wealth disparities.

Who *should* be benefiting from the wealth that companies create is rarely discussed in corporate boardrooms. The answer is assumed. As CEO of a publicly traded firm, Bill Howard will encounter general agreement—from his board, the financial markets, the business press, business schools, and the courts—that maximizing shareholder value is the noblest aim of his company. He is fulfilling his moral obligation, his fiduciary duty, to serve the company's owners. Bill will thus have built-in incentives, and social permission, to take advantage of his borrowers, to work against the interests of his depositors, to pay his employees as little as possible, and to line his own pockets to the maximum extent.

It's little surprise that in the grip of this system logic, a lender like Ameriquest was happy to give the Haroldsons a mortgage ill-suited to their needs. This was less a human transaction between two people than the mechanical workings of a globe-spanning system aimed at extracting as much financial wealth as possible. The system was doing what it was designed to do.

A THING APART

The tornado-force pressure of wealth creation has historically created a powerful pull in the world of finance. The stock market that began as a servant to industry—a tool to help fund new companies—ultimately subjugated business to its power, says Lawrence Mitchell, dean of Case Western Reserve School of Law, in *The Speculation Economy: How Finance Triumphed Over Industry*. Beneath the angelic countenance gracing the New York Stock Exchange, this temple came to house a fierce and exacting god of commerce. As the Industrial Revolution proceeded, Mitchell wrote, the stock market "quickly came to be the main thrust behind business, the power behind the boardroom," driving the decisions of business and the path of the nation's economic development.

The magnetic force of this place shifted the goals of
industry from the manufacture of goods
to the manufacture of stock.

Businesses were no longer created to serve the living community. They were created to manufacture financial wealth. Along the way, ownership shifted from the human hands of company founders into the anonymous hands of the marketplace, where people might "own" companies they'd never set eyes upon.

Ownership was no longer a tangible, enduring relationship with something real. It took on a machinelike quality, creating buckets of commodity earnings like widgets off an assembly line. The logic of it, in Mitchell's language, turned the financial marketplace into "a thing apart, an institution without face or form whose insatiable desire for profit demanded satisfaction from even the most powerful corporations it created." Its winged power to spin the capital extracted from business transactions into greater and greater wealth became an unstoppable force—a vortex of wealth creation too powerful to resist.[10] Finance became the master force, Financial Purpose the purpose of the economy itself.

If the behavior of banks has to do initially with how hungry their owners are, Wall Street turned insatiable hunger into a permanent, impersonal condition. The stock market embodied a starkly new kind of ownership, reduced to a single laserlike focus: the quest to extract financial wealth in infinitely growing quantity.

As Bill Howard told me, "When you're public, you have a different constituency," a financial constituency. That changes the culture of a bank. If Beverly Cooperative Bank had gone public, he said, he could no longer have a mission of serving the community. His mission would be to create returns for stockholders.

Yet as powerful as the magical force of Wall Street is, it alone can't fully account for the mess we're in. Because it isn't new. When my brother first worked at Salomon Brothers in the 1970s, the magic of the multiple was already an old story. Something—or some things—happened in recent decades to dramatically change the way financial firms behaved and the way borrowers like the Haroldsons behaved. New forms of alchemy were set loose. And one of those new forms of alchemy was speed.

SPEED TAKES OVER

From the subway stop where I get off, it's a few short blocks to 84th and Madison, where I meet Michael at Le Pain Quotidien for breakfast one morning. As we take our seats in the back at a battered wooden table, I ask him to talk about the changes he saw in his three decades on Wall Street—to explain why and how things had become so much faster and more fierce.

The small specialists' firm my brother joined, Adler Coleman, was a partnership. Salomon Brothers, Lehman Brothers, and Goldman Sachs were all partnerships in those days. Their primary focus was on long-term investments, Michael tells me. "A lot of things played together to create a more short-term focus," he says.

A major element of the shift was a change in ownership design. These partnerships—Salomon, Lehman, Goldman Sachs—all became publicly traded firms. "That's certainly one of the key reasons why we got into the mess we got into," Michael says. "When I was there, we took a lot of risk, but because firms were partnerships, we were using our own money. If all of a sudden you're using someone else's money, they end up taking all the risk while you make all the money. That's going to change your behavior dramatically. You're going to get riskier and riskier."

Another element of change was the removal of fixed fees on trades, which meant that trading became cheaper and volume increased. This went hand in hand with a shift in how stocks were valued. "When I started as a trader, we traded in fractions," Michael explains, "one-eighth and one-quarter, three-eighths, a half." A stock might be priced at ten and a quarter ($10.25) or ten and an eighth ($10.125). Over time, prices went to pennies. "You make a lot of money when you trade at one-eighth. You don't make any when you trade at a penny," he says. Since traders were pocketing less on each trade, they sought greater volume in order to make money. The pieces were falling into place for the volume and speed of trading to soar.

Michael felt the increased velocity in his job as auctioneer on the floor. His job was to match buyers and sellers of a particular stock, finding the price on which they agreed. As the speed of trading took off, "it got to the point where my mind was way ahead of my mouth," Michael says. "As the order flow is coming in so rapidly—buy this, sell that—I'm giving directions to a clerk at a terminal. But by the time a price is coming out of my mouth, it's too late, because another order has come in and the price has changed. When I got older," he says (and "old" in the trading world meant 50-ish), "my mind wasn't as fast. That's when I knew it was time to leave."

The pressure Michael felt was rising throughout the stock market, as the specialist system was giving way to computerized trading. In his early years at the Exchange, the number of shares trading in a given day might total 25 million. He left in 2002, and by the end of that decade, trading reached an unfathomable 6.2 *billion* shares in an average day. The open outcry system, the verbal, human exchange that Michael took part in, was morphing into the ethereal new form of electronic trading. Liquidity— the ability to move into and out of equity investments with ease—was becoming instantaneously at hand, as a perpetual sea of buy and sell orders moved about the globe at close to the speed of light.[11]

The phenomenon of *high-frequency trading* was taking shape, at speeds that made the blink of an eye seem slow. Velocity leaped far beyond the capability of any auctioneer's human utterance, coming to be measured in thousandths of a second (milliseconds), even millionths of a second (microseconds).[12] The metamorphosis occurred because traders developed ingenious new strategies for financial alchemy. One strategy was *latency arbitrage*, vacuuming up the tiny price differences that occurred in the infinitesimally small time lags between the sending of an order from one trading platform and its arrival at another. Another strategy might simply be called *deception*. Traders issued fake orders and canceled them a nanosecond later to get a sneak peek at prices that people would accept ($26.10? just kidding; $26.11? just kidding; $26.12? just kidding; $26.13? deal). In some trading models, deceptive bids, or canceled orders, represented up to 99 percent of all bids placed.[13]

High-frequency trading came to account for close to *three-quarters of all stock trading* in the United States. Firms employed robot computers to do daily battle—buying and selling securities tens of thousands of times *per second*—using algorithms, or computer codes, programmed some-times just to trick other algorithms into doing trades, in the high-stakes gambling of Casino Finance.[14]

OWNERSHIP BECOMES ITS OPPOSITE

The whole thing is like an absurdist drama. Only it isn't. This is virtu-ally the entire infrastructure of the US economy: the so-called ownership shares in all public companies, which is to say, the liquefied value of the buildings and the products and the revenue flows of the vast majority of the economy. Mortgages on homes like 56 James Court are bound up in the madness, even if it's hard to tell how. Mostly homes have become little bits of revenue streams—little bits of interest payments and closing costs and late fees and outsized prepayment penalties—which feed the swirling rivers of earnings that make the vortex spin. To keep it spinning, those riv-ers of earnings must grow every year. That means executives must generate more fees, more mortgages, faster trading. It's a world—probably the only world—in which the Haroldsons' five mortgages in five years make perfect sense.

Even at companies that don't practice high-frequency trading, stock ownership has become more short term. One study of 800 institutional fund managers found that the typical holding period for stocks is a year and a half. For nearly one in five institutional fund managers, stocks are held an average of a year or less.[15]

The very concept of ownership, in its origins thousands of years ago, was about the end of nomadic wandering and the advent of a permanent rela-tionship with the land. The human quest was about seeking, as Rainer Maria Rilke put it, "something pure, contained, narrow, human—our own small strip of orchard between river and rock."[16] That's ownership. It's about finding our place, settling down. As I'd seen it in my father's life, and the lives of my grandfather and uncles, owning a company meant nursing it through good times and bad, being responsible for it and for the people who worked there. But in the world of Wall Street, "ownership" is the opposite of permanent. It's the opposite of responsible. It has become a force that unsettles lives, helping to throw people like the Haroldsons and millions of others out of their homes.

That transformation happened when, in the division of ownership, in the breaking of property into its dual identities of real asset and financial asset, *the financial side came to exert too great a force.* The lure of wealth creation and the strength of the financial whirlwind became too great. The living balance was lost. What mattered now was Casino Finance, the world of "liquidity"—of placing bets, extracting wealth, and getting rid of ownership, over and over again, as fast as the human mind could imagine.

HEADING OUT

As Michael and I head out of the restaurant, an older man at a nearby table lays an arm on Michael's sleeve. "I couldn't help overhearing what you were saying," he says, looking up into my brother's face. He refers to a comment that Michael made about earlier days on Wall Street, when traders he worked with day in and day out had no tolerance for deception. "Your word was your bond," Michael had told me. "If you were dishonest, it was very, very hard to make it up. You had to resolve issues immediately. It wasn't like you could say, let's go talk for a few minutes," he'd said.

"I also worked on Wall Street for many years," the gentleman says to Michael, "and you're right, your word was your bond. That's the way it was. But it's not anymore."

A new ethos had taken hold, and it made people like my brother and this gentleman recoil. Wall Street has always been about making money, but in recent years that aim became massively accelerated and over-the-top aggressive. The whole scheme of equity trading—the process of trading "ownership" shares—became programmed warfare. And that entire system was on autopilot. Moving at top speed. If it had become routine to trick and deceive other traders at the upper reaches of the system, who were invisible and needed never be dealt with again, how much less visible were ordinary people like the Haroldsons, whose mortgages were many steps removed? The tangible world of home ownership, the real world, was receding to the vanishing point.

The banks that the Haroldsons dealt with were not all publicly traded—yet when they sold off their mortgage loans, they sold them to financial firms that *were* publicly traded. In the end, the twig of ownership from the Haroldson house ended up as another spinning electron in public financial markets. As mortgages were churned out, they were sold to bigger financial firms that specialized not only in lending but in trading—trading mortgages, trading equities, trading derivatives, and so on.

Most of that trading in the United States—more than *90 percent*—is generated by just six big, publicly held financial firms. Two are JPMorgan Chase and Morgan Stanley, the twin offspring of the House of Morgan, that exclusive club across the street from the Exchange. The others are Goldman Sachs, Wells Fargo, Bank of America, and Citigroup.[17] The willingness of these big financial firms to buy and repackage loans served as a lubricant, an accelerant to aggressive mortgage lending throughout the nation. These were the titans of Wall Street that kept mortgage lending turning in its widening gyre.

The capital formation process that these giants set in motion was another form of financial alchemy. It involved speed, and that speed helped create a new phenomenon of size. The size of institutions "too big to fail" is part of it. But from a systems perspective, there's something else at work that's even bigger. We might call it, simply, overload.

....

FOUR

OVERLOAD

The Expanding House of Claims

Heading from New York back to Boston on the Acela train, I found myself turning over in my mind something Michael had said. It was about investment banking firms' changing their ownership structures from partnerships to publicly traded companies. I'd been so engrossed in our conversation about speed, I'd glossed over that point. But I realized how critical it might be. Why hadn't I heard others talking about this?

Back home, I dug around on the Web and found an academic paper exploring the changes in culture that occurred when Salomon Brothers went public in 1981, Lehman Brothers in 1984, and Goldman Sachs in 1999. Authors Richard Freedman and Jill Vohr of the Stern School of Business at New York University said this ownership shift had gone hand in hand with a dramatic change in the investment banking industry, from relationship banking to transactional banking—from customers' having a long-term relationship with a single bank to an approach of searching around constantly for the best deal. They also said the shift in ownership structures accompanied disturbing trends at these firms: greater internal conflict, more greed (if that seemed possible), shorter tenure among employees, and an increasingly short-term focus.[1] It was a telling portrait of what it meant to become a publicly traded firm.

Casting around further, I discovered that Michael Lewis wrote about this ownership shift in *The Big Short*—his look at who profited amid the 2008 meltdown. In his closing pages, he observed that "you could trace the biggest financial crisis in the history of the world back to a decision" made by John Gutfreund, when, "in 1981, he'd turned Salomon Brothers from a private partnership into Wall Street's first public corporation." Had it remained a partnership, Lewis wrote, the firm would not have leveraged itself so dangerously, taking on $35 of debt for every $1 of assets it held, as Salomon Brothers had. No partnership, Lewis wrote, "would have sought to game the rating agencies, or leapt into bed with loan sharks," like the firms that did predatory mortgage lending. "The short-term expected gain would not have justified the long-term expected loss."

When a partnership becomes publicly traded, somebody else takes all the risk, and you make all the money, my brother had said. Lewis said the same thing slightly differently. When Gutfreund took Salomon public, he and the other partners "not only made a quick killing, they transferred the ultimate financial risk from themselves to their shareholders," he wrote. Risk taking accelerated. And when risky loans turned sour, more than a trillion dollars of the stuff was ultimately transferred to US taxpayers, Lewis continued, as the Federal Reserve stepped in to purchase bad sub-prime mortgages from banks.

Lewis concluded: "Combing through the rubble of the avalanche, the decision to turn the Wall Street partnership into a public corporation looked a lot like the first pebble kicked off the top of the hill."[2]

What started the financial avalanche was a change in ownership design—a shift from partnership to publicly traded company.

Partnerships like Goldman Sachs and Lehman Brothers were not the only ones making that shift. When big banks gobbled up locally owned banks, when mutual banks converted to public ownership, and when the not-for-profit New York Stock Exchange was sold to Euronext, more and more of the financial sector flowed into that single ownership design: the publicly traded corporation. It's an ownership design on autopilot, controlled by gamblers shooting chits around the globe thousands of times per second.

Its essence is insatiability. However much money these companies make one year, they need to make more the next. This design is also about institutionalized irresponsibility. The aim is to get somebody else to bear the risk. Thus the logic of the whole system led to a point where folks turned to creating toxic loans after all the reasonable loans had been made. Who cared, as long as the garbage could be thrown in someone else's backyard? Then at some point, the whole world filled up with garbage.

The big banks kept the machine running—buying bad mortgages from predatory lenders with one hand, repackaging and selling them to investors with the other. What kept the big banks themselves in overdrive were the reinforcing feedback loops that governed their ownership design. It was all aimed at financial wealth creation. What could be better? And yet at some point, it tipped over into something else, for a reason that the system logic could not begin to encompass:

The house of financial wealth had grown too large.

After decade upon decade of siphoning more and more financial wealth, spinning it out into larger and larger bodies of assets, the global house of Wall Street had come to overshadow the Main Street base on which it stood. Yet in a system engineered to create that growing superstructure, it was impossible to see that its swollen size was now the problem.

PHANTOM ASSETS

To picture this state of affairs, it's useful to think of two economies. As economic historian Fernand Braudel observed, "We tend to see the economy as a homogenous reality," when in fact two economies existed as far back as the 15th century. The one most written about is the market economy, also called the *real economy*. It's where people own houses and make and sell real things.

But there's a "second shadowy zone, hovering about the sunlit world of the market economy," Braudel wrote. This is the *financial economy*, where financiers manipulate exchange to their advantage—where "a few wealthy merchants in eighteenth-century Amsterdam or sixteenth-century Genoa could throw whole sectors of the European or world economy into confusion." Instead of being about creating things that people need, the financial economy is about accumulating power, Braudel wrote. It's where a tiny financial elite creates or benefits from anomalies, zones of disturbance, to amass vast wealth. The financial economy "represents the favoured domain of capitalism ... the only *real* capitalism," he concluded. "Without this zone, capitalism is unthinkable: this is where it takes up residence and prospers."[3]

The financial economy is in essence a *collection of assets*: stocks, bonds, loans, mortgages, and the rest. These are all *claims against the real economy*. Every dollar of debt owed by one party is held by another party as an asset. The second party has a claim against the first. Thus the Haroldsons owed $462,500 on their final mortgage, and investors held those same dollars in their portfolios as assets. Those assets were claims against the Haroldsons' income and against the value of 56 James Court, which could be seized and sold as a way to repay the debt. Similarly, assets in the stock market— shares of stock—are claims against the value of companies.

All forms of financial wealth are claims against something real. That real thing—the house, the company—is the true wealth.[4]

The financial economy can be pictured as a sphere dwelling above the real economy and drawing on its energy. In the early 1980s, these two worlds were in rough parity. The sum of global financial assets was roughly equal to global GDP. There was roughly a dollar of assets (claims) for every dollar of flows through the economy. But as the pursuit of wealth extracted more from the real economy—more mortgages, more fees, more profits, more bits of wealth that Wall Street wove like spun gold into substances of larger size—the sum of financial claims expanded massively. By the end of 2005, according to an International Monetary Fund analysis, financial claims reached nearly *four times* global GDP. There were roughly four dollars of claims for every dollar of GDP.[5]

The Haroldsons' outsized $462,500 mortgage was one speck of sand in one brick in that overbuilt house of claims. But it told the tale. A couple that in 2002 held a $233,000 mortgage had within four years come to owe a debt nearly twice as large. As the couple spun out of one mortgage and into another, then another, then another, there was an artificial swelling of

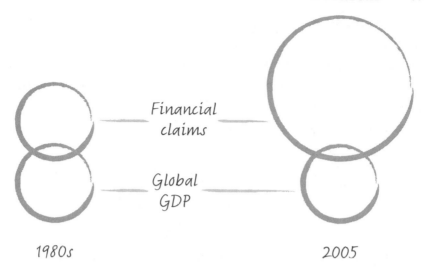

Financial
claims

Global
GDP

1980s   2005

FINANCIAL ECONOMY AND REAL ECONOMY

claims against the house. Because those claims were beyond anything the hamstrung couple could pay, they became unsupportable.

It was 2010 when 56 James Court was finally sold. I discovered this when I revisited the register of deeds site— about a year after my visit to the house with Orion—and found that a real estate agent had nabbed the house for just $206,000. Only with this new transaction was the identity of the long-invisible owner finally revealed. The dismemberment of ownership and subsequent legal messes had so clogged the system that it had taken years—as the house stood empty and weed-choked—before the details of the transactions had posted to the register of deeds.

But at last, there it was: the Haroldsons' final mortgage had been held by Aegis Asset-Backed Securities Trust. It was a structured investment vehicle concocted by Aegis. There was no single owner of the single mortgage on this one house, just a nest of connections—a black box into which mortgages were placed, where they were blended and mixed, out of which issued little bits of claims on the stuff that investors could hold as assets. It was a microcosm of the shape of the whole system. Aegis, which had written the Haroldsons' final mortgage (as well as two earlier mortgages), had apparently tried to emulate the big guys, doing its own slicing and dicing and reselling of mortgage derivatives. In the process, it went bankrupt.

The reason, no doubt, had to do with the fact that some of the trust's mortgages turned out to be phantom assets. Half of the Haroldsons' last mortgage was thin air. Investors thought they "owned" more than $200,000 in claims that in the end would never be paid. In the larger system, there were millions of similar cases.

Derivatives may have been the straw that brought the structure down. But the real problem was more vast.

> *The global superstructure of assets had come to*
> *exceed the load-bearing capacity of its foundation*
> *in the real economy.*

The collapse of the mortgage on 56 James Court was one of the first signs of trouble with that overstressed foundation. But the whole edifice was set for a fall.

THE SILENT GROWTH OF "FINANCIALIZATION"

The mammoth swelling of claims against the real economy was the result of a process known as *financialization*. It is often defined as *the shift in an economy's center of gravity from production to finance*. More broadly, author Kevin Phillips defined financialization as a process in which financial services take over "the dominant economic, cultural, and political role in a national economy." It's not clear who coined the term. But it's a phenomenon that, as Phillips remarked before the meltdown, long remained underresearched and underanalyzed.[6]

In the United States, it was the turn of the millennium when, as Phillips put it, "[m]oving money around ... surpassed making things as a share of the US gross domestic product." Beginning in the 1980s, financial deregulation encouraged the finance, insurance, and real estate sectors—collectively, the FIRE sector—to interweave in so many holding companies that it became routine to see it as a single sector. By 2000, revenues of that sector reached 20 percent of GDP. Manufacturing slipped under 15 percent. That was a massive change from the postwar years, when making things represented close to 30 percent of GDP, while financial services was a relatively small 11 percent.[7]

In terms of profits, the shift was more dramatic. By 2004, Phillips observed, financial firms took in nearly *40 percent of all US profits*—while manufacturers got just 5 percent. At the root of financialization was a single factor: debt.

> *The United States had shifted from manufacturing stuff to manufacturing debt.*

This was how the financial economy had grown so large. The growth of debt occurred not only in the United States but globally, and it involved much more than home mortgages. As economist Nouriel Roubini wrote in *Foreign Policy*:

> The credit excesses that created this disaster were global. There were many bubbles, and they extended beyond housing in many countries to commercial real estate mortgages and loans, to credit cards, auto loans, and student loans. There were bubbles for the securitized products that converted these loans and mortgages into complex, toxic, and destructive financial instruments. And there were still more bubbles for local government borrowing, leveraged buyouts, hedge funds, commercial and industrial loans, corporate bonds, commodities, and credit default swaps. ... Taken together, these amounted to the biggest asset and credit bubble in human history.[8]

If debt expansion had been building for decades, its final swelling took place as the wealth engine of the stock market was stalling. In 2000, the dot-com bubble burst, leaving the NASDAQ composite index a decade later trading at less than *half* of its peak value.[9] A not-dissimilar fate met the Dow Jones Industrial Average. From 1980, when the Dow stood at 1,000, it tripled within a decade, and tripled again in another decade—hitting the astonishing height of 10,000 at the century's end. Yet there it slowed to a crawl. In the first decade of the new century, it would not surpass 11,000 for any extended period.[10]

There were reasons for that sense of siege at the New York Stock Exchange. Something was happening. Or rather, something had stopped happening. The wealth engine of the stock market was sputtering. As stocks bounced wildly in the years following the 2008 crisis, the price/earnings ratio—that magical brew that multiplied the value of earnings many times over—was losing its potency. In the first decade of the 2000s, the P/E ratio of the S&P 500 (an index of large companies) reached the extraordinary level of 30. By 2010, it had fallen to 15.[11] The magic of the multiple was shrinking. The alchemy of Wall Street appeared to be approaching invisible limits. At least temporarily.

WHEN MORE MEANS LESS

If investors see these breaks in a once-steady upward climb as a misfortune—and hopefully a temporary one—systems thinking offers a different perspective. One of the signature insights of systems thinking is this:

There will always be limits to growth.

No living system grows rapidly forever. Yet this is how linear growth is conceptualized—as a straight line heading upward. As James Gleick wrote in *Chaos: Making a New Science*, "Linear relationships are easy to think about: the more the merrier."[12] The truth is, a system that attempts to grow in that way will hasten its arrival at its own limits.

A quantity growing exponentially toward a limit will reach that limit in an unexpectedly short time.

The Dow triples in a decade, triples again in another decade, and then boom—it hits some kind of ceiling. The NASDAQ soars and then crashes. In a linear mind-set, more can always be followed by more. But in nonlinear reality—the reality of living systems—more can sometimes lead to less. As Gleick wrote, "Nonlinearity means that the act of playing the game has a way of changing the rules."[13]

In a linear relationship, Donella Meadows explained, you put 10 pounds of fertilizer on your field, and your yield goes up a couple of bushels. You put on 20 pounds; it goes up a couple more bushels. There's a straight line of increase. But in nonlinear reality, "the relationships between cause and effect can only be drawn with curves or wiggles, not with a straight line," Meadows wrote. If you put 200 pounds of fertilizer on your field, your yield won't go up at all. Put on 300, she continued, and your yield will *go down*—because you've damaged the soil with too much of a good thing.[14]

But limits are an uncomfortable fit in the financial mind-set. Even after the bursting of the NASDAQ bubble, the exhaustion of the Dow, the explosion of the housing collapse, the near-meltdown of the global economy, and years of economic misery that followed, the giant California pension fund CalPERS was still projecting future annual earnings of 7.75 percent on its investments. In truth, over the previous decade, it had earned on average less than half of that, according to Richard Riordan, former mayor of Los Angeles. But financial models don't draw the future in curves and wiggles. They draw straight lines.[15]

So it was that as the wealth engine of the stock market stalled, there were still buckets and buckets of financial wealth sloshing around the globe seeking places to earn that 8 percent, and the financial sector continued its search for new ways to absorb it all. Part of the answer was the swelling of debt. Banks sent credit card offers by the armload into homes. They urged families like the Haroldsons to turn rising home values into cash through refinancing and home equity loans. Companies piled debt on themselves with a record issuance of junk bonds. And governments built up debt as they ran deficits to pay for tax cuts, defense spending, and ultimately the massive bailout of financial institutions.

DEREGULATION AND DESIGN

On the consumer side, that torrential flow of money up into the financial sphere was unleashed in part by the abandonment of usury laws. Left behind was the ethical notion that there might be limits of decency and fair dealing to how much finance could extract from the pocketbooks of ordinary people. On the side of industry, the process was enabled by deregulation of many kinds. There was the dismantling in 1999 of the Glass-Steagall Act, which had separated banking from more speculative activities. Interstate banking restrictions had also been lifted, and massive bank mergers followed, leading to the demise of many community banks and the emergence of superbanks like Citibank and Bank of America. Beside them rose other towering presences, operating outside the reach of financial regulation: the investment banks, hedge funds, and private equity firms in the *shadow banking* sector, where much financing activity migrated.[16]

The whole process was aimed at transforming every conceivable molecule of economic value into a financial asset. It was Financial Purpose on a planetary scale. In truth, it was the *transformation of real wealth into financial wealth*—the shifting of assets from one side of the ownership equation to the other, from the real wealth of ordinary people to the financial assets of the elite.

This is what Occupy Wall Street would call the 1 percent problem. The relatively modest assets of the 99 percent, like the Haroldsons, were being transformed into debt, to be held as the assets possessed in large part by the 1 percent. After decades of this silent ownership shift, the top 1 percent wealthiest came to own more than half of the assets in the United States and 70 percent of all financial assets.[17]

Deregulation set the process loose. Yet beneath deregulation lay a deeper issue. *What had been deregulated?* Had it been the local knitting circle or the YWCA that was set loose, global economic crisis would not likely have been the result.

> *What had been deregulated was the essential architecture of extractive ownership—that institutionalized drive to maximize financial gains.*

Extractive design didn't create that drive. It began in the human heart. But extractive forms of ownership took financial wealth creation as a starting point, wrapped themselves around it, called it their purpose, measured progress toward it, rewarded it, and sought to remove all barriers that stood in its way. What began as a human impulse—one among many impulses—became an institutionalized, collective force of massive scale. The design of extractive ownership became, in essence, the design of the economy. It was a global engine driving toward a single goal. And deregulation removed the brakes.

The financial economy became swollen to four times gross domestic product (GDP) because all the energies of the system were focused on moving wealth up into the financial sphere. The aim was to liquidate and absorb the value of the real world, to keep the gyre of finance turning. Generatively designed financial institutions—community banks, CDFIs, credit unions—kept their energies rooted in the real economy. Their aim was to meet the needs of life, to build real wealth. But one form of ownership was devouring the other.

As financial ownership became swollen, real ownership was transformed into a kind of debt peonage, where a couple like the Haroldsons might pay and pay and pay, and in the end own nothing. Between 2000 and 2004, home values soared by 40 percent, but homeowners ended up with a *lower percentage of equity ownership* in their own homes.[18] The gains in home values went to creditors. What happened to the Haroldsons happened not only to countless others, but also to the GDP of the global economy. Yet the aim of extractive ownership remained the same: to create still more financial assets.

There was also that other part of the operating system: *minimize risk.* This was the next force I needed to trace to complete this design journey. If extractive ownership had a natural tendency to kick the system into overdrive, there was another tool of ownership that made folks feel secure operating in that hyper-risky way: derivatives. The question began to formulate in my mind: how could I pay a visit to the abstract world of derivatives?

LOSING TOUCH WITH REALITY

I check my map to pinpoint where I am to meet my friend for lunch: the Boston Stock Exchange building, a 20-minute walk from the Tellus Institute, across the Boston Common to the Financial District. I'm on my way to see John Katovich, a longtime participant in the Corporation 20/20 project and one of the most creative thinkers I know, in both traditional and generative forms of finance. One of the founders of Katovich & Kassan Law Group in San Francisco and the former chief counsel for the Pacific Stock Exchange, John was for the moment chief regulatory officer at the Boston Stock Exchange.

He had moved to Boston because that exchange agreed to let him explore the creation of a local stock exchange and a socially responsible stock exchange, in return for John's helping them with their regulatory needs. But within a few months of his arrival, the Boston Stock Exchange was sold to NASDAQ. Its operations were moved out of Boston. John found himself chief regulator of a piece that remained: the Boston Options Exchange, the hub where stock options were traded. As it turned out, he would move back to the Bay Area a few months after our meeting. But for a brief window of time, his presence in Boston offered me, serendipitously, a way to take a renegade insider's tour of the world of derivatives in the form of their plain vanilla variation: the stock option.

Stock options are among the simplest forms of derivatives, which I thought might make them a reasonable stand-in for that larger family of financial vehicles *derived from*—a step (or two or three) removed from—securities like stocks and bonds. Visiting the exchange where stock options are traded seemed a way to find the ground beneath the esoteric financial instruments that played such a fateful role in the life of the Haroldsons. Entire libraries have been written about derivatives and their role in triggering the financial crisis. But what I'm after in this visit is something physical: I want to see what derivatives trading looks like to a person standing somewhere on the earth.

As the Boston Stock Exchange comes into view, I see that it isn't nearly as grand as the New York Stock Exchange. It's 12 stories of creamy white granite, with its own understated elegance—for example, in the lamps on either side of the entrance featuring sculpted figures in flowing robes of bronze. Pulling on that entrance door, I find it locked. Around the corner is another entrance that stands open; inside, men in hard hats and tool belts walk around. The former stock trading floor is being transformed into a bank. The foreman points me to a third entrance, where I enter a narrow marble foyer and take the elevator to the second floor. A small sign on the wall reads, "BOXR: Boston Options Exchange Regulation."

John meets me, and we walk together to the market operations center—"the central control room," he calls it. It's a quiet room with beige carpet, where a few guys sit in swivel chairs. Occasionally they glance at multiple screens where numbers blink. This is the exchange where trades on 215,000 different stock options are cleared. Through these computers 10 million contracts a day flow. Among other things, John tells me, "We're measuring the health of the system." They are at that moment "measuring latencies"—the speed with which orders are executed. Latency is the time between when an order is typed in, somewhere in the world, and the instant it is posted to the system and executed. "In the old days it was one minute," he says. "Now it's 10 to 15 microseconds" (millionths of a second).

A stock option, John explains, is the right to buy or sell shares of a particular stock at a preset price during some month in the future. "Google has maybe 500 different options," he says. If Google is trading at, say, $450 per share, someone can lay down maybe $5 (the price fluctuates constantly) for the right to buy 100 shares of Google at $460 a share in November. There are likely 499 other variations on this. Which makes sense, sort of.

"You can close your position without ever having owned or touched the actual stock," John adds. Here my ears perk up. "In fact, *most of the time you don't touch the stock*." Options, in other words, are only tangentially related to reality—the "reality" being the momentary price of Google, or any other stock. When you buy an option on Google for which you pay $5, you don't actually need to use that option to buy or sell Google stock. Instead, you might sell the option itself for $10 and pocket the profit. The option itself is the thing you own.

In effect, you're trading little invented pieces of real estate in time. When that tiny piece of real estate opens its doors in November, you can hypothetically stand on it and buy those shares of Google. But in the *vast majority of cases*, you don't. Options are their own universe of financial value, above and beyond the value of the underlying stock. They're something else for traders to own and trade and make money on—like baseball cards, carrying a value entirely apart from the players (such as Google).

For all those financial assets swirling in the financial economy—all those bits of extractive ownership zooming around, searching for a place to land and extract their due—derivatives are a new landing pad. They're a new architecture for extraction, allowing the business of "creating wealth" to stake ownership claims in a new realm. There is the foundational world of the real economy. On top of that stands the financial economy. And above the financial economy floats this more fictional and hence more vast and boundaryless new frontier: the world of derivatives.

THROUGH THE LOOKING GLASS

Stock options are a tiny sliver of this new sphere of value, which has become massively swollen in the era of financialization. The stock option is just one form of derivative, and there are hundreds of other forms, with more being invented all the time. As a whole, financial derivatives comprise a sphere of uncertain size and unimaginable complexity. Charles Morris summed it up nicely in *The Trillion Dollar Meltdown*. While basic financial assets—stocks, bonds, loans, mortgages—before the crisis grew to four times global GDP, on top of that house of claims, derivatives swelled to *ten times* global GDP.[19]

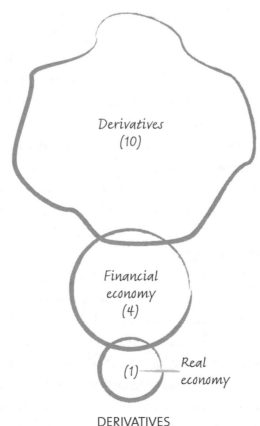

DERIVATIVES

There were reasons why Aegis and Community First Bank were eager to make risky loans to people like the Haroldsons, who in anyone's wildest dreams would never be able to pay them back. Chief among those reasons were two kinds of derivatives. The first was collateralized debt obligations (CDOs). When a mortgage firm issued a mortgage and sold it the next week to, say, Goldman Sachs, that firm sold it again to investors—but first it worked its alchemical magic, turning dross into gold. It placed a batch of mortgages in a blender, sliced and diced them, and then sold off various layers. Investors could buy the cream at the top, the dregs at the bottom, or the stuff in the middle. Investors weren't buying particular mortgages; they were buying *aspects* of mortgages. This was part of what had obscured the ownership of the Haroldsons' home. CDOs were one type of derivative implicated in the meltdown.

There was a second type. It was the reason why investors were blissfully content to buy the dregs at the bottom. It was a form of insurance called a *credit default swap*. It meant that if mortgages turned out to be worthless, the holder could collect on the loss. It was like owning a house and buying fire insurance.

Here's where things get truly weird. It's possible to buy credit default swaps *even when you don't own the entity holding the underlying assets*. These are derivatives called *naked credit default swaps*. With these, in essence, you can buy insurance on a home you don't own. Metaphorically, there can be one house with a hundred insurance policies against it. Then if the house burns down, a hundred people will have to be paid. The payout will be *a hundred times the value of the house*. Now, if this isn't *Alice in Wonderland*, I don't know what is. And it's only one example of the shenanigans going on in the world of derivatives.[20]

A similar derivative is the *synthetic* CDO, which is an investment engineered to behave like a particular basket of mortgages, except—voilà!— there is no underlying basket of mortgages.

Now, consider for a moment. All financial assets are at one time born as claims against something real. A mortgage is a claim against a house. A share of stock is a claim against a company and its stream of profits. Simple derivatives, like the option to buy Google in November at $460, are one step removed from real assets. But then, quietly, at some unheralded moment, the thin thread connecting derivatives to reality was severed. Derivatives were engineered into existence—like *naked* credit default swaps and *synthetic* CDOs—that were claims against thin air.

In the long evolution of capital creation, these derivatives represented an unseen solstice, a moment when the lengthening days of wealth creation reached a zenith and began the turn toward something else, not the creation of wealth but its decay. They were so complicated that few knew any line had been crossed. Some derivative contracts can run to multiple pages in length. Yet as long as only a small number of houses were burning down—as long as mortgages weren't yet going bad—investors were happy to buy this through-the-looking-glass stuff, thinking themselves sophisticated in doing so.

THE FLAW IN THE FORMULA

The problem with the system traces to the organizing principles of extractive ownership. Selling mortgages beyond the point where they make any sense is about *maximizing financial gains*. Nothing in that core rule says, maximize gains only when it makes sense in the larger system. Building concern for the common good into this stuff is considered naive.

The only risk that extractive design cares about
is risk to the self.

That's the flaw. For when the financial sphere is four times global GDP, the moves of finance are like the moves of an 800-pound gorilla deciding where to sit. Some small atom of "self" is no longer the appropriate unit of reference. At work is a global system of market governance: a system of governance and a system of worship, both. When that system is intent on maximizing the gains of the few and disregarding impact on the many, the results can be catastrophic. But extractive ownership design doesn't concern itself with this.

It assumes that risk can be managed at the level of the individual firm or portfolio, using diversification of assets, or derivatives. If an enormous gain for Aegis means certain and massive loss for the Haroldsons, well, tough. What happens to little people is off the radar screen. Thus it was that hard-nosed businesspeople and sophisticated investors drove the world economy to the edge of a precipice, imagining all the while that they were doing what any prudent person would do. They were following the fiduciary duty to maximize gains for investors.

Derivatives in one sense are something new. But in another sense, they're the old system of extractive ownership spinning itself out in ever-newer forms—a Koch snowflake growing larger and larger.

A statement by Ron Chernow, author of *The House of Morgan*, a book about J.P. Morgan, put it all in perspective. "Wall Street for a number of years has been gripped by a quiet crisis," he said, just days after Lehman Brothers collapsed in a fiery heap in September 2008. "Beneath all the financial wizardry, beneath all the financial engineering, there has been an *increasingly desperate search for new sources of profit.* [italics mine]."[21] That's the best simple description of derivatives ever uttered. If assets like stocks and bonds can't spin off wealth fast enough to satisfy investor appetite, it's because they have the pesky habit of remaining tethered to the real world. Ultimately, the best way to satisfy the need for more is to *remove oneself from reality.* That means engineering things *derived from* reality. In the end, it means losing touch with reality.

As John and I take our seats in his office, he shows me how all this looks to a trader. "If you pull up your Thomson Reuters screen, you get a snapshot of some things going on," he says, turning his computer monitor so that I can see it. "This is a snapshot of the world market." On the screen are rows and columns of numbers, many blinking and shifting. One particular entry, 458.04, turns into 458.02, then 458.11, and then again 458.04, in a second or two. That's Google.

"Do you see how fast it's moving?" he asks. "That's actually slow, I would say. Each one of those changes of numbers—.04 to .02 to .11 and back to .04—that's rapid-fire change of price. But underneath that, there are probably thousands of transactions all happening at each one of those prices."

I ask him, is the crazy speed at which it's moving part of the problem?

In a way, yes, John says, because speed creates perpetual pressure for ever-rising financial gain. Yet even with the manual systems of 30 years ago, he says, we could have had a major disaster. The problem is that people have lost touch with one another.

"We don't trade with each other on an interpersonal basis anymore; we trade against this screen," John says. "When my attention is always on immediacy, and I'm a broker out there making a loan to someone I know I'll never see again, I don't care about that person. And the guy behind me writing the loan, he's telling me everything is fine. So even though I know this loan is bizarre, I'm going to do it anyway, because I'm out to make a buck. Everyone in the chain is under the same pressure to produce. Not just the mortgage broker but the CEO of Bank of America, the bank itself, the lawyers who designed the collateralized debt obligation structures, Moody's (a ratings firm), etc."

The result is the creation of loans and other financial products that make little sense. John talks about an old friend who became a mortgage broker in the go-go years, "a wheeler-dealer, a fast talker." John and a colleague asked the fellow if he could write a mortgage for another friend who'd dropped out of society and done nothing for years but travel, live in India, learn the ways of the Buddha. "As a joke, we said, 'Bill, can you get him a mortgage?' He got him a million-dollar mortgage."

"And the guy had no income?"

"He hadn't had any income for 15 years," John says.

"Did he have assets?"

"Not many."

"Wow."

BEYOND PICKET FENCES

The financial system is like an engine that can speed up but not be slowed down. "If you build an engine that can go an unlimited amount of revolutions per minute, it will explode," John says. When early steam engines were built, engineers understood that and added governors to slow them down. "An engine without a governor is not sustainable. But that's what we have right now." Attempts at governance, from the 1930s onward, have been in the form of regulations applied externally. Yet you can't change a system effectively with rules applied from the outside. Adding rules that are fundamentally at odds with a system's own internal guidance system is like putting a picket fence in front of a speeding locomotive. The fence doesn't change the nature of the machine. From a systems perspective, the principle is simple:

Locate responsibility within the system.

This is what CDFIs, credit unions, cooperative banks, and genuine community banks do. These models tend to encourage more responsible behavior by employees, because the notion of serving the community is designed into their fundamental structure. Working to promote and spread these generative alternatives is a very different approach to change. It's about moving, over the long term, toward an economy where responsibility is located within the system.

Promoting these models doesn't immediately solve the problems of the existing financial system. New and better regulations are still needed. But if we as a culture were to more deliberately try to build the generative economy, we might accomplish two things. First, we'd give the energies of the system someplace to flow. As John put it, "You build an alternative standing alongside the existing system so that people can migrate there." Second, we might begin to change the conversation profoundly. By creating a new concept of economic activity, the legitimacy of the current Casino Finance system begins to erode—ultimately creating the cultural readiness for a deeper shift of the whole system.

What, at its core, should that new system be about? This is a question I put to John. If he could design a new financial system, where would he begin?

"I'd start by emphasizing that money is an abstraction," he replies. "All the instruments we trade are abstractions. If I were going to redesign the system, I'd stay closely connected to the real. It would have as its cornerstone a connection to real things."

FIVE

COLLAPSE

The Eroding Middle-Class Base

That reminded me: What happened to the Haroldsons? To bring this journey to a close, I needed to find out what happened to the family on the other side of the ownership equation—not the financial side but the real side. It was time to try again to track them down.

When I'd previously searched for the Haroldsons on the Web, I'd found so many people with similar names that I couldn't call them all. I thought a call out of the blue might not do much good, anyway. I hoped for a personal introduction. Checking back with Orion, I get the name of someone he knows who owns a two-flat across from the Haroldson house, a woman I'll call Toni. When I phone her, she picks up immediately. "I never knew the Haroldsons because they'd already left when I bought my house," she tells me. But she can put me in touch with a Jamaican family, Luis and Alva, who lived next door to the Haroldson house for 25 years. She mentions another neighbor, a retired gentleman, Giuseppe, who's lived on the street for 30 years.* "Call me in a few days," she says.

When I do, there's good news. Luis and Alva have a niece who is friends with the Haroldsons' grandson. They'll be seeing him soon and will pass along word that I want to talk. I ask Toni if she has a phone number for the Haroldsons. "We're working on it," she says brightly. How about a number for Luis and Alva? Toni laughs and says she never needed it. "You just have to show up and knock on their door."

A few weeks and a few unanswered calls later, I finally catch up with Toni again by phone. As soon as I identify myself, she launches in: it's a

---

* Names have been changed to protect privacy. Details are real.

busy day, she's on her way out the door, she's losing her tenant, she has calls to return. "Listen, honey, I'm not going to be able to help you," she says, her tone kindly but exasperated. If I want to know more about the Haroldsons, it looks like I'll have to show up at Luis and Alva's and knock. Later that week, that's what I do.

From the Stonybrook T stop, I walk the few blocks and mount the pebbly concrete steps, seeing a "For Sale" sign in the yard of 56 James Court. "New renovation," it says. The porches have been rebuilt, the trim painted white, new gray siding added, double-pane windows and air conditioners installed. In the yard—freshly mown now—a dozen tiny shrubs nestle in fresh mulch. Walking to the back, I peer under the porch to find it swept clean, no one living under there anymore. I tap on the siding. Plastic. The firm listing the home is in the business of "real estate, mortgages, insurance"—one of the holding companies in what Kevin Phillips called the FIRE sector (finance, insurance, real estate).

Heading next door, I climb the steps and ring the bell. Footsteps sound in the hall.

"What do you want?" a man's voice asks.

I find myself speaking to a peephole. I say that his neighbor Toni referred me, and I'm researching the foreclosure of the house next door.

"No one lives there," he says quickly. It's the previous owners I'm looking for, I begin, but he cuts me off. "It's not my house. I don't have nothing to say about it." I hear footsteps retreating.

Standing there holding the Whole Foods bag with the chocolate-dipped gingerbread cookies I'd planned to offer—over tea in a sunny kitchen, I'd imagined—I begin to feel vaguely ridiculous. Yet undaunted. Perhaps at Giuseppe's I'll have better luck.

I find the second-floor flat where he lives and knock. Then knock again. Through the glass door, wooden stairs gleam under fresh polish, and at the top of them a dog arrives, barking. I knock once more and then turn to leave. As I let myself out the gate, I turn and see an older man peering at me from the second-floor window. Then he's gone.

Down the street, I run into a young woman in blond dreadlocks coming out of Toni's yard with a small boy in tow—apparently the tenant moving out. I raise a hand and she stops to chat, telling me she's lived there less than a year.

"The neighborhood has become increasingly violent," she says. There've been a dozen shootings in the last year.

"Were they killings?"

"At least four were. We're leaving, moving to Florida."

As she heads off, the reality of Toni's situation sinks in for me more deeply than before. This landlord and homeowner is under enormous strain, as is her entire neighborhood. She might be at risk of losing her home. It seems less urgent, somehow, to trouble her yet again about a former neighbor she's never met. I leave a package of chocolates atop the rusted mailbox on Toni's cluttered porch, with a note thanking her for her help, and set off for the T stop.

THE COLLAPSE OF A MIDDLE-CLASS LIFE

Out of ideas about how to proceed, I turn to a colleague with a better understanding of public records and ask him to undertake a deeper search for me. Before long, a document arrives. It has the Haroldsons' new address and, wonder of wonders, Michael Haroldson's phone number. There's more. My friend has found that the Haroldsons are both in their 60s, and Michael is a retired firefighter. Realizing that I won't get the personal introduction I'd hoped for, I send a letter off, explaining who I am and what I'm researching, asking if they're willing to talk. A week or so later, I phone and leave a message. And wait.

Enough time passes that I give up. Then one day the phone rings. "This is Michael Haroldson," the gentleman says, in a voice like a baritone in a gospel choir. Yes, he's willing to meet. He suggests after ten some morning, because by then the four kids they have running around will be off to school.

Their new place turns out to be just 13 miles south on Highway 107, in a large apartment building. After parking my car, I get buzzed in by a security guard, who points me toward their unit—down a maze of corridors freshly carpeted in institutional beige. Michael meets me at the door, and Helen soon joins us. Both are youthful looking, though the circles under Helen's eyes show strain. I soon see one reason why, as a bright-eyed toddler wakes up from his nap, and Helen carries him in to join us.

"He'll be 11 months tomorrow," Michael announces.

"Well, happy birthday," I say, as the little one climbs up on the couch with me. He's one of four grandchildren the Haroldsons are raising, ranging up to age 12. As I hand Michael the box of fresh cookies I've brought, he talks about how they've come to find themselves in the role of caregivers (asking me not to share some of those family details). We move on to talking about Michael's career as a firefighter. I've done some Google searching and discovered that he received a Distinguished Service Award.

"Yes," he recalls. "There'd been a stabbing in front of my mother's house, and two kids were lying there, bleeding. I went to work on both of them, with no gloves, trying to suppress the bleeding. I saved one of the kids. The other died." The killer, he found out later, was standing across the street the whole time, watching him. He'd gotten other awards as well, he says, including firefighter of the year.

Helen, too, is in a helping profession. She's a nurse's assistant at a hospital where she's worked for 34 years. Because of the kids, she now works just two days a week. In sum, this is a couple, retired and semiretired, raising a second family on a firefighter's pension plus dribs and drabs from part-time work. Their situation has its seeds back at 56 James Court, when they found themselves unexpectedly responsible for two grandchildren.

"You lived in that house on James Court for 13 years," I begin.

"Almost 14," Michael replies. He moves unself-consciously into talking about how they lost the house, why they cycled through five mortgages in five years. Their son had needed a place to live and moved into the rental unit downstairs. He was out of work. Michael and Helen ended up supporting that family.

"When the kids needed things, it was expensive," Michael says. So they refinanced the home to pay off some bills. And then did it again. And again.

"When you refinanced, they gave you a check. Do you remember for how much?" I ask.

"It wasn't that much," Michael says. "Maybe $14,000. Between $9,000 and $14,000. We did that four times, I think it was."

If his recollection is right, they pulled perhaps $50,000 or so in cash out of the house. Yet their mortgage debt climbed by an additional $250,000. That told me the mortgages that the Haroldsons took on likely contained abusive terms. My research showed that, in general, subprime mortgages often contained features like teaser interest rates that quickly reset to double or triple the amount, prepayment penalties of $8,000 to $10,000 or more if loans were paid before their full term, high charges for brokerage fees, and monthly payments often higher than a family's total income.[1] Before our meeting, I'd estimated that with these charges, as well as closing costs of maybe $5,000 per mortgage, the five mortgages that the Haroldsons went through in five years could easily have extracted fees totaling $100,000 out of the home's equity. It sounded as though it might have been a lot more than that.

"Were there prepayment penalties involved?" I ask. They both look at me blankly. "Were there variable interest rates, the kind that can go up over time?"

"They went over things briefly, but it wasn't fully explained," Michael tells me. "We would think we'd be getting a lower interest rate, but instead it went up."

"You don't know why the rates went up?"

"No."

"Were you aware that your total debt was going up?"

"We were just aware that our monthly payments were going up," he says. The payments started at around $1,800 a month and then went to $2,400, then $2,800, $3,200, $3,300. "It was overwhelming," he says.

I ask about Aegis, where they'd gotten three mortgages. Michael says they went to the company's office and spoke to a person who seemed nice. "He was young and a fast talker," he adds. They dealt with him more than once. "He told us, don't worry about it, we can do this, we can do that. Basically, he was saying what I wanted to hear."

"Did anyone tell you that when you refinance so quickly, every 12 months or so, you're losing a lot of money?"

"No. When we'd have financial difficulties, we'd call them up. Once we got maybe $5,000." Michael leans forward and his voice quickens. "But even $5,000, with the kids, would come in handy."

It was little wonder that mortgage brokers had been eager to write subprime mortgages. The profit potential was enormous, and the hands ready to grab it were lined up all the way to Manhattan. As Charles Morris described it, those brokers "were creating 'product' for an assembly line that flowed from mortgage banks to the CDO machines, run by firms like Merrill Lynch and Citigroup—swelling Wall Street bonus checks."[2]

These days, the Haroldsons seem to live pretty much month to month, as about half of American workers do. They likely have little to tide them over in hard times, in savings or investments. Most assets, 83 percent globally, are held by the wealthiest 10 percent.[3] This family isn't in that category. Like the vast majority of American households, they're in the bottom 90 percent of wealth holders—those with thin or no asset holdings—among whom 73 percent own less than $10,000 in stock.[4]

Living largely hand to mouth—probably spending more on bank overdraft fees than on fresh fruits, as the typical American family does—they had no cash to hire a lawyer for the refinancings.[5] When foreclosure faced the Haroldsons, a workable loan modification by a caring banker wasn't in the cards—as it hadn't been for millions of others. The Obama administration had encouraged banks to help borrowers stay in their homes, but few loan modifications had been done. Having the misfortune of getting Ocwen as their servicing agency, they dealt with a firm that had earned that F from the Better Business Bureau. Their phone calls might have reached someone in India with little knowledge of how to help the hamstrung couple and little incentive to do so.

THE DIFFERENCE BETWEEN WEALTH AND CASH

Like many, the Haroldsons had walked into this situation because of the tantalizing cash on offer. What they didn't grasp (or didn't focus on) was the fact that they were liquidating an asset. They may not have known the difference between *wealth* and *cash*. Left untouched, their home would have *created wealth* over time as it rose in value. But because they'd turned that value into borrowed cash, they lost wealth. The cash had to be paid back, plus interest, plus closing costs, plus brokerage fees, plus prepayment penalties. Meanwhile, their slice of real ownership was depleted. Mounting debt remained.

Not being equipped to think about this chain of events, the Haroldsons focused instead on *monthly payments*. If they could afford the payment and get cash in hand, well, why not? To a family pinched by expenses, such a deal seemed a godsend. They didn't fully comprehend that owning something—really owning it, free of debt—is the path to prosperity. It was this gap in economic literacy that the financial sector drove a Mack truck through. Along with millions of others, the Haroldsons went beneath the wheels.

At least they still had each other and had been spared divorce. Pretty much everything else was lost—the home they'd owned for 13 years, the equity that might have yielded them a little comfort, the neighbors and friends they'd enjoyed. They also lost their credit rating, and in the end, they declared bankruptcy. Their life on James Court had pretty much collapsed.

The larger social order around them was also experiencing collapse. The rising violence and fear I encountered in their former neighborhood was seen across Boston, as home break-ins between 2009 and 2010 soared 24 percent—and as much as 60 percent in Roxbury, a neighborhood bordering theirs. Boston Police superintendent-in-chief Daniel Linskey blamed soaring crime on the bad economy.[6]

Beyond Boston, collapse threatened the economy at large, with unemployment and underemployment plaguing a massive 17 percent of Americans in the early years after the meltdown, and with youth unemployment in some European nations higher still.[7] One in four US children—one in eight Americans overall—relied on food stamps to stave off hunger.[8] Across Europe, government and business leaders struggled to avert the collapse of the euro zone, as debt woes and economic crises struck Iceland, Greece, Ireland, Portugal, Italy, and other parts of the continent.

THE EROSION OF WAGES

Debt, in a way, was only a symptom of those multiple crises. A deeper issue was inequality. Had the Haroldsons' son not lost his job, had Helen made more money, the family might not have needed to go so deeply into debt to stay afloat. Their plight wasn't unique. Income for the majority of Americans had been flat for 30 years. According to Census Bureau figures, a male worker in 2007 earning the median male wage took home less, adjusted for inflation, than the typical male worker three decades earlier.[9] In the roughly 20 years leading up to the recession in 2008, an astonishing 56 percent of the growth in income in the United States went to the richest 1 percent.[10]

Had the share of income going to the middle class been larger, consumers wouldn't have taken on so much debt to maintain their lifestyle. Had the wealthy gotten a smaller share, they wouldn't have bid up asset prices so high.[11] From a systems perspective, the problem is an economy that's hitting the limits of its normal functioning.

Deregulation freed corporations to do what they're designed to do, which is to maximize gains for shareholders. At a larger level, this means that the entire system becomes focused on increasing the assets of the wealthy. Yet many of those assets are the debts owed by the middle class. With middle-class incomes flattening, there's less ability to pay off those debts. Thus the upward movement of wealth, from the real economy up into the financial economy, is constrained. Left to do what its basic design dictates, the extractive economy becomes overburdened with claims from above and undermined by the collapse of wages from below. The problem is that the system is designed to serve the few and not the many.

Yet in the downturn following the crisis, the system continued to follow its core logic: to increase profits for wealth holders and to decrease wages. When corporations found it difficult to increase sales, they nonetheless enjoyed record profitability. They accomplished this neat trick by cutting expenses, which in large part meant wages—also known as jobs.

Companies used tactics like not rehiring, employing temporary rather than full-time workers, increasing workloads, and shifting jobs overseas. As a study by Northeastern University's Center for Labor Market Studies showed, the result in one typical six-month period, a year or so after the meltdown, was that pretax corporate profits rose a massive $390 billion, while wages went up a tiny $70 billion.[12]

If this pattern seems particularly perverse at a time when working people are losing their homes and their jobs, it isn't new. But there's a curious piece to it. In the larger scheme of things, this pattern—maximizing profits for owners, minimizing wages for workers—has been at work since the days of the robber barons. Why had it suddenly become a problem in the larger system functioning? Why had the collapse of a few families like the Haroldsons triggered such a massive system response?

THE THRESHOLD EFFECT

The answer has to do with thresholds. Thresholds are the reasons why a system might suddenly jump into a kind of behavior not seen before. As systems theorist Ervin Laszlo noted, processes often don't work in unbroken, linear ways. Things build up until a critical threshold is reached, and then sudden change is triggered. Think avalanche or mudslide.

When management of a system is intent on a single variable, success can create exponential growth followed by collapse. That's the *threshold effect*: a point when a system flips from one state into another state, which is often degraded. There's a disturbance, yet the system's response is out of proportion to the size of that disturbance. In natural systems like forests or farming, one process that triggers a threshold effect is the human striving for *maximum sustained yield*. As ecologist C. S. Holling wrote, "Placing a system in a straitjacket of constancy can cause fragility to evolve." Managing for a steady increase of one variable can cause instabilities to silently build elsewhere. Intensive management of forests can yield increased wood production, but create monocultures more vulnerable to injury from industrial air pollution. Bovine growth hormone given to cows can increase milk production, but make cows less healthy and shorten their lives.[13]

Keeping a system from flipping into a degraded state means respecting limits. It involves recognizing a simple systems insight:

Systems behave differently when at or near limits.

Economist Herman Daly put it this way: "As in physics, so in economics: the classical theories do not work well in regions close to limits."[14] Because of the excesses of financialization, the economic system was at or near limits, with financial claims four times GDP while millions of families were getting by on food stamps. These were logical outcomes for the design of extractive ownership. The constancy of seeking maximum profits for a financial elite caused instabilities to build, making the whole system vulnerable to collapse.

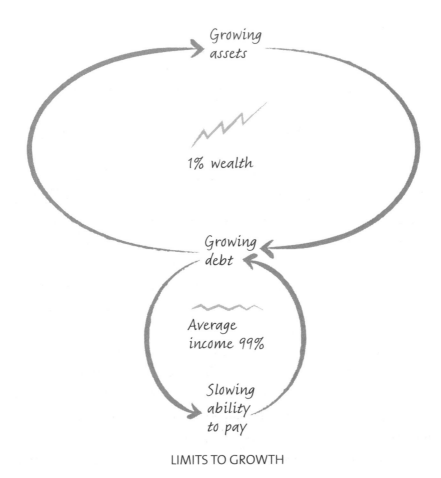

Growing
assets

1% wealth

Growing
debt

Average
income 99%

Slowing
ability
to pay

LIMITS TO GROWTH

If the ecological concept of thresholds seems compelling, is it simply an analogy or something more? Is it accurate to apply systems thinking to the mathematical world of finance?

This is a question I pose one day to my Tellus colleague Rich Rosen, a physicist who also closely studies economics. There's no doubt that the 2008 crisis was a case of overshoot and collapse, he tells me. But he adds that it's hard to say there was a single, clearly defined threshold that was passed. With the financial system, he says, "there isn't as clear a set of limits as you can define with physical systems." (Even with physical systems, it's often hard to tell precisely where limits are, he adds.) Debt grew dramatically in a few short years in the United States, but why did it collapse at one point and not another? The answer was probably tied up with *inequality of income distribution*, Rich says. At different levels of income inequality, different levels of debt would be sustainable.

"The constraint is the ability to pay back," he says. "That functions as a kind of physical limit."

The financial world operated with an implicit assumption that financial wealth could grow indefinitely, independent of GDP and independent of wage levels. And in theory, Rich says, he can imagine a scenario where that might happen: Wealthy people would bet against one another, and speculative activity would grow.

"But that's not how it's worked," he continues. "In fact, in the real world, where the rich have gotten richer relative to the rest of the population, that means somehow they're siphoning money from the rest of us." With the wealth gap widening and the average person's income not keeping pace, "the evidence seems to me pretty compelling," he says. "This is not rich people betting against each other, but extracting from the rest of us."

"Is that like one species eating all the ground cover so there's less for other animals?" I ask.

"It's more like a cancer cell, which has an ability to grow out of control where there isn't enough of an immune system to keep it in check," he says. "Cancer cells grow and kill the biological organism." But there's a limit to how far wealth extraction can go, he adds. Living systems out of balance find ways to right themselves. Something shifts. "At some point, people get rebellious," he says. He adds what seems to me a good summary lesson of the whole mess.

"A fairer system is a more resilient system."

Here is a kind of secular morality, a word for the social limits we're hitting: *fairness.* An economy built on fairness, on designs aimed at a fairer distribution of wealth, is likely to be more resilient. If we are to avoid threshold effects (also called economic crises, which seem to be occurring every couple of years), it means managing not just for profits or growth but also for resilience. *Resilience* is the capacity of a system to bounce back from disturbances with its structures essentially intact. The opposite of resilient is brittle, prone to breakdown.

The economic system's instability is related to its moral code. In an interdependent global system, overloaded with financial claims, the absence of fairness becomes dangerous. Limits of decency and fair dealing turn out to be real limits. Ethical limits and limits of system resilience are showing themselves to be the same thing. An unfair system will ultimately snap beneath its own weight. And it did.

The collapse of the Haroldson family's finances is a part of what triggered the threshold effect of economic crisis. I'd finally been able to sort out the ownership tangle around their home—tracing how the twig of ownership they signed over had passed from mortgage lender to mortgage lender, was sliced and diced by Aegis, and was placed in a structured investment vehicle, pieces of which had been sold to investors. When the Haroldsons' mortgage had gone bad, one splinter of the twig of ownership had passed to MERS, which began the foreclosure, and another splinter had gone to Ocwen, which earned fees overseeing the house as it stood empty. I'd seen how this disaggregated ownership system had fed a growing force of financial extraction and how that force had been building—hurtling toward a limit that the financial world could not conceive existed.

The resulting crisis is still sorting itself out. If housing prices in the United States have experienced collapse, much of the phantom wealth on the other side of the equation is still on the books. People are still pretending that those assets are real, trying to get those claims paid.

The Haroldsons, I discover, are still on the receiving end of those demands. Near the end of my visit, Michael mentions casually that he's still receiving bills from Ocwen telling the couple that they owe money—despite their bankruptcy. "Every month a statement comes," Michael says calmly, although I am incredulous. He goes into the back room to retrieve one, and I see that it is dated years after they lost their home. The statement says the Haroldsons owe close to $200,000.

"Are they calling you?" I ask.

"No," he says. "Just the statements. We pretty much ignore them."

I say that I wish I could personally offer help, and that if I can find someone who might assist them, I'll let them know. Reluctantly, I stand to go. Helen asks me a final question.

"Did you notice the big tree in the front yard of the house?" she says. "We planted that when it was a little branch. We used to go out in the winter and tie it up to a stake, brush off the snow. Now it's a huge tree." Her eyes shine with pride.

"That's something you deserve to feel good about," I say, as I shake hands to leave. "That tree will be there for a long time to come."

There are many things I still don't know about the Haroldsons' situation—many legal and financial details that attorneys could wrangle over. But I can say one thing with reasonable confidence, which is that they weren't treated fairly. That wasn't the only reason they lost their home. But it seemed a key reason. It was a key reason why the larger economy came close to collapse. It's said that the flapping of butterfly wings in São Paulo can lead to a hurricane in Miami. The same might be said of mortgage fees unfairly charged, or contracts won through deception, which can trigger a hurricane in global financial markets. At its limits, an unfair system is an unstable system.

Some will say this family made unwise choices and is bearing the consequences. That's true. But had they made the unwise choice of buying bad meat from a careless slaughterhouse, we wouldn't lay the blame on them. Our society doesn't allow the sale of tainted meat. Yet tainted mortgages remain legal and were in fact encouraged by the design of extractive ownership.

Back home after my journey to the Haroldsons' apartment, I visit the website of that financial, insurance, and real estate company whose sign stood in the yard of the family's former home. Its site shows photos depicting refinished wood floors and new appliances, indicating that the renovation of 56 James Court has been inside as well as out. The home has been divided and is being sold as two units. One lists for $289,000, the other for $279,000. I do a quick calculation. The real estate agent who bought the neglected house, after it stood empty for years, paid $206,000. Following renovations of, oh, let's say $100,000, the amount put into the house would total around $300,000. The listing price is now $568,000. That means that the new owners will be pocketing around a quarter million dollars: not a bad profit, going to (surprise) the FIRE sector.

II

Returning
to Earth

Ecological Values as the Seedbed
of a Generative Economy

Redesigning the models of ownership that form the base of our economy isn't a mechanical, legal exercise. Ownership designs embody a worldview and a set of values. The dominant designs of our day are built around values of individualism, growth, and the pursuit of maximum financial wealth. An emerging ecological sensibility is shaping a new set of core values, such as sustainability, community, and sufficiency. This values shift creates the seedbed for new kinds of generative ownership and a profoundly new kind of economy. Instead of being rooted in the ethereal world of finance, this new economy finds fertile soil in the living earth and in human community. Some of the most compelling models embodying this new worldview are found in ownership of the commons, which is the focus of the journeys of part 2.

....

SIX

WAKING
UP

From Maximizing Profits
to Sustaining Life

I once taught a course at Schumacher College in southern England titled "Can the Earth Survive Capitalism?" I began the class by talking about problems with the current design of our economic system—particularly financialization and extractive ownership design (though I wasn't yet using that language)—and I planned next to move to solutions about the redesign of corporations. But I found the class wasn't ready for that next step.

Their minds were on "collapse." That was the word I heard bandied about in hallways and over dinner, as I came to realize that many of these students—schooled as they were in deep ecology—were convinced that what lay ahead was total ecological collapse, after which we would, if we were lucky, regenerate our civilization at the village level. Schumacher College is near Totnes, the first of the "Transition Towns" in the UK that are preparing locally for a post-carbon world. Local change excited these students, and with good reason. Yet they seemed to subconsciously imagine that the larger economic system—corporations, the stock market, banks—would somehow implode and be vaporized, for they couldn't picture it all ever really changing. It seemed easier for them to imagine the collapse of civilization itself.

"There are two worldviews in this room," I said, as I set aside my lesson plan and opened up an hour for unplanned discussion. "I think it's important that we put them on the table." One is a view of total social collapse. The other is a view of transformation—not the advent of some utopia but a kind of muddling through to a new social order that would arise out of the one we have. "You don't want to plan on total collapse," I said. "If it comes, we won't be tending our community gardens. We'll more likely be dealing with a new form of fascism."

In the hour of freewheeling talk that followed, we brainstormed about the larger transformation needed in our civilization—all the shifts that would be required in law, values, sources of energy, sustainability technologies, international governance, the rebuilding of democracy, the reinvigoration of communities, and more. What was needed, we agreed, was an entire change of worldview—a new way of thinking about our relationship to the planet and to each other.

With that larger context in mind, we were able to move into discussions about corporate redesign. Soon I found them debating questions of governance and whether employee ownership should be required for all firms. Some of these students were just out of college, while a few had spent decades inside major corporations, but all were able to grasp the issues of ownership design. As a teacher, I came away satisfied—yet also somehow troubled.

STEPHAN'S QUESTION

Something was lacking, not in their understanding but in my own. My thinking to that point had focused on the design of corporations and capital markets. But something in that approach had begun to seem vaguely out of focus to me.

Midweek, the class went on a field trip that was a traditional part of the Schumacher experience. It was a trip I'd taken before, where a question had been asked that stayed with me. It was a question much larger than corporate redesign:

*What kind of economy is consistent
with living inside a living being?*

The question was posed inside a forest not far from Totnes, where we'd gone on a trip led by the college's resident ecological scientist, Stephan Harding. Taking us on a path deep into the forest to a clearing beneath a leafy canopy, Stephan instructed us to form pairs and take one another by the hand, blindfolded, to experience the forest by touch. I was led to a tactile encounter with a soft, round, cushiony living being that was rooted in the ground—about as large as a cantaloupe and soft as a kitten. But, disturbingly, I could not name it.

When I removed my blindfold, I saw it was "only" a mound of moss. But it moved me, unaccountably, and brought tears to my eyes. It was an experience of intimacy before words. An experience, I would call it, of kinship.

Stephan instructed us, then, to go off alone for a time, and I sat by a creek, feeling something wordless opening in me. As we gathered together again and took our seats on fallen trees, Stephan stood and gave a lecture on deep ecology—that school of thought that recognizes no distinction between the human and natural worlds, that sees all human activity as a subset of the living system of the earth.

Deep ecology and systems thinking are closely related. They're two different lenses into the same mind-set, one that sees living systems as the preeminent guide we need for designing all physical technologies and social systems. This view starts from a notion of humans not as masters and owners of the earth but as members of it. Everything we think we "possess," everything we create or build, is not *on* the earth but *of* it, as an arm is part of the body.

"Matter is sentience. Sentience is matter," Stephan said. Picking up a leaf from the forest floor, he went on, "This leaf is a subject. The world is a communion of subjects. Everything has interiority."

It was at the end of the lecture that he posed the question. It was a question he himself could not answer, he explained, but he hoped we could begin to do so, because—and he looked at me as he said this—it was a question on which the future of life on earth depended. *What kind of economy is consistent with living inside a living being?*

DETOUR THROUGH THE COMMON

It was a question that took me many years to understand. There was something basic, utterly simple, that I couldn't grasp. I needed to journey far
from the language of corporations and capital markets to find the answers.
I returned from Schumacher and soon found my work at Tellus moving
into a new phase as I joined a Ford Foundation initiative looking at how
the wealth of rural communities could be kept local. That project drew
me into research exploring a variety of ownership designs that worked in
partnership with the natural world—managing forests, running farms,
harnessing the wind, fishing for lobsters. All of them involved designs governed by local communities.[1]

I'd thought that class at Schumacher marked the conclusion of my
long journey into understanding the design of ownership. Instead I found
myself at the beginning of a new journey. It was about ownership and governance of the commons. Many of the largest challenges looming ahead for
human civilization are problems of ecology: climate change, acidification
of oceans, deforestation, soil erosion, peak oil, loss of species, groundwater
depletion, and more. What is the role of ownership design in causing these
problems of the commons and in potentially alleviating them? No quest to
understand ownership could be complete, I realized, without some grasp
of these answers.

It was the second part of the question—potential solutions—that
initially drew my attention. Building on my Ford work, I began looking
widely, and among the most striking ownership models I found were the
community forests of Mexico. That nation had become a global leader in
forest stewardship by granting ownership rights to local communities,
many of them indigenous, tribal peoples—like the Zapotec Indians of
Ixtlán de Juárez in southern Mexico.

Three decades ago, the Zapotec tribe won the right to communally
manage forests previously exploited by state-owned companies. Over
time, the problems that bedeviled other forests in Mexico, like deforestation and illegal logging, became relatively unknown at Ixtlán. The reason
is that community members have incentive to be stewards of the forest,

since forest enterprises employ 300 people doing work such as harvesting timber, making wooden furniture, and caring for the forest. In this design of commons governance, the forest is not walled off as a pristine preserve, nor is it clear-cut to enrich absentee owners. It's a *working forest*, with control in the hands of those with an incentive to look out for the long-term interests of both the human community and the natural world.

This is Rooted Membership at work—operating hand in hand with Living Purpose. The forest is not seen as an object whose sole purpose is permitting owners to extract maximum amounts of financial wealth. It's a living forest, a community of trees and humans. The purpose is to live well together, maintaining the living forest and supporting the human community. Because governance rights are in the hands of humans rooted to that place, they have a natural incentive to be good stewards. And they are able to carry out their mission because they govern the forest; it's Mission-Controlled Governance.

In Mexico today, I discovered, community forests represent an astonishing *60 to 80 percent* of all forests. Worldwide, more than a quarter of forests in developing nations are managed by local communities. Community forests hold promise as a key tool in fighting deforestation, which accounts for nearly one-fifth of all greenhouse gas emissions. But here's the truly remarkable part: the story of community forests, like the story of cooperative banks, remains virtually unknown. Even within Mexico, the phenomenon is largely invisible.[2]

Another large-scale solution is found in the ownership model of the *conservation easement*. It leaves property in the hands of private owners while allowing development rights to be held separately—generally in the hands of an environmental organization or the state. The aim is to permanently prohibit development on particular pieces of land by attaching voluntary, legally binding easements to the property deeds. Easements have been used to protect wetlands, conserve watersheds, preserve agricultural land for family farms, and protect migratory corridors for animals—as with the Malpai Borderlands Group, a ranchers' organization in Arizona and New Mexico, which has preserved nearly one million acres of unfragmented open space for wildlife.

Conservation easements are a cheaper way to stop development than outright purchase. And they yield tax advantages for owners. Throughout the United States, many millions of acres are under the protection of conservation easements. And the concept is spreading to Latin America, Canada, Australia, the Pacific, and the Caribbean.[3]

A similar model I explored is the community land trust, where families own their homes and a community organization owns the land beneath them. There are hundreds of examples in the United States, and more are forming in the wake of the housing crisis. I also studied catch shares, ownership rights to the use of fishing grounds, which were first used to help ailing fisheries in Australia, New Zealand, and Iceland, and later to revive red snapper in the Gulf of Mexico and halibut in Alaska.[4]

These models represent an intriguing twist on the disaggregation of ownership—the idea that ownership is a bundle of rights, which can be unbundled and distributed in novel ways. They show that the problem is not disaggregation itself but the purpose behind it. When the Haroldsons gave a twig of ownership rights to a mortgage lender, which wielded it against them, extractive purpose was the problem. With community land trusts and catch shares, twigs of ownership are given to parties with Living Purpose. And in these cases, disaggregation helps create solutions.

What these models show is that an economy consistent with living inside the living earth is an economy that effectively joins the interests of humans and the natural world. At work in many of these models is a kind of organic reciprocity. When ownership rights are in the hands of those whose self-interest depends on the health of the forests, the fish, and the land, they have a natural tendency toward stewardship. Self-interest and the interests of the whole become one and the same. Rooted Membership, Living Purpose, and Mission-Controlled Governance are among the ownership patterns that make this possible.

COMMON OWNERSHIP IN A NEW KEY

Something else struck me. Many of the models I found in rural areas put ownership in the hands of low-income people. One design particularly close to my heart is the *resident-owned community*, which was first devised in New Hampshire and later spread across the United States. It had its genesis in 1983, when residents of the Meredith Center Trailer Park faced eviction because an out-of-state developer wanted to buy the land beneath their homes. With a loan from the New Hampshire Community Loan Fund, residents bought the park themselves.

That stroke of ingenuity, or grace, or whatever it was, grew into the loan fund's Manufactured Housing Park Program, which uses a cooperative ownership model to help people in mobile homes and other kinds of manufactured houses purchase the land on which their homes stand. The process works a legal transformation in the nature of their property. Manufactured homes previously viewed by banks as personal property (in the same category as a car or a boat) become *real estate.* That means they get better loan terms. It also means, as studies show, that residents plant more flowers, attend more school conferences, enjoy higher property values, and move less often. By owning the land where they live, a community of low-income people becomes a communion of subjects, their homes no longer a collection of objects viewed by an absentee landlord as a way to extract maximum rent.[5]

Here again is Rooted Membership at work—bringing a transformation not in an ecological community but in a human community, through locally rooted, collectively held ownership. At the heart of it is Living Purpose. And the design is fed by Stakeholder Finance, where capital becomes a friend, not a master.

It's intriguing to me that the resident-owned community model was devised by a financial institution. It wasn't a big bank with executives striving to make multimillions for themselves. Yet this loan fund has nearly $70 million under management. And it pays investors up to 4 and 5 percent interest annually, at a time when bank certificates of deposit are paying a fraction of that.

The founding director of the New Hampshire Community Loan Fund—still at the helm after more than 25 years—is Juliana Eades. I met her at a conference one day. What struck me was how approachable she seemed and how much she laughed. She had short gray hair, wore not a trace of makeup, and was at ease in simple cotton slacks when nearly everyone else was wearing a suit. Juliana is as far from a banker type as you can get. I talked with her for half an hour and came away not knowing that she was the president of the fund. When I asked about her position, she simply told me that she'd been there since the beginning.

Her organization isn't seeking to build an empire by taking possession of all these mobile home communities, or by putting mortgages on them and then flipping them so that someone else can extract their value. Instead, the goal is to help regular nonfinancialized folk enjoy the benefits of full ownership. When the model proved itself in New Hampshire—with 90 resident-owned communities experiencing zero defaults—a new organization, ROC-USA, was created with the aim of taking the model nationwide.

At work is a remarkable sensibility. Instead of a clutching after more and more for the self, this approach to ownership embodies a letting go, a spreading of the bounty. It's generative ownership at its best: ownership as embodied generosity, yet financially hard-nosed at the same time. These people aren't getting a gift; they're buying land. The loan fund isn't in the business of philanthropy; it makes loans that are paid back with interest. The end point is common ownership, by common folk—regular people, members of the working class.

LOCAL DOMINION

Yet another model proving workable is *community wind*. The best example of this is Denmark, where a grassroots movement launched the drive to put up wind farms. Many turbines erected in the 1980s and early 1990s were owned by the wind guilds, and today cooperatives still own a substantial portion of installed capacity. When in 2009 Denmark passed legislation encouraging wind development, it required new wind projects to offer at least 20 percent ownership to locals. Similar arrangements are working in

Germany, where half of renewable energy generation is owned by farmers and other regular citizens.[6]

Common ownership of wind creates a powerful benefit: it reduces the community resistance that wind often encounters with absentee ownership. This has been seen in Germany, Canada, and other nations besides Denmark. Community ownership is a way to "democratize electricity," wind specialist Paul Gipe told me. Yet in the United States, community wind is just beginning to be more widely known. "Only a few of us on the fringe are talking about community wind," Paul said.[7]

In the states, community wind generally takes the form of municipal ownership—ownership by local communities. Wanting to see this model up close, I join some friends one cloudy Thursday afternoon at Rowe's Wharf in Boston for the 45-minute ferry ride to the wind installation in Hull. In 2001, the small town of Hull put up the East Coast's first commercial-scale turbine, and that is what my friends and I are journeying to see—along with 350 other people who've bought $10 tickets for the cruise led by the Mass Energy Consumers Alliance. We stand in line close to an hour before boarding the *Freedom* vessel, taking our seats finally inside the ferry's large central room, where the crowd is festive, as though we were at a church barbecue or a state fair. This is the seventh or eighth trip to Hull that Mass Energy has run.

"We probably should have had a second boat, because we had to turn people away," an organizer says over the loudspeaker.

At our destination, Pemberton Point, we disembark and walk to the turbine. There the organizer asks, "How many of you have touched a wind turbine before?" Many step forward. My friends and I stand and watch.

"I hope we look back on this in 20 years and think of it as quaint," Susan says.

Katherine goes to look and returns to say, "Not a lot going on in there. A ladder and a box."

"A hundred yards away, you don't hear anything," the organizer announces. We stand 50 feet away and can hear it, but it isn't loud. "It's about the sound of a dishwasher," Susan says.

I spot one of the citizen organizers who led the effort to put up this turbine, Andrew Stern, and step forward to chat with him. "How did it all begin?" I ask. "When you started, what did you do?"

"You call up and schedule a meeting," he says. "You have a lot of doughnut and coffee meetings" with people like the plant manager and a town selectman.

When he approached them, I ask, what did they say?

"They didn't say no," he replies with a laugh.

This turbine has been built because there are local people with authority over electricity generation—people you can sit down with over coffee. It has been built, in other words, because the community owns the power plant. As a small sign on a chain link fence tells us on the way out, this turbine is owned by "Town of Hull Municipal Light Plant."

To my mind, this place is in sharp contrast to Salem, where the local electric plant (a coal plant) is owned by Dominion, a publicly traded company headquartered in Richmond, Virginia. Our citizens' group in Salem has long hoped to see the plant shut down and wind power possibly built there. But the local manager has no authority over such things. And the CEO at Dominion, Thomas Farrell, isn't someone we can get on the phone. Even if by some miracle he flew in for doughnuts (an infinitesimal chance, given that the Salem plant represents a speck of the company's $15 billion in revenue), he likely would remind us that his duty was to shareholders, not to Salem.

It's not that Dominion lacks resources to spend on wind. A few years earlier, Farrell managed to find a massive *$6 billion* lying around that he spent buying back company stock (at a time when the company was telling Salem that it couldn't afford to pay the property taxes it once had paid).[8] There's one community that Farrell responds to, and it isn't local.[9]

Hull is different. There the process of building a wind development involved the community. In 1997, teachers Malcolm Brown and Anne Marcks led citizen meetings, and the planning carried over into the curriculum of Marcks's senior high school physics class. Brown, a retired philosophy professor and one-time member of the Hull Municipal Light Board, told *E* magazine, "The Hull experience shows it is easier to win approval for wind projects if the benefits are enjoyed close to home, flowing to local residents transparently and directly. This way the project is ours, not theirs. We're the investors and we're the beneficiaries."[10]

WAKING UP

There are many ways that generative designs contribute to solving problems of the commons. Community wind helps eliminate roadblocks to clean energy. Resident-owned communities spread wealth. Conservation easements preserve natural places. Community forests prevent deforestation. After studying these designs, it dawned on me why my original approach was off target. In the face of these radically different designs, the monoculture of profit-maximizing corporate design began to seem an industrial-age artifact—suited to certain circumstances, toxic in others. As ubiquitous as that design is, I began to get a glimmer that its day might pass—when we the people wake up.

I began to see why the idea of redesigning the corporation is out of focus. Years had passed since I'd listened to Stephan in the forest, but I finally got it. You don't start with the corporation and ask how to redesign it. You start with life, with human life and the life of the planet, and ask, how do we generate the conditions for life's flourishing?

I saw why I'd had a hard time answering Stephan's question, about the kind of economy best suited for living inside a living being. The set of answers looks different, depending on where you stand when you ask the question. If you stand inside a large corporation like Dominion and ask what kind of economy we need, the answers are about incremental change from the existing model. The only way to start that conversation is to fit your concerns inside the frame of profit maximization ("Here's how you can make more money through sustainability practices"). Asking corporations to change that frame is like asking a bear to change its DNA and become a swan.

If you take the more radical stance of standing inside the law and ask how to change the profit maximization mandate—which we at Corporation 20/20 explored at length—you find yourself in the sunless thicket of corporate governance (directors' duties, common law, Delaware court cases). I and my colleagues spent years wandering in that thicket, and I saw the tendrils of things-as-they-are ensnare the feet of the most intrepid explorers. Few who enter that thicket emerge with sanity intact.

Those approaches aren't how the founding generation of America began. They didn't start with complicated arguments about the law or tell the king that caring for the peasants would improve his return on investment. They articulated truths they held to be self-evident. That's what Stephan did in that forest. He said simply:

> *"A thing is right when it enhances the stability*
> *and beauty of the total ecosystem.*
> *It is wrong when it damages it."*[11]

That's right as rain. It's another piece of the secular morality that can guide us: the sustainability of the larger system comes first. Everything else has to fit itself within *that frame.* What kind of social architectures are consistent with a living world where all beings can flourish?

A NEW PARADIGM EMERGES

This is the perspective of the whole, and it's the perspective from which Stephan spoke. "The economic system is waging a massive war on nature," he said. "We can talk new business systems as much as we like. But unless we have this perspective"—putting the good of the whole first—"we're not going to make it." When the whole is damaged, all are damaged. When it flourishes, all can flourish. This understanding is basic to systems thinking, which stands upon a fundamental insight:

There are no separate systems.

This was key to the radical re-visioning of science that physicists confronted in the early 20th century, when systems thinking was first introduced. In the mechanistic worldview of Descartes and Newton, scientists conceived of matter as made of separate particles. But at the atomic and subatomic level, physicists encountered a strange new world, which confronted them with the wrenching necessity of constructing an entirely new view of reality. Physicist Fritjof Capra wrote:

> In their struggle to grasp this new reality, scientists became painfully aware that their basic concepts, their language, and their whole way of thinking were inadequate to describe atomic phenomena. Their problems were not merely intellectual but amounted to an intense emotional and, one could say, even existential crisis.[12]

They realized, in the end, that the universe isn't made up of things at all, but of patterned flows. "What flows is a mysterious, nonindividualized something we call energy," Ervin Laszlo wrote in *The Systems View of the World*. Some of the energy flows twist themselves into relatively stable patterns, which allows "things" to emerge, "like knots tied on a fishing net," he went on. These are the particles of matter. Whirling energy appears in the relatively stable patterns of electrons, which join to form larger patterns called atoms. Atoms twist into chemical molecules; molecules form cells. Cells build into organisms, and organisms join in "superorganic communities" both ecological and social—such as forests, towns, corporations. These living communities unite to form the global system of Gaia, the living earth. The whole has "the character of a vast system of balanced energies," Laszlo wrote, "acting in some discernible form of cohesion."[13]

This dramatic shift in worldview led Thomas Kuhn to the notion of *paradigm shifts*—when the concepts by which a community describes reality are deeply rewritten. Expanding on Kuhn, Capra spoke of a *social paradigm*, the constellation of concepts, values, and practices shared by a community that forms a vision of reality around which the community organizes itself.[14]

The paradigm now receding, Capra went on, has been with us for centuries and consists of entrenched ideas and values—including the idea of the economy as a mechanical system, of life as a competitive struggle, and of progress as unlimited economic and technological growth. "Last but not least," Capra wrote, is the notion that it's natural that "the female is everywhere subsumed under the male."[15]

Paradigms, values, and worldviews are not free-floating concepts but become embedded in institutional designs. A paradigm shift in capitalism faces us today. The signals are everywhere around, in financial and ecological crises. Yet the old worldview remains entrenched in the ownership designs of corporations and capital markets. Mutely, these designs enact the view of economic activity birthed with the industrial age: a view of business as a machine, feeding in "natural resources" and "human resources" in order to output goods and services. In capital markets, the view is of corporations as objects owned by shareholders, their purpose the churning out of endless streams of earnings like an assembly line.

DOMINION

This is the paradigm of dominion—the dominion of humans over the natural world, of male over female, of whites over other races, of capital over labor. *Dominion* is from the Latin *dominium*, meaning "ownership," which is from *dominus* ("master"). In the words of 18th-century British legal theorist William Blackstone, ownership confers upon the owner the right to "sole and despotic dominion."[16] That is the traditional view of ownership. It is the root concept for the whole paradigm.

Generative designs for ownership of the commons silently embody a different model of ownership—not about dominion but about belonging. It's about a sense of belonging to something larger than oneself, a common whole. And this is a matter not of sentimentality but of literal truth. It's a matter of biological reality. The life in which we all participate—the life of the forests, the fish, the land—makes our lives possible. The notion of isolated individuals, dwelling securely in some financial sphere above the rest of us, is a fantasy. It's a biological impossibility, for life in isolation does not exist. "Sustained life is a property of an ecological system rather than a single organism or species," as biologist Harold Morowitz put it.

"Life is a property of planets rather than of individual organisms."[17]

If new designs for ownership of the commons are more grounded in reality, that doesn't mean they're the whole answer for how to build a new economy. The models I studied aren't panaceas. Some people say catch shares are a bad idea rather than a good idea. Municipal utility officials are often deaf to citizen input. Conservation easements in their agricultural form—designed to protect farmland from development—often fail to stop the long decline of farming communities.[18] Community loan funds operate in businesslike ways, but most still need grant income.

These models aren't perfect. They're not some magical tool to end all problems of the commons. Climate change can't be stopped by changing ownership designs; other kinds of faster action by government are needed. At this moment in time, what commons ownership designs represent are tools of awakening. Our minds have been so colonized by the paradigm of industrial-age capitalism that we've lost the ability to imagine other ways of organizing an economy. These humble designs remind us that there are many ways. After the long flight of fantasy of financialized capitalism, generative ownership designs for the commons are ways to begin coming to our senses. By the bye, they work.

I had found the answer to the first question I'd set out on my journey into the commons to investigate, about the role of ownership designs in solving problems of the commons. What I planned next to explore was the other part of my question: what was the role of ownership design in *causing* problems of the commons? I knew where to begin that journey. The answer had something to do with a core concept in the industrial paradigm: the idea of growth.

SEVEN

THE
ISLAND

From Growth to Sufficiency

I hold the e-mailed printout of directions in one hand as I steer with the other. Left after Kingdom Hall, three-tenths of a mile on a dirt road, left at the Red Arrow Road sign on the tree. Turning onto the dirt road, I find myself driving through a forest that feels odd, but it takes me a moment to realize why. This stand of oak trees is clearly not young, but the trees have not grown tall. They retain the height of perpetual youth, yet bear the gnarled, wizened countenance of age—their adaptation, my host will later tell me, to the winds on this island of Martha's Vineyard and to the sandy soil in which they grow.

"Our house is the last one on the left next to the pond," the note says. I pull into a gravel parking lot, beyond which stands a cluster of two-story, cedar-shingled houses, weathered to that comfortable New England gray. Sixteen of them are nestled together in the forest, with porches facing inward, toward a central courtyard. But "courtyard" is too fancy a name for this long common area, covered with greenery that is natural rather than manicured. Meandering down the middle of it is a dirt walking path. The place has a palpable air of ease and serenity.

Out of the house by the pond—one of the larger houses in the grouping—steps my host, John Abrams, with salt-and-pepper beard and wire-rims. John is an old friend from my days at *Business Ethics* and a longtime participant in Corporation 20/20, but this is the first time I've been to his home. He strolls with me down the dirt path and shows me around. Neighbors call out greetings as we pass, and kids ride by on bikes.

"Even three-year-olds can be left to play here on their own," John says, "because there are no vehicles in the inner space and so many eyes looking out." This is Island Cohousing, the community where John lives, and which his firm, South Mountain Company, built.

Some homes have an ownership framework ensuring that they remain affordable for low-income residents, while others have traditional ownership designs, but I can't tell the difference. Each house is constructed substantially from salvaged and certified sustainable wood. Some have solar panels. And the homes are tightly insulated, he explains, which means they're cool in the summer and warm in the winter.

"They all have composting toilets," he continues. "It was one of the riskiest decisions we made in building the place—would people buy houses with no-flush toilets? Would authorities approve them? Would banks finance them? In all cases, the answer turned out to be yes. People went for it." The houses are sized for comfort rather than ostentation. They range from two-bedroom to four-bedroom, the largest about 1,700 square feet.

John takes me through the common house, with an expansive screened-in porch and generously sized rooms on the first floor, bedrooms upstairs. This shared space, he says, "allows us to have smaller homes." Here, community members throw parties and put up out-of-town guests. It's where weekly potluck dinners are hosted and yoga classes taught.

Over dinner, John and his wife, Chris, talk about how they came by accident to live on this small island off the coast of Massachusetts—only 100 square miles in total—which serves as a resort community of second homes for the wealthy. The two were "bicoastal hippies," John said, and came out to help his parents build a house, then just stayed. And kept on designing and building, working with others to create South Mountain Company.

A tour of that company is the ostensible purpose of my visit. It's one of the rare companies I've found that consciously practices slow growth. I've made this journey because I want to experience the living answer to a simple question:

*What does a company look like that has
moved beyond growth?*

What allows some companies to disregard the growth imperative, while others seem trapped in it as in a vise grip? I want to see the answer up close in this one place. Island Cohousing seems a sideshow. It is only later that I realize it is in fact far more.

ENOUGH

The next morning, I take the same route to the housing community and continue a short distance beyond, for South Mountain Company occupies part of the same 36-acre plot as Island Cohousing. Soon the headquarters of this $8 million, 33-person business comes into view—a two-story cedar-shingled structure that looks less like an office than a lodge. Its interior has an air of relaxed comfort, with rugs over wood floors and high ceilings with exposed beams of blond wood. The table in the conference room, I notice, has legs in their original shape of branches, stripped of bark and sanded but not otherwise industrialized. Outside John's office sits an overstuffed leather chair that invites me to sit.

As I wait for John, an employee comes into the building and stops to chat with the front desk person, saying he's been in the parking lot listening to the end of an interview with Lawrence Ferlinghetti. He proceeds to describe that interview at some length. It is 9:15 a.m. and no one seems concerned that this person is "late" to work.

John and I sit in his office and talk a long time that day, the forest visible outside his window and the sun streaming in. He points out the wind turbine that the company put up, which—along with solar panels—supplies 90 percent of the firm's electricity. At lunch we drive around to see places the company built. We visit a house designed to approach zero net energy, which can feed excess energy from solar panels into the grid and is heated only with a pellet stove. He takes me by "Jenny Way," a cluster of ten homes that includes the first LEED-certified platinum single-family affordable homes in the nation (LEED stands for Leadership in Energy and Environmental Design).[1] One source of wood for homes like these is logs salvaged from the bottom of rivers—"sinker cypress," John calls it.

In this resort community where real estate is extraordinarily expensive (I saw an ad for a "two-bedroom walk to the water" priced at $5 million), the company uses some profits from building high-end homes to create affordable houses. It offers employee housing assistance and led the development of the nonprofit Island Affordable Housing Fund. South Mountain maintains long-term relationships with its clients, offering "post-occupancy care." If a cabinet door fails to work after ten years, it gets fixed. I meet separately with a number of employees, including designer Derrill Bazzy, who started there as a carpenter. He talks about how many clients became close friends.

"My son's godparents are clients, and we're godparents to their kids," he says. "When there's a certain comfort level within a company, it's easy to extend that out to customers."

Most compelling to me are the company's unorthodox policies on growth. These originated in 1994, after the firm took on projects that doubled its revenue and meant adding employees. As John describes it in his writing, "The company was shot through with anxieties, dissatisfactions, and stresses. There seemed to be a general sense we had grown too much, too fast." To gauge it better, he called a staff meeting. He hung a chart on the wall and drew a vertical line down the middle labeled, "Maintain present size." On the left it said, "Decrease size," and on the right, "Continue slow growth." Employees were asked to each place a sticky dot somewhere to indicate their preference.

When everyone stepped back, most dots clustered near the center, a significant number were scattered to the left, and several were smack in the middle. The consensus, John wrote in his book, *Companies We Keep*, was, "We should back off on the accelerator a little, adjust ourselves to our recent growth, err toward caution, and slow down a bit." Since then, the company has held similar growth meetings every few years. At one point it kept revenue flat for nearly a decade. And it often turns away work that doesn't fit its values or plans.[2]

South Mountain is free to take this approach because of its ownership structure. This is an employee-owned and employee-governed firm. The people who feel the effects of growth can control it. Employees make up the board of directors, and they feel no need for outside board members. Because the company finances itself with its own profits, it has no outside investors. Employee-owners choose to focus not on *more* but on *enough*— in John's words, "enough profits to retain and share, enough compensation for all, enough health and well-being, enough time to give the work the attention it deserves, enough to manage, enough headaches, enough screw-ups."

Another word for *enough* is *sufficiency*, wrote Thomas Princen in *The Logic of Sufficiency*. It's different from the industrial ideal of efficiency, which is the notion that more, faster, cheaper, is always better. Sufficiency, Princen said, is "the sense that, as one does more and more of an activity, there can be enough and there can be too much."[3] Sufficiency is natural in living systems. It arises as an operating principle in this company because membership is rooted in the living hands of employees, and because Mission-Controlled Governance gives voice to those employees.

THE STICKINESS OF GROWTH

South Mountain's comfort with slow growth is far outside the mainstream of business. In extractive ownership design, the operating principle is that the continuous growth of financial income is the ultimate good. If all of corporate America squeezed into John's room and placed their sticky dots, they would cluster massively to the right—in territory labeled "continue rapid growth forever." Over the years, I'd seen that imperative lead to the ethics crises at Enron, WorldCom, Adelphia, and other companies. Rather than admitting that growth in profits had become difficult, they cooked the books to keep the fantasy alive longer. The same mentality led investment banks to push expansion into subprime mortgages, for they were loath to admit that all the appropriate lending was finished.

Pursuit of growth is why Dominion spent an unfathomable $6 billion buying back its own stock—a paper maneuver designed to remove shares from circulation so as to drive up the price of remaining shares. It produced nothing in the real world: no wind turbines, no natural gas plants, no solar energy installations. What it produced was a bump in stock price. At Dominion, that bump meant the CEO walked off that year with $15 million, largely due to stock options. Yet Dominion's stock price soon deflated. In less than two years, the stock traded *lower* than before the buyback. This energy company spent $6 billion on thin air. It did so at a time when the future of the planet depends on our energy choices. It was Nero fiddling on a planetary scale.

In the short run, Casino Finance and Governance by Markets can work wonders, for a few. In the long run, they can make a mess for everyone. Dominion and Enron behaved as they did because of their ownership design. It's the way extractive, industrial-age ownership links earnings to capital markets, and the way those markets spin molecules of earnings into larger bodies of wealth—transforming a dollar of earnings, through an inflated P/E ratio, into $20 or $30. This magic holds an irresistible lure, because it "creates" financial wealth beyond anyone's wildest dreams. CEOs are the ones who keep it going. But if every CEO at every major firm were abducted by aliens tomorrow, others would simply step in. Nothing would change. The problem isn't so much individuals as it is the ownership design that encourages, amplifies, and rewards their behavior.

Could a CEO of a publicly traded company wake up one morning and decide, well, enough revenue and profit; let's slow down and stay at a nice plateau of prosperity? Could such a firm, in other words, become a steadystate economy writ small? Not without all hell breaking loose.

The multiplier effect holds together only when investors expect future earnings to grow. If earnings flatten or decline, the process goes into reverse. Stock prices collapse. CEOs are handed their head on a platter. Others are brought in to get the growth machine roaring.

Keeping stock price inflated isn't the only reason why companies like growth; they want to capture market share, achieve economies of scale, and so on. But the financial markets create an *addiction* to growth, transforming a preference into a white-knuckle need.

Growth is an imperative of finance,
not of business itself.

"The real key is keeping business private," John says to me. "As soon as you become a public corporation, your social mission is done. You cannot resist the pressure of Wall Street."

THE MACHINE STUCK ON HIGH

Most public discourse about growth focuses on issues like climate change, consumerism, and policymakers' fixation on GDP. But those bigger issues are inseparable from what happens inside of companies. Take consumerism. Whenever a consumer buys something, some other party is selling that thing. Those transactions aren't happening at garage sales. The selling is done by companies. The sales revenue of major corporations represents most of global GDP.

The fit between consumption, company focus on growth, and the swelling of GDP is a tight one. It's all one process. Pressure for growth arises at all three points—at the individual, company, and national levels. Yet the pressure may be most intense in companies and financial markets.

Corporations and capital markets are the internal combustion engine of the capitalist economy. They're where it hits the ground and goes. And where it spins out of control. When companies aim to limitlessly grow profits, they sometimes kick themselves into high gear and run beyond normal tolerances. Gaskets blow out. Engines overheat. Pedestrians get run over. Inside the company, the pressure leads to overwork, anxiety, layoffs, outsourcing, wage cuts, reductions in health benefits, and accounting misstatements. Outside the company, the pressure ripples through the economy like an electric charge down a wire—pushing customers to buy more than they need, families to take on more debt than is manageable, ecosystems to absorb more waste than is possible.

What keeps the pressure on high is extractive ownership design. Since ownership shares of big firms mostly trade on public markets, these companies are driven by the same algorithm of growth at any cost. The output they create adds up to an economy too large for the carrying capacity of the biosphere. As Fritjof Capra put it, "It's an alarming thought that organizational systems are now the main driving force of ecological systems."[4]

Most people don't recognize that ownership design plays a large part in driving the whole thing. People see the urge toward wealth accumulation as akin to gravity. And greed does arise naturally in the human heart. But so does compassion. Extractive ownership design singles out one natural impulse and institutionalizes it, normalizes it, magnifies it.

In the short run, profit-maximizing companies can help a rapid transition to an ecologically cleaner economy. But in the somewhat longer run, that transition might represent a brief moment in time. If human civilization and planetary ecosystems are still functioning well 50 years from now (not a small if), what about the next 50 years? And the next 100 or 200 or 1,000 years beyond that? What kind of economy will be suited for ongoing life inside the living earth? Will it be an economy dominated by massive corporations intent solely on growing earnings? That doesn't seem likely. When you take the long view, the question turns itself about:

Can we sustain a low-growth or no-growth economy indefinitely without changing dominant ownership designs?

That seems extremely unlikely. Probably impossible.

METEORS HITTING THE EARTH

The biggest challenge of getting outside the growth paradigm is recognizing how much we're in it. Since the end of World War II, we've been living in an inconceivably massive explosion of economic growth.

"People living in an explosion are different, just as people living in a war zone are different," my Tellus colleague John Stutz says to me. "The normal reaction to an explosion is to take cover and wait for it to be over." By contrast, we assume that our explosion will go on forever.

John, who has a PhD in mathematics, studies numbers the way others study cookbooks. He's a student of growth. A researcher he often turns to is Angus Maddison, who put together estimates of global GDP back to the year one. (Some people sit around and do this stuff.) Maddison's figures offer a geological-scale perspective on growth. And they're eye-opening. One afternoon in my office, John explains how, compared with earlier eras, growth since 1950 has been off the scale.

"We've been through 50 years of growth so massive, it's distorted the whole experience of the species," he says. "Suppose your salary went up every year by $100,000. Then one year you got a raise of $50,000. You'd be really angry. That's the kind of distortion that has set in, where the smallest falloff in growth rates seems a catastrophe."

On a global scale, GDP changed very little in the first 1,800 years of the common era. Then with the start of the Industrial Revolution in 1820, growth began to pick up. Global GDP swelled to eight times as large by 1950. But in 1950, growth lifted off like a rocket, from slightly over $5 trillion to a jaw-dropping $51 trillion in 2008. The output of 1950 was about 10 percent of this new level. The remaining *90 percent* of global GDP appeared in just under 60 years.[5]

As John put it, "It's as though a town that spent 100 years building a few houses suddenly woke up one morning and built New York City in a day."[6]

To make this kind of exponential economic growth visible, different people have created thought experiments. Here's one I dreamed up. Imagine we're in a movie theater, watching a two-hour film graphically depicting the growth of global GDP. On the screen is a simple frame with 100 squares, representing 100 percent of economic activity in 2008. Two thousand years will pass in two hours. When the lights go down and the film begins at year one, we watch as a single square slowly fills in. This takes an hour and three-quarters. We are at the year 1750—just before the American and French revolutions. Economic activity equals 1 percent of the activity in our era.

We watch as an additional four squares fill in. This takes about ten minutes and represents a century and a half. We're at 1913—just before the start of World War I. The pace picks up. Another two minutes and we're at 1950. We've gone from the time of Jesus to the time of Dwight D. Eisenhower, and 10 squares are now filled.

In the final three minutes of the film—from 1950 to 2008—*90 squares* rapidly fill in. Economic activity is now *nearly ten times* what it was in 1950. This is roughly the span of one human life: my own.

But the filmmaker has a bonus. She steps onto the stage to explain: "Let us assume that growth in the next two decades, up to the year 2030, is about 2 percent a year in the rich world and somewhat higher in the developing world. Let's watch how the next minute and a half of earth time would unfold." She invites us to look around, and we watch as a second entire screen fills up, and activity spills onto a third screen, in the blink of an eye.[7]

By 2030—roughly when my kindergartener niece will be a few years out of college—global economic activity could be *more than double* what it is today. That activity (if it proves possible) would occur on our one planet, which is already in ecological overshoot. If it's reasonable to compare the impact of current human economic activity to that of a meteor hitting the earth, as some have, then in the coming two decades, we could see the impact of a second massive meteor. What about the next 20, or 100, or 1,000 years beyond that?

"Islands are laboratories," John Abrams wrote. "Islands are semi-closed systems. When you get off the boat or the plane and set foot on the Vineyard, you know immediately that you are in a place with limitations." The fixed boundaries create the conditions for innovation. "Challenging the false gospel of unchecked growth," as John calls it, is part of South Mountain's experiment in living well within limitations.

And there's a second part: learning to live well when the growth stops. This was the new reality that hit South Mountain Company in the wake of the 2008 crash and the housing bust that followed. "The year 2009 was our year of reckoning," John wrote in a company review. This employee-owned company had to contend with the unthinkable: not enough work for all. In a rigorous effort to avoid layoffs, the firm turned to furloughs, wage cuts, major marketing efforts, and employee skill building. But by

January 2011, five long-term employees (two of them former owners) were no longer with the firm.

The large volume of work the company had enjoyed for so long was shrinking. South Mountain had begun shifting to smaller jobs, more renovations, and more energy work. As the company reinvented itself, John wrote, "we came to realize that we wanted to get smaller *even if we didn't absolutely have to.*" Heresy upon heresy. Here was a firm that not only challenged the gospel of growth, it willingly (if somewhat painfully) opted to shrink—and to do so in the most humane way possible.

Learning to live well within limitations. This is what I saw in action in my visit to Martha's Vineyard: what it might mean to begin adapting to the emerging possibility of no growth, slow growth, or "degrowth," as some are calling it. But South Mountain Company, it turned out, wasn't the most interesting of John's post-growth experiments. It was at Island Cohousing that I most vividly saw something truly different—not simply the absence of growth, but the *presence* of something else. Call it sufficiency. Call it well being. It's about allowing ourselves to slow down and just live. John's willingness to live simply at Island Cohousing was all of a piece with his willingness to share ownership with employees and to accept that his company needed to shrink. It's all the same value system. Sufficiency goes hand in hand with fairness and community, because when we're no longer hell-bent on squeezing out every possible dime of increased earnings for ourselves, we can begin to notice other people's needs. When we're moving more slowly, satisfied with what we have, it's easier to treat other people well. It begins to seem foolish to financialize every molecule of property in order to infinitely grow our financial assets.

This sufficiency approach is institutionalized, normalized at Island Cohousing. Families own their individual houses and land, but the forest and common areas are held jointly. The people living there agree that these common areas are not intended to be for sale (though they could be, if three-quarters of the owners vote for it). In addition, the homeowners voluntarily agree to covenants about how to live together: agreeing to honor ecological design and to make some homes available to low-income residents. Individual freedom is honored. Yet the interests of the community are taken care of *by design*. Not the design of legislation. The design of common property.[8]

REINVENTING THE COMMONS

The idea of holding land in common for the community is an old idea. It's still seen in the British tradition of the town common in New England. Mexico once had the ejido system, involving village control over communal lands. Traditions of common land ownership were known in ancient China and Africa. In Israel, there is the Jewish National Fund, a public but nongovernmental institution established over a century ago to hold land that would, in the words of its founder, be "the property of the Jewish people as a whole." Today the fund still holds title to substantial land in Israel, overseen by trustees who lease portions to kibbutzim and others who use it in the public interest.[9]

Native American tradition embraced the most expansive notion of common holding, based on something closer to kinship than ownership. Because they saw the earth as a mother, the sacred ground of all beings, Indians found it inconceivable that one person could claim exclusive possession of land. The story is told of warrior chief Tecumseh and his incredulous reaction when white settlers suggested that natives sell land.

"Sell the country?" Tecumseh said to them. "Why not sell the air, the clouds, the great sea?" To American Indians, owning the land was incompatible with being a member of its living community. But in the design of Island Cohousing, the seemingly contradictory notions of individual ownership and relationship to the whole are reconciled.[10]

Island Cohousing and other similar experiments help reawaken an ancient wisdom about living together in community, which was lost in the spread of capitalism. Historian Karl Polanyi, in his 1944 work, *The Great Transformation*, traced the crises of capitalism to the fact that it "disimbedded" economic activity from community. He said that throughout human history, economic activity had been embedded in society, part of a larger social order that included religion, government, families, and the natural environment. The Industrial Revolution upended this. It turned labor and land into market commodities—inputs into the great machine of industry. They were to be "bought and sold, used and destroyed, as if they were simply merchandise," Polanyi wrote. But these were fictitious commodities. For they were none other than human beings and the earth.[11]

The economic aspect of land—its price in the market—is only one of its many facets. Land is the foundation of life. It's the planet, the seasons, the source of sustenance. To turn it into a commodity, governed only by market forces, is to threaten the web of life that depends upon it.

A place like Island Cohousing runs this process in reverse. It decommodifies the land, putting it again under the control of community—through a design that is sensitive to market forces but not subject to them. It re-embeds economic activity in cultural and ecological context. It re-embeds ownership in community.

With a silent intelligence, such designs show how the deep blueprints of cultural understanding can be rewritten. It's part of the "metaphysical reconstruction" that E. F. Schumacher said would be needed to transform our economy. When property is designed in a generative way, it's no longer about sole and despotic dominion. It isn't about standing apart from the objects we own and squeezing every penny from them. It's about being interwoven with the life around us.

FROM OBJECTS TO RELATIONSHIPS

The "shift from the parts to the whole is the central aspect of the conceptual revolution we now need," Fritjof Capra said. In classical Newtonian mechanics, the behavior of individual parts determines the behavior of the whole. But in systems thinking, the whole determines the behavior of parts.

In the new reality that physicists conceived at the turn of the last century, they recognized that subatomic "particles" are not things but *interconnections among things*. As Henry Stapp put it, an elementary particle is "in essence, a set of relationships that reach outward to other things." What we call a part is simply a pattern in a web of relationships. "The shift from the parts to the whole can also be seen as a shift from objects to relationships," Capra said.[12] A shift from dominion to community.

The choice between growth and no growth isn't the place to begin redesigning economic activity. The place to begin is with relationships: to each other and to the living earth.

On the night I'd first arrived and had dinner with John and Chris, I was struck not only by the welcoming sense of community at Island Cohousing but also by the simplicity of the home where this company president lived. When John drove me around that next day, he took me past the house where he and Chris had lived before, which was larger and more valuable than their current home. Their cohousing home was simple. Four bedrooms. And on the first floor, one combined kitchen, dining, and living space. The staircase post was a bare branch from one of the wizened oaks on the property, stripped and sanded but not otherwise industrialized. There was a single rug on a bare wood floor, some simple furniture. That was it. John and Chris don't have a glitzy lifestyle—not because they can't afford it but because they don't want it. In relationship and in community, they seem to have found what they sought.

This is sufficiency at work—a genuine sense of having enough, feeling satisfied. Another term for sufficiency is happiness.

Still, as compelling as Island Cohousing and South Mountain and the other commons designs are, I feel that I'm seeing mostly an atomized, individualized version of the generative economy. What holds it together? How can it begin to cohere into an actual economic system? This is my next quest. I want to see, in one place, a whole social ecosystem of generative design.

....

EIGHT

BRINGING
FORTH
A WORLD

From Individualism to Community

The ground crunches beneath my feet as pavement gives way to dirt, dirt gives way to beach, and the beach slopes to the water where the Gulf of Maine stretches to the horizon. A small white lobster boat pulls into the dock below. Nearby, a handcrafted sign nailed to a tree tells me this is the North End Lobster Co-op—one of the more than 20 lobster cooperatives found in Maine. All around stand towering piles of lobster traps, six high, each as large as an end table. Behind me, a clutch of lobster boats are stacked in shelves, out of the water for the season. Winter is coming on, and most co-op members have stopped lobstering, though a few hardy souls will remain at it all year. A yellow dog comes loping up offering greetings, its owner nowhere in sight.

After the high-end little utopia on Martha's Vineyard, I've come to the coast of Maine for a reality check. Can generative economic models be set in motion in the state that is the poor cousin of New England? And if so, how? What's the larger system design that makes it possible? It seems to me that this lobster co-op, where people make an estimated $30,000 to $50,000 a year from hard manual labor, might offer some useful lessons.

With me is Keith Bisson from Coastal Enterprises, Inc. (CEI), of Wiscasset, Maine—the *community development corporation* (CDC) that helped a group of five lobster fishermen obtain $380,000 in financing to buy this place in 2002. The co-op now has 24 lobstermen as members, and activity from this property supports more than 40 families.

"A lot of those guys used to fish on the town wharf," Keith tells me. They had to haul their own bait and fuel every day. When they went to buy bait, he continues, "they'd be taken advantage of by wholesalers." Owning land gives them guaranteed access to the water, as well as a secure place for winter storage of boats and traps. They've built a bait cooler on-site, allowing them to store a ready supply. Buying bait collectively, they get better prices. They've also arranged for a lobster buyer to come regularly to the co-op—in the busy season, every day—so that lobsters are moved efficiently.

"Access to water is important," Keith says. "It's hard for working folks whose livelihood is dependent on water to afford to buy waterfront property." Of the 5,300 miles of shorefront in Maine, only 25 miles are still in use for fishing and marine industries. To preserve that land as working waterfront, CEI helped this lobster cooperative put a *working waterfront easement* on the property. Modeled after a conservation easement, this innovative ownership design was created by CEI and funded by a state bond program to the tune of $6.75 million. Some two dozen working waterfronts have been preserved, allowing hundreds of fishing families to support themselves. The easement is a covenant that attaches permanently to the property deed, guaranteeing that land will always be used for commercial fishing. Essentially, it involves selling development rights to the State of Maine. This lobster co-op received a check for $135,250—yet it maintains ownership and use of the land.[1]

Still another powerful ownership design represented here is Coastal Enterprises, a private nonprofit corporation with a generative mission. As a CDC, it traces its roots to the 1960s civil rights movement. Its founder, Ron Phillips, is a former seminary student who veered away from the ministry to pursue social justice through economic development. CEI isn't a traditional development agency, offering tax breaks to lure big corporations. Its mission is to create healthy communities in which everyone can reach his or her full potential. It focuses on creating local ownership and local wealth. A particular focus—as its name implies—is coastal activity. Fishing.

With a staff of 85, CEI operates also as a community development financial institution (CDFI), with more than $700 million under management. It's one of the 1,000, found in all 50 states, and it's particularly innovative in designing social and ecological covenants into transactions. Fishery borrowers are asked to sign agreements to take part in a Fishtag project, collecting scarce biological data.[2] A manufacturer borrower might be asked to commit to an Employment and Training Agreement (ETAG), to hire the unemployed, or to offer training to immigrants.[3] In short, CEI practices Stakeholder Finance, where capital is a friend to the community.

BEYOND MARKETS AND STATE

Here, clinging to the rocky shores of Maine, is the generative economy groping its way into being. People are making a living in difficult circumstances and modeling an inclusive economy along the way. The ecological commons is benefiting dramatically. At a time when the vast majority of the world's fish stocks are overexploited, the Maine lobster industry remains vibrant. Since the late 1980s, catches have been at record levels, despite intense commercial activity. While groundfish stocks—such as cod and halibut—support only 50 fishing boats in the Gulf of Maine, those same waters support 5,600 lobster boats.[4] The Maine lobster industry is often cited as an example of successful collective action in "common pool resource management."

"Collective action dilemmas have received an enormous amount of attention from social scientists, primarily because they describe so many of the most vexing problems plaguing humanity," wrote James Acheson in *Capturing the Commons: Devising Institutions to Manage the Maine Lobster Industry*.[5] The problem is "the tragedy of the commons," as Garrett Hardin described it in his 1968 essay. Hardin said that if there were a common pasture on which everyone could graze cows, soon the land would be overgrazed and become worthless. The only solutions, he wrote, were state control or private ownership—"either socialism or the privatism of free enterprise."[6]

But in 2009, Elinor Ostrom won the Nobel Prize in economics (the first woman to do so) for research showing that old dichotomy to be false. All over the world, she and her colleagues found communities that spontaneously devised ways to manage the commons successfully. These include irrigation systems in the Philippines, forests in Africa and Asia, grazing systems in Switzerland, and groundwater regimes in California. As Ostrom wrote, many of these involve "rich mixtures of 'private-like' and 'public-like' institutions defying classification in a sterile dichotomy." She titled her Nobel lecture "Beyond Markets and States."[7]

Something fascinating is at work in the Maine lobster industry. Going beyond old notions of traditional private property versus state intervention, a whole range of new economic architectures are in use. Alternative ownership designs play key roles. But they do so inside a larger frame of supportive infrastructure—a *social ecosystem* of generative design.[8] The law operates in the background to help bring this economy into existence and hold it in place—yet its role is more innovative than top-down regulation. A panoply of supportive institutions and rules have evolved here mostly from the ground up—with "ground" meaning the bottom of the ocean, where lobster live and breed, and from which fishermen scratch out a living.

I'd come to Maine to experience two things on this, my final journey through the commons. First, I wanted to see a living example of the role of government in supporting a generative economy. Second, I wanted to see a whole family of generative ownership designs *in situ*. I wanted to categorize the various models and see it all operating as a whole system. I hoped to capture in this one place a sense of the social ecosystem of the generative economy.

THE FISHERMAN SCIENTIST

I make a date to talk with Ted Ames, the fisherman-scientist who won a 2005 MacArthur award (the so-called genius award), and I catch up with him in his office at Bowdoin College in Brunswick, where he's serving as visiting scholar for a year. He is a small man with youthful energy and the weathered face of someone who's spent years on the water. In the mid-

1990s, he and his wife, Robin Alden—at the time, commissioner of the Maine Department of Marine Resources—helped put in place an innovative plan to protect the lobster industry, which Ted calls "a collaborative, ecosystem-based approach."

There was a time, he tells me, when the lobster industry in Maine was in the same state of collapse as other fisheries are today. "In the 1930s, the bottom fell out of lobstering," he says. Canneries were buying and processing all sizes of lobsters, and there were no regulations restricting what could be caught. Small lobsters and broodstock were being taken, which was decimating the next generation of lobsters. Big boats had also begun auto-trawling in the Gulf of Maine—a massively extractive approach that destroyed habitat and damaged traps. Lobstering had become "too efficient, too industrial," Ted explains, if you wanted to preserve habitat to grow another crop. A new law was passed in 1947, which in Ted's words said, "Thou shalt not catch lobster in Maine with anything but a lobster trap."

It was part of a series of ecological ground rules that evolved over time in Maine. The use of traps protects habitat. Other rules prohibit the taking of egged females, protect juveniles until they are appropriately large, and protect older lobsters known to be good broodstock. Lobstermen were instrumental in lobbying for all these rules, some of which evolved out of best practices already in use.

Yet ecological rules alone weren't enough. Attention was also needed to *social architectures*, for the issue was not only *what* could be taken but *how* and *by whom*. Tending to such matters was the aim of the 1995 regulations. As the lobster industry recovered and became steadily productive, it was under increasing pressure from big boats and new technologies. To rein that in, in 1995 the legislature passed the zone management law, which does three things: it establishes individual trap limits; it controls entry into the industry; and, most innovative, it delegates a good deal of authority to local lobstermen, through the zone management system.

The law divides the coast into seven zones, each run by a council elected by licensed lobster fishermen. The zones contain districts of lobster license holders who elect representatives to their zone council. These councils are technically advisory to state authorities, but their recommendations are generally adopted. They have certain areas of oversight. They can establish trap limits, differing from zone to zone, as long as they don't exceed the state maximum. They help determine rules controlling entry into the industry, such as educational or apprenticeship requirements. And they have a voice in other matters dear to a lobsterman's heart, such as how many traps can be hung from a single buoy.[9]

"It's called democracy," Ted says. "Isn't that a novel concept?"

It is strikingly novel, in more ways than one. The law stipulates that lobster fishing in inshore waters can be done only by *owner-operated boats*. Large corporate-owned boats are still needed in offshore waters, Ted says, because only big boats can operate safely there. But corporate boats can no longer fish for lobster in sensitive coastal waters, where breeding occurs. It's a powerful use of ownership design as a tool to protect both commons and fishing communities. According to James Acheson, the ownership rule is explicitly intended to prevent corporations like Shaftmaster Corporation—which operates out of New Hampshire, using big trawlers with hired captains and crews tending large numbers of traps—from coming to Maine and dominating and destroying lobster grounds.[10]

Big boats like those "could clean out one area and move to another," Ted says. "The business plan for that kind of operation is completely different from the small-scale operator, where boats are invariably owned by individuals or families." The ownership rule is supplemented by another provision requiring an apprenticeship period. No one can obtain a lobster license without working two years on another lobster boat, where stewardship traditions and lobstering etiquette are learned.

These rules set the stage for the zone councils. Voting for these councils is one-person, one vote—very different from the corporate world, where voting rights are proportional to wealth holdings. This empowers fishermen with small and medium-sized operations. As Acheson wrote, "These men had grown tired of watching 'big fishermen' or 'hogs' take a disproportionate amount of the lobsters and cause huge trap tangles in the process." In passing trap limits for their zones, the little guys rein in that behavior.[11]

FRAMING THE GENERATIVE ECONOMY

Both lobsters and fishing families thrive in Maine, because the system works at many levels to restrain extractive behavior and encourage generative behavior. There are many kinds of rules here, but operating in the background, as a kind of wire frame supporting the system, are different kinds of ownership architectures. As Acheson wrote:

> According to the law of Maine, all of the oceans, lakes, and rivers are public property. Ocean waters are held in trust by the state for all citizens. All ocean beaches to the high tide mark are owned by the state, and all citizens have legal access to them.[12]

At this level, the overarching ownership concept is the ancient notion of *trust*: holding something in trust for the common good and for future generations. As trustee, the state of Maine calls on the property concept known as *usufruct*—the temporary right to use property belonging to someone else, as long as the property isn't damaged—to create rules for right of access. In a sense, Maine holds the bundle of twigs of various property rights. And out of that bundle it separates usufruct rights, allocating certain of those rights to small owner-operators, leaving a different set of rights to corporate owners.

This *law of the ocean* is one supportive frame here. Another frame is provided by various *enterprise ownership designs*, such as cooperatives, CDCs, and CDFIs. Because of those sturdy background patterns, Coastal Enterprises can emerge as a CDC/CDFI, another part of the ecosystem of support for lobstermen.

CEI, in turn, devised a new contractual form of ownership design with the *working waterfront covenant*, which helps keep waterfront property in the hands of fishing families. Fishing families themselves join together to form groups like the North End Lobster Cooperative, which helps them to thrive in a competitive environment. At various points, these ownership designs emerge from the background like knots on a fishing net, shaping the energies of the system into stable patterns that tend to create generative outcomes.

What is explicitly restricted in this picture is extractive design. Large corporate boats can operate only in designated areas. Instead of permitting limitless liberty to absentee owners for the seeking of wealth—by hired hands indifferent to local custom—Maine set spinning a new governing pattern. It operates by generative principles, like the principle that the right of extraction has limits. That the right to make a living comes before the right to make a killing. That fairness for the many is more important than maximizing by the few. That sustaining the prosperity of larger living systems, both human and wild, is the root condition for the flourishing of all. And that these new economic principles are to be grounded in governance of, by, and for the community. *Fairness, sustainability, community:* the fundamental values of the generative economy are all at work. Through design.

As a fisherman and the son of a fisherman, Ted Ames doesn't use such lofty terms. "It's worked—that's the neat part," he says. "When basic rules are vetted by fishermen themselves, you get a different dynamic." Although there's a powerful state role in this social ecosystem, much of what arose in Maine came from fishermen, their practices, their lobbying efforts, their needs—and by extension, from the living needs of lobsters.

The notion of lobster zones has its genesis in a history of territoriality in the Maine lobster industry that goes back generations. A newcomer can't just show up and start throwing traps in the water without incurring the wrath of locals. By time-honored tradition, lobstermen use small areas near their home harbor, working waters their families have worked for decades, which they defend vigorously.

As Acheson wrote, "At some point, usufructory rights strengthened into a sense of ownership, giving people justification for defending the areas against the incursions of others." The lobstering territories were ownership in embryo. This territorial system, he continued, is "the root institution governing the lobster industry, making possible the generation of other kinds of rule systems." The territorial system, Acheson said, "helped produce a sense of stewardship and one of the most effective conservation programs in any fishery in the industrialized world."[13]

EMERGENCE AS A PATH
TO LARGE-SCALE CHANGE

In the Maine lobster industry we see a process that systems thinking calls emergence. Instead of imposing abstract, large-scale concepts from the top down, the governing policies in this case emerged from the community. As Fritjof Capra emphasizes, effective change needs to be a living process. In natural systems, he observes, transformational change happens when traditional patterns reach "critical points of instability," creating a crisis that is resolved by the spontaneous emergence of new ordered patterns. It's known as *self-organization*, or, simply, emergence. "Creativity—the generation of new forms—is a key property of all living systems," Capra says. "Life constantly reaches out into novelty."[14]

Seeing the emergence of a new economy as a natural process is different from thinking of the competition of two ideologies vying for dominance, which is the paradigm of capitalism versus communism. Change as an emergent process doesn't mean the absence of crisis or conflict. Both were present in Maine. And it doesn't mean that some universally beloved outcome is reached. Solutions adopted in Maine generally favored one group at the expense of another. These things are natural in social systems. What emergence does mean, as an approach to policy, is starting small, proceeding organically, scaling up existing practice, and trusting that a creative solution is present in the very circumstances causing a crisis. Emergence also means that solutions may first appear not in politics but in business. One role of policy is to formalize and scale up what has emerged.

We can see this process at work in the development of other generative designs, such as *microfinance*. It began with the single example of Grameen Bank in Bangladesh making tiny loans to poor women and eventually mushroomed into a massive global industry. Microfinance today has its own rating agencies, consultants, conferences, institutes, and billions upon billions of dollars in lending. Central Asia alone is home to more than

1,000 microfinance institutions. In India, the number of microfinance clients grew tenfold over four years to surpass 10 million.[15] The process of emergence mirrors that of evolution, where nature discovers designs through trial and error. A variety of new designs are tried out, and those that succeed are replicated and spread.

In social systems, as Meg Wheatley from the Berkana Institute suggested, the formation of networks is central to emergence—like the networks and institutes supporting microfinance. "We don't need to convince large numbers of people to change," Wheatley wrote; "instead we need to connect with kindred spirits" who share a common vision. In this way, separate, disconnected local actions begin to spring up simultaneously. When they "connect with each other as networks, then strengthen as communities of practice, suddenly and surprisingly a new system emerges at a greater level of scale." Powerful emergent phenomena can appear without warning, such as the organic food movement. What can't be accomplished by politics or strategy just happens.[16]

What can block emergence is the lack of clear mental models. Resource depletion often occurs, Elinor Ostrom and her co-authors wrote, when governments adopt schemes to privatize or centralize resource management in ways "that undermine or destroy communal rights." Problems arise, she continued, "because the state does not recognize or support informal common-property regimes." Lacking a simple mental model that allows them to see what's going on, government leaders blunder.[17]

The lack of clear design parameters can allow emergent phenomena to go astray in other ways—as happened with microfinance. In recent years, a few lenders shifted out of nonprofit status and sold ownership into public stock markets. The Mexican microlender Compartamos did this in 2007, and SKS Microfinance in India followed in 2010. In the pursuit of higher profits for shareholders, these banks raised interest rates and began pursuing debt collection more aggressively. As Muhammad Yunus explained, empathy once shown toward borrowers disappeared, and "borrowers came to believe that lenders were taking advantage of them." In India, some stopped repaying their loans, and a full-blown crisis in the field erupted. Microfinance took a wrong turn because it lacked design parameters. If the industry were to adopt ethical standards limiting extractive ownership—as the Maine lobster industry did—it might pave a resilient path to excellence again.[18]

NAMING AIDS SEEING

Much of the work of creating clear mental models is a process of naming. In the broad field of generative ownership design, this work isn't yet far advanced. The sheer abundance of designs makes it hard to see that a unified phenomenon is at work. It can help to think in terms of a single *family* of generative design. Within it we can separate out different broad *categories* and *subcategories.* But since boundaries between these often aren't clear, it can also be helpful to think in terms of *patterns of design,* as a way to reveal common shapes in the profusion (these patterns are discussed in greater detail in part 3).

In my work, I've seen four broad categories of generative ownership design—many of which I saw in Maine. Rather than a definitive categorization, consider this a loose grouping, possibly a starting point for further work by others.

1. **Commons ownership and governance.** Here, assets are held or governed in *common.* The ocean, a forest, land, a park, a municipal power plant (like Hull Wind) is held or governed *indivisibly by a community.*

2. **Stakeholder ownership.** This is ownership by people with a *human stake in a private enterprise*—as opposed to a purely speculative, financial stake. It includes cooperatives, partnerships, credit unions, mutual insurance companies, employee-owned firms, and family-owned companies. But for these models to be generative, their purpose must be life serving (not all mutual, employee, or family ownership can be considered generative).

3. **Social enterprise.** These organizations have a *primary social or environmental mission* and use business methods to pursue it. They can be nonprofits, subsidiaries of nonprofits, or private businesses. Social enterprises sometimes blur the line between for-profit and nonprofit.

4. **Mission-controlled corporations.** These are corporations with a strong social mission that are *owned* in conventional ways (often with publicly traded shares), yet they keep *governing control* in mission-oriented hands.

They include the large foundation-controlled companies common across northern Europe. A family or a trust can also be in control.

The law governing ocean waters in Maine is an example of commons ownership. The lobster cooperatives are a form of stakeholder ownership. Coastal Enterprises, Inc., is an example of a social enterprise. These different enterprises use different ownership designs toward similar ends—to create the conditions for life.

Generative design, in essence, means kinds of ownership that have a Living Purpose, with at least one other design pattern that serves to hold that purpose in place (otherwise, what you have is not a design but only a good intention). With Hull Wind, the most important design pattern is Mission-Controlled Governance. The aim is not to maximize profits but to generate electricity for a community at an affordable price; the enterprise is governed with that end in mind. With lobster cooperatives, Rooted Membership is the defining element; the people who use the facility own it—they're the members. They also govern it. As a community development financial institution, Coastal Enterprises practices Stakeholder Finance to carry out its mission; its aim isn't extracting financial wealth from communities but helping them to thrive. Yet it makes loans, not grants. It blurs the line between for-profit and nonprofit, because it uses business methods to pursue a social purpose. As a CDFI, Coastal Enterprises is also part of an Ethical Network of other CDFIs, sharing similar goals (CDFIs are formally recognized in federal law).

If there are more kinds of generative design than many people realize, the scale of activity is also larger than might be supposed. In the United States, more than 130 million Americans are members of a co-op or credit union. More Americans hold memberships in co-ops than hold stock in the stock market.[19] Worldwide, cooperatives employ more people than all multinationals combined.[20] In Colombia, SaludCoop provides health care services to a quarter of the population. The Japanese Consumers Cooperative Union serves 31 percent of the nation's households. In Spain, the Mondragon Corporacion Cooperativa is the nation's seventh largest industrial concern. Cooperatives account for 71 percent of fishery production in Korea, 40 percent of agriculture in Brazil, and 36 percent of the retail market in Denmark. Cooperatives represent 45 percent of the GDP of Kenya and 22 percent of GDP in New Zealand.[21]

Or take employee ownership. In the United States, the National Center for Employee Ownership reports that there are 11,300 employee-owned firms, with some 14 million participants. And in Europe, large companies have nearly 10 million employee-owners. Employee ownership has been increasing in such countries as Spain, Poland, France, Denmark, and Sweden.[22]

Granted, not all of these companies are generative, if they don't have a generative mission (and many may not). But their impact on employee well-being can still be significant. Workers in US firms with employee stock ownership plans have been shown to have 2.5 times the retirement assets of comparable employees at other firms.[23] And there may be a greater potential for generative activity when companies are majority employee owned; one estimate put the number of such companies in the United States at 2,000 to 3,000, with about 1 million employees.[24]

BRINGING FORTH A WORLD

Generative design is such a large domain, how has it managed to remain so invisible? The answer has something to do with naming—in systems thinking, *cognition*.

According to the Santiago Theory of Cognition, developed by Humberto Maturana and Francisco Varela, humans do not perceive the external world in a direct way but instead filter it through our own internal maps. As we encounter new situations, we alter those internal maps. That's how learning occurs. Through this process of building up our internal model, we construct the world in which we live. As Fritjof Capra wrote, cognition "is not a representation of an independently existing world, but rather a continual bringing forth of a world through the process of living." The act of knowing brings forth a new world inside us. When I learn to identify a particular bird, I begin to see it more regularly. I perceive something I'd missed. Naming helps us to see.[25]

The process is more than individual, because language represents *shared reality*—the world of culture. Human consciousness is a social phenomenon. When a culture lacks precise words for things, we have difficulty perceiving them. At one time, we lacked language for sexism and racial discrimination. The bringing forth of this new language helped a new world to emerge, where women and racial minorities gained power. Words have impact when they name something on the edge of emergence in the collective awareness, some collective impulse seeking recognition and release.

When Grameen Bank makes microloans to help the poor and a whole microfinance industry mushrooms into existence, some collective impulse is seeking release. When Elinor Ostrom tells us that communities all over the world are managing the commons successfully, it's as if a spring of cold water has burst forth. Something we needed has been named, and now we can see it. Because we see it, we can bring forth more of it. This can happen with the models and processes of the generative economy. What begins as an experiment in one place can be replicated and spread, like shoots of a new forest rising up.

After I talked with Ted Ames, he returned to his work at Penobscot East Resource Center, the nonprofit that he and his wife founded. Its website told me he was rigging up his boat to go fishing for the summer and fall seasons.[26]

I found a paper he'd talked about, where he suggested that lessons from the Maine lobster industry could be applied to fishing for cod, haddock, flounder, and other groundfish. The approach would involve coastal management units of reasonable size, with inshore areas collaboratively managed by local councils. Spawning grounds would be protected by prohibiting big corporate boats and requiring "habitat-friendly gear." Translation: thou shalt not fish with anything but a hook and a line.[27]

Depleted fisheries in the region have potential for renewal, he'd said to me, because several dams are coming down in rivers where groundfish used to swim, and hundreds of miles of old spawning habitat will be reopening. No one has so far taken his plan seriously, he said. But he remains hopeful. "I think you could re-create a lot of the original abundance that existed here," he said. "We have an uncanny ability to screw things up, and also the ability to make things better."

III

Creating Living Companies

The Five Core Elements of Generative Ownership Design

All acts of design are governed by a pattern language. Patterns recur when the language we use to make our world becomes widely shared. Among the most basic elements that create patterns of ownership are purpose, membership, governance, capital, and networks. These form a simple language of ownership design. With these elements, we can create a variety of kinds of ownership, just as ordinary language allows us to create a variety of sentences. In their generative form, these elements are Living Purpose, Rooted Membership, Mission-Controlled Governance, Stakeholder Finance, and Ethical Networks. Employed toward creating the conditions for life, these elements combine to form a sturdy framework for living companies. Should these kinds of companies one day become a new norm, they might serve as root and branch of a generative economy, where all life can flourish for generations to come. The search to see these design patterns at work in enterprises of substantial size shapes the journeys of part 3.[1]

NINE

LIVING
PURPOSE

Creating the Conditions for Life

One of the most extraordinarily alive companies I know is a tiny children's bookstore in Minneapolis called Wild Rumpus, where I love to take friends and family in the same spirit with which I might take them to visit a museum or a treasured church or a sacred grove of trees. To visit this store is an event. We often make a morning of it, and inevitably we linger. I show my niece the mice under glass in the floor, a hidden warren of life literally beneath the floorboards. I tell her, watch for the chickens—they're funny chickens without tails, and with heads that are barely visible, so they look like bits of white fluff walking about. And then there are the cats, the Manx cats, the world's friendliest cats, who submit to nonstop petting by children all the day long, remarkably without complaint. It is the animals who draw me to this place, and once there, I browse amid the books, taking home a journal for myself, an early Christmas gift for a nephew, or a bookmark for my partner. I have a sense of ownership about this store. I feel at home there, always. It is alive. It is a place that has what architect Christopher Alexander calls that "sleepy awkward grace which comes from perfect ease." I leave with a sense of gratitude.

What makes the place alive, one might imagine, are the animals. Yet this bookstore is very different from the Rainforest Café across town, out at the Mall of America, which also features animals. Granted, they're stuffed animals: plush parrots hanging from perches, calling out their mechanical "caw" when you walk by. Wild Rumpus is also very different from

PetSmart, which has animals, live ones, all in cages down neat rows on immaculate linoleum floors.

The difference is more than the animals. It's a spirit, a sense of aliveness, not only in the animals but in me when I'm in the place, and in everyone I've ever taken there. I've visited a lot of companies in the field of socially responsible business, and I've felt this spirit at other places, large and small. I've seen it driven out of companies more times than I can count. In my third set of journeys, I wanted to pin down more precisely what it is, what makes it happen, what keeps it alive over time, what kills it.

What makes a company a living company?

What makes an enterprise not just responsible, or ethical, or in possession of the right legal charter, but literally alive, a place where you want to go and where you feel alive when you do? Respect for the living community of the earth is a critical starting point, but by itself it's not enough. Living companies are about more than sustainability, as it's commonly understood. In business terms, sustainability too often means greening a product line but keeping the growth machine revved on high, keeping the people who make and sell the products in a state of subordination, and treating customers like sources of profit and little more.

There is a broader sensibility in a truly living company that I wanted to see in action. It has to do not only with *physical technologies* but also with *social architectures*: how companies themselves come alive in a human, social sense. What I wanted to see in this set of journeys was how the living relationships that compose a company become living processes. Not deadening processes, like what the machinery of mortgage creation became, but living systems that feel alive to those within them and that help create the conditions for life all around.

THE QUALITY WITHOUT A NAME

The question I ask about the social architecture of companies is one that Alexander asks about the physical architecture of buildings: what makes them come alive? He explores the answers in his seminal work on architecture, *The Timeless Way of Building*, published in 1979 and a classic still widely read today. He begins:

> There is a central quality which is the root criterion of life and spirit in a man, a town, a building, or a wilderness. This quality is objective and precise, but it cannot be named. The search which we make for this quality, in our own lives, is the central search of any person, and the crux of any individual person's story. It is the search for those moments and situations when we are most alive.[1]

Alexander called this root criterion "the quality without a name." It cannot be named precisely, he said, for it is never the same twice, always taking its shape from the particular place where it occurs. We often call this quality *aliveness*. We might also use words like *whole*, *comfortable*, or *free*, he said. He suggested further, perhaps *egoless* or *eternal*. I would add the word *genuine*.

"It is a subtle kind of freedom from inner contradictions," Alexander wrote. "A system has this quality when it is at one with itself; it lacks it when it is divided. It has it when it is true to its own inner forces; lacks it when it is untrue to its own inner forces." We know this quality when we encounter it in a person, he continued, for when a person "is true to himself, you feel at once that he is 'more real' than other people are." When our world has this quality, people can be alive and self-creating. When the world lacks this quality, he says, people cannot be alive but will be self-destroying, and miserable.[2]

To define this quality in a building or a town, Alexander suggested we begin by recognizing that every place is given its character by the patterns of events that keep happening there. Each building and town is made of these patterns in space and of nothing else. The more living patterns there are in a place, "the more it has that self-maintaining fire which is the quality without a name." We feel this quality, he continued, in "some tiny gothic church, an old New England house, an Alpine hill village, an ancient Zen temple, a seat by a mountain stream, a courtyard filled with blue and yellow tiles among the earth." To unlock the secrets of how to generate this quality, "we must first learn how to discover patterns which are deep, and capable of generating life." And then we must find ways to speak to one another about these patterns. We need a language to describe them: a *pattern language*.

While buildings are made of patterns in space, companies and organizations are made of *patterns of relationships*. A person walks into Starbucks and orders a decaf soy latte, and the employee makes it fresh, by hand. An investor buys stock in a company, and its executives measure success as a rising stock price. I walk into Wild Rumpus and show my niece the mice. The patterns that compose an enterprise are made from the patterns of interactions among various parties: owners, investors, employees, customers. When I walk into a bank, I don't go behind the desk and start printing out loan documents and deciding on interest rates. That's the banker's role. As an investor, I don't tell a company's workers how often they should wax the floors. That's their work.

The patterns of events that happen at Beverly Cooperative Bank are distinctly different from those at Aegis. Making a loan to a neighbor, keeping that loan on the books, dealing with the borrower when he or she hits a hard time—this is a pattern of relationships true to its own inner forces. It is a system rooted in a particular place, focused on a Living Purpose of serving that human community. It is a system capable of resolving its own forces, maintaining its own energies, and benefiting most everyone involved. It's a very different pattern of relationships than what is at work when a mortgage broker for Aegis writes a loan for the Haroldsons with terms they don't understand and then sells off that loan to investors, knowing it may go bad. That's a company not true to its own forces. It is setting forces loose that will be resolved only when the Haroldsons lose their home, when investors suffer a loss, and ultimately, when Aegis itself goes bankrupt.

The very different patterns of relationships of these two financial firms are held together, most fundamentally, by a *set of values*, and by a *purpose* based on those values, which is institutionalized in the organization. Aegis is focused on financial wealth for its owners. Beverly Cooperative Bank is focused on the ongoing life of the bank and the community.

When an enterprise says it's focused on the community and actually is focused on the community, it is free from contradiction. When systems are free from inner contradictions, Alexander said, "they take their place among the order of things which stand outside of time." They become *eternal*. What makes them eternal, he said, is their ordinariness.[3] Beverly Cooperative Bank need not be, and is not, a heroic institution. It's not a national leader in all things socially responsible. It's a bank going about the real business of banking, much like a tree going about the business of being a tree. It's simply itself. By being a genuine bank, it is naturally in service to the community, for this is the reason why communities allow banks to exist.

Living Purpose—being of service to the community as a way to feed the self—is the *sine qua non* of all generative ownership design. It is the single irreducibly necessary core of every generative enterprise. We see Living Purpose at work in the design of the Maine lobster industry, in the work of Grameen Bank, in the community forests of Mexico, in the community ownership of Hull Wind, in the employee ownership of South Mountain Company.

THE HIDDEN FORCES OF FINANCIAL PURPOSE

These entities may or may not have a formal mission statement framed on a wall somewhere. As systems theorist Donella Meadows observed, "A system's function or purpose is not necessarily spoken, written, or expressed explicitly, except through the operation of the system." She said the best way to determine a system's purpose is to watch how it behaves. Purpose isn't about rhetoric or stated goals. It's about behavior.[4]

System purpose reveals itself over time
as a series of events.

A system is true to itself when the values it espouses—like ethics, sustainability, and community service—are consonant with its behavior over time. Enron had a lovely code of ethics, which had virtually nothing to do with its behavior. It was a company harboring "hidden forces," to use Alexander's term. As he wrote, "when a person's forces are resolved, it makes us feel at home, because we know, by some sixth sense, that there are no other unexpected forces lurking underground." By contrast, when a system is not true to itself, it will have hidden forces operating in the background. "When a place is lifeless or unreal, there is almost always a mastermind behind it," Alexander wrote. "It is so filled with the will of its maker that there is no room for its own nature." It is divided against itself.[5]

I saw unexpected forces lurking underground at companies many times when I was publishing *Business Ethics*. To take one example, I watched apparel and footwear companies adopt ethical codes of conduct for their suppliers, going so far as to send auditors to factories overseas to gauge compliance. The aim was to set up a feedback loop that said, respect wage laws, treat workers decently. And the players involved seemed sincere. Yet their work was subtly counteracted by a stronger feedback loop operating in the background, which sent a contradictory message. Its signals reached suppliers when buyers from the same companies said, deliver your goods to us at the lowest possible price, on the fastest possible schedule. Low costs and fast schedules do not create conditions conducive to worker well-being. Yet suppliers knew their income depended on meeting buyer requirements. Buyers' signals arrived, so to speak, with checks attached.

Money speaks more loudly than ethical codes. And money is what feeds company income statements, which are based on a model of maximizing income and minimizing costs. With publicly traded companies, these financial statements link to financial markets, where the feedback loops say, keep profits/earnings growing in order to keep stock price climbing. Stock prices, in turn, link to stock options for executives. Needless to say, this financial feedback loop is stronger than the weak feedback loop of an ethical code, no matter how sincere the auditors.

Maximizing financial gains lurks in the background of publicly traded companies because it's in their fundamental ownership frame. Most basically, it is the heart of their purpose. Ethics training, corporate social responsibility (CSR), and sustainability programs too often don't penetrate to the heart of the matter. They don't alter *company purpose*. This is the reason why I watched whole industries grow up in ethics training,

CSR programs, and the rest—only to marvel at how profit maximization remained impervious to every kind of ethical code thrown at it.

THE ROLE OF LAW

For many years, I believed the problem was in the law. I wasn't alone in that thinking. Still today, the idea that public corporations have a legal duty to maximize gains for shareholders remains the conventional wisdom. It's widely accepted by business and policy elites in the United States and much of the rest of the world, and has been the dominant theory of corporate purpose since the 1990s. *But it isn't true.* That's the view of an increasing number of legal theorists, including Lynn Stout, professor of corporate and securities law at Cornell Law School. In her new book, *The Shareholder Value Myth*, she states that United States corporate law does not require, and never has required, directors of public corporations to maximize shareholder wealth.

This supposed duty rests on incorrect factual assumptions, she continues, including the erroneous idea that shareholders "own" the corporation. In truth, what shareholders own are *their shares*, not the corporation itself, Stout says. The notion that corporations have a legal duty to maximize profits for shareholders is simply an ideology. And it's an ideology that's increasingly outmoded, under challenge by new scholarly articles appearing almost daily, Stout observes. "As a theory of corporate purpose," she adds, "it is poised for intellectual collapse."[6]

Much more can be said about the legal debate around corporate purpose. Be forewarned: this is the thicket from which few emerge with sanity intact. For those intrepid souls willing to venture deeper into this territory, I recommend Stout's book.

While legal scholars wrangle, others are working to establish a new, more generative corporate model—the *benefit corporation*—with a broader purpose baked into its governing legal documents. Benefit corporations, as recognized in the laws of a few states, aim to benefit society and the environment in addition to their shareholders. A slight variation on the model is the B Corporation, created through a private certification process that requires companies to declare a social purpose in their governing documents and to meet independent standards of social and environmental performance.[7]

The broad concept of the benefit corporation is based in part on the ideas of Leslie Christian, president of Portfolio 21 Investments. During her long participation in Corporation 20/20, I watched as she formulated and launched a new kind of company called Upstream 21, an Oregon holding company that buys and holds small, local companies committed to sustainability. Oregon state law—like the law of many US states and the law of many nations around the world—says that corporate directors must act in the best interests of the corporation and its shareholders. Working within that framework, Upstream 21 adopted articles of incorporation that say the "best interests" of the company embrace not only shareholder interests but also those of the environment, customers, suppliers, and local communities. The firm also changed voting rights, so that those with a living stake in the firm—such as employees and initial direct investors—have more voting power than those who might purchase company stock secondhand. Voting rights diminish when they pass from direct investors to investors in the secondary market.[8]

Drawing on the language of purpose devised by Upstream 21, the founders of B Lab—Jay Coen Gilbert, Bart Houlahan, and Andrew Kassoy—created a standard template for a new kind of company, built around this expanded purpose. They designed and added a set of social performance standards. And from Heerad Sabeti, a social entrepreneur leading the work for new kinds of social enterprises, they obtained permission to use the name he devised: the "benefit" company.[9] In 2010, Maryland became the first state to pass benefit corporation legislation, formalizing this new option in law. Other states soon followed, including Vermont, New Jersey, New York, Virginia, Hawaii, and California, with many others expressing interest.[10]

Within two years, some 500 companies signed up to be B Corporations, including a few fairly substantial companies, like Seventh Generation, a national distributor of household products for green living, with $150 million in sales. Here, however, is where the plot thickens.

UNTO THE NEXT GENERATION

Seventh Generation was cofounded more than 20 years ago by Jeffrey Hollender, someone active in Corporation 20/20. He was one among many founders of socially responsible companies who wrestled with the challenge of keeping their social legacy alive as their companies grew larger, brought in investors, and began passing leadership to the next generation. It was a challenge that we at *Business Ethics* dubbed the "legacy problem."[11] Few of the companies I'd studied solved it to their full satisfaction.

Many once-idealistic companies found their social mission under pressure once they went public or were sold to publicly traded companies. There was Ben & Jerry's, sold to Unilever against its founders' wishes; Aveda, sold to Estée Lauder; Stonyfield Yogurt to Groupe Danone; Kashi to Kellogg; Tom's of Maine to Colgate; Odwalla to Coca-Cola. I remembered hearing the founder of Odwalla, Greg Steltenpohl, speak at a meeting after he'd sold his firm, commenting ruefully, "I used to be in the business of making great juice; now I'm in the business of making money."

Jeffrey Hollender seemed to have the challenge under control. For six years, Seventh Generation had been a publicly traded company, but in 1999 Jeffrey took it private again, because he found that the costs and pressures of being public outweighed the benefits. He remained at the helm—personally committed, in the words of a company "Corporate Consciousness Report," to embracing "a model of deeper business purpose, where economic growth is merged with social justice."[12] For Jeffrey, I knew that commitment was real. When he signed up Seventh Generation as a founding B Corporation, it seemed he was on his way to solving the social legacy problem. As he wrote in his book *The Responsibility Revolution*, "Perhaps there's no surer way for a company to live up to the authentic imperative … than to become a B Corporation."[13]

Then the day came when I was helping organize a meeting on company design and Jeffrey was scheduled to join us but had to back out at the last minute. New leadership was being brought in, he explained over the phone, and he needed to tend the home fires, because he found himself engaged in a struggle for the company's soul. Within a few months, news reached me that in late 2010, Jeffrey had been pushed out of the company he'd cofounded.

Even though Seventh Generation was no longer publicly traded, it succumbed to the pressure for growth and profit maximization. It had brought in a mainstream-minded new CEO plus $30 million in outside investments and had set the course for a plan to take the company from $150 million to a massive $1 billion in sales. Growth like that can be crushing to employees in a firm.[14] And as Jeffrey recognized, a company intent solely on growth may not always be focused on the rigorous choices needed in ecological sourcing, nor prepared to make the occasional sacrifices required to be truly sustainable. He and the board had serious philosophical differences about issues like transparency, employee ownership, and how best to create shareholder value. In addition, Jeff told me, his board didn't consider him a "professional manager," despite his record in growing the firm to $150 million. Ultimately, the board ushered him out the door.[15]

Speaking publicly about the whole experience later, at the Sustainable Brands conference in June 2011, Jeffrey said he'd failed to put the right ownership design protections in place. "I didn't institutionalize values in the corporate structure," he said. "I took too much money from the wrong people. I failed to give enough of the company to the employees who would have protected what we'd built."[16] One lesson of the story seemed clear:

> *Benefit corporation language in company documents*
> *isn't enough.*

Lynn Stout is right. The problem is not primarily in the law. Changing the legal language of articles and bylaws does not necessarily touch a company's true purpose.

Let me hasten to add: The benefit corporation movement is without doubt a huge step in the right direction. It represents a vital codification of an emerging new sensibility. The B Corporation certification builds consumer awareness, brands responsible companies, and creates a potential learning community of companies. As society becomes more familiar with the concept of benefit corporations, the concept could also help create the cultural awareness that will facilitate further systemic reforms. The benefit corporation model is vitally important.

And as it exists at this point, it is not a complete design. It's like a house with an excellent floor but no ceiling and only one partial wall: a good place to start building but not a finished structure. My sense is that the creators of the B Corporation are smart guys, interested in developing the model over time. Perhaps what's needed is a larger set of standards analogous to a building code, similar to the LEED standards for green buildings. In the same way that LEED buildings are rated silver, gold, and platinum, ownership designs might receive similar graduated ratings for progressive design excellence. Meanwhile, single enterprises might adopt B certification as a floor and build their own design additions on top of it.[17]

> *The test of benefit corporations will be*
> *how well they succeed, over time,*
> *at those moments when founders lose control.*

One of these moments is when a company brings in substantial capital or goes public. As a temporal pattern, we can call it a time of Capital Infusion. The second moment is when the founder retires or sells. We might name this the temporal pattern of Founder Departure. These are the moments when the forces of finance have the chance to exert their magnetic influence, pulling good companies out of their previous orbit. The power of finance is that nearly irresistible lure of the potential to pocket massive amounts of financial wealth. The gale-force winds of this opportunity can be resisted only by those clearly focused on something more compelling, who have a guiding star so clearly in view that they know who they are and where they're going. And this allows them to put in place sturdy structures, rooted firmly to place, embodying that Living Purpose—*with other design protections also built in.* Good people empowered by good design: that's the aim. And no single design pattern constitutes a complete system that can accomplish it. As systems thinking tells us:

> *Resilience arises from patterns of many feedback*
> *loops, operating through different and redundant*
> *mechanisms—so if one fails, another kicks in.*[18]

On the B Corporation website is a powerful statement that says benefit corporations "are required to make decisions that are good for society, not just their shareholders."[19] It's a worthy goal, but the B Corporation model isn't there yet. Company founders will need to lead the way in making these designs more robust if they are to ensure that social mission is sustained into subsequent generations, past the founders' era.

It's one thing to have a truly living company when you're a tiny children's bookstore and the founder is still at the helm. That's analogous to the situation at virtually all B Corporations. It's something else again to keep that spirit alive when the company raises substantial capital or needs to help equity investors get their money back. Or when founders want to cash out. Or when the company grows large.

Even in the most ideal economy of the future, large companies will surely be needed. There's an argument to be made—as E. F. Schumacher did so eloquently—that small is beautiful, that the best companies may always be relatively small. This is an important topic for further research: is there an optimal scale for generative companies? I hope colleagues in the field of ownership design take up this question and find the definitive answer. But it's a conversation for another day.

What I hoped to solve, in my final set of journeys, was a different question: are there companies substantially larger than mom-and-pop shops, where the founders are long gone, that are truly living companies?

Are there large companies that have solved the legacy problem?

Some activists and theorists would suggest that this question is the wrong one, that the real issue is how to force all major companies into responsible design. They want to start with law, with regulation. My instincts tell me to begin instead with *positive models*. The energies of a system can't organize themselves around a negative (don't do this, don't do that). We need a positive vision of generative design that is so strong, it exerts it own magnetic power, drawing people in—just as the vision of democracy has magnetized people around the world. The seeds of this design are there in small, local, living companies. But if we can't solve the issue of keeping the souls of these companies alive past their founders, how can we possibly hope to make real change at large companies across the entire system?

What we need may not be a complicated legal formula but clear, simple descriptions of patterns that all of us can use. As Christopher Alexander wrote, we need languages "with the patterns in them so intense, so full of life again, that what we make within these languages will, almost of its own accord, begin to sing."[20]

Is it possible that these patterns are already alive and working at large firms? This seemed to me a critical test of the whole idea of generative design. Do such firms exist—and if so, what makes them work? If legal language doesn't complete their designs, what does? Firms that hint at the answers, I began to discover, are found all over the world. One I wanted to see—one I found utterly compelling—was the John Lewis Partnership in London. What I'd heard about this firm left me wondering if it was simply too good to be true. Was it?

TEN

ROOTED MEMBERSHIP

Ownership in Living Hands

"I was at my old job at Safeway for 18 years, and I had one bonus in those 18 years, for 50 pounds (US$82)," Emma tells me. When that store closed a few years back, this 30-something woman, mother to one young daughter, took a job down the street at a Waitrose near King's Cross station. She and I are standing inside that store and talking on this particular day, not far from the queen's palace in London. The store is part of a chain of UK supermarkets owned by the John Lewis Partnership (JLP). Emma works as a clerk on the floor, tending the cash register and straightening shelves. For that job at Waitrose, she gets a bonus every year; a recent one totaled 2,000 pounds (US$3,264). "I spent some on a holiday in the Canary Islands," she tells me. "It was my first holiday in four years."

The butcher at the meat counter who steps aside to talk with me—a middle-aged gentleman named John*—wears a white linen fedora, a crisp white shirt beneath a green-striped apron, and a bow tie. He explains that they are all required to wear a hat. But wearing a tie every day is his choice. "I just feel more dressed," he tells me. People notice touches like that at Waitrose, where pay raises are given for performance, including things such as "being a tidy person," John says. He tells me about his sister, Carol, who also works at Waitrose and has just been diagnosed with cancer. "They've been really good," he says, referring to the company. "There's a

---

* Both Emma and John asked that only their first names be used.

budget set aside for people like this. She's been off for three months, and they're holding her job. They tell me to tell her not to worry."

When employees at Waitrose and other JLP stores face a personal or family emergency like John and Carol faced, they can seek a grant or loan from the Committee for Financial Assistance. That committee, composed of and elected by employees, controls the special budget that John referred to, making decisions outside the chain of management. Help from that fund—plus the commitment to hold Carol's job—took "the money side of worries away," John says. She's had two major operations in less than a week. "When I came in today," he added, "the first thing the manager said was, 'How's Carol, how's she doing?'"

The clerk Emma and the butcher John are owners of the store I am visiting. They are among the 76,500 employee-owners of the John Lewis Partnership, the largest department store chain in the United Kingdom, with 35 department stores and 272 Waitrose grocery stores. Revenues of this company are £8.2 billion (US$13.4 billion). That means that if this were a US company, placed into the Fortune 500 list of the largest corporations, it would settle in at around 180.[1] This is higher than Monsanto and ConAgra. And it's a company 100 percent owned by its employees—or as this firm calls them, its partners.

The business is owned solely for the benefit of those who work in it, and they possess a number of ownership rights. First, the purpose of the company is to serve their interests, the "happiness" of all its members, through "worthwhile and satisfying employment in a successful business." Second, they share in the profits every year. And third, they have a formal voice in how the company is governed.

MEMBERSHIP: DEFINING WHO'S IN, WHO'S OUT

I've come for this visit because I want to see this company up close. The patterns of its ownership design seem genuine, but I want to get a better sense of it all, to see if it's real. "[P]eople can get into the most amazing and complex kinds of disagreement about the 'ideas' in a pattern, or about the philosophy expressed in the pattern," Christopher Alexander wrote. Yet "to a remarkable extent," he continued, people "agree about the way that different patterns make them feel."

> *"Go to the places where the pattern exists,*
> *and see how you feel there," he advised.*

When a pattern is made from thought, it makes us feel nothing. When patterns arise from the actual forces of a situation and successfully resolve those forces, we can feel that balance. The reason, Alexander said, is that "our feelings always deal with the totality of any system."[2]

In my time at *Business Ethics*, I developed a pretty good nose for determining whether companies passed the sniff test, whether they seemed genuine in pursuit of a generative mission. I'd read a good bit about this company, and we'd invited one of its executives, Ken Temple, to attend one of our Corporation 20/20 meetings. I was intrigued. When I found myself in London on other business, I decided to add a few days to experience this place in the flesh, to see if it had the soul of a living company.

At the John Lewis Partnership, ownership design starts with a clear and profoundly different mission. This firm has a written constitution, printed up and publicly available, which states that the company's purpose is to support "the happiness of all its members." Now, let me pause and note: this is the only major corporation I've found that declares its purpose is *to serve employee happiness.* This is so, at JLP, *not* because it boosts returns for shareholders. At the John Lewis Partnership, employee happiness isn't a path to some other goal. It *is* the goal.

And it's more than a statement in the company's legal documents. It's embodied in another critical design pattern: the way in which membership boundaries are defined. If it's true that there are no separate systems, only subsystems of the single system of the earth, it's equally true that life depends on boundaries, on things like cell walls and membranes. No living system is a formless soup of energy. No company is a boundaryless entity embracing all living beings, equally serving all stakeholders. Each company has a clearly defined set of members.

Who *is* the company? Who has the right to a claim on its surplus? Who has a right to what's left over, should its assets be sold and its debts settled? These are questions about what we traditionally call ownership—what we can call *membership*, to distinguish it from other aspects of ownership design.

If the ultimate perquisite of being an owner is the right to pocket some of the profit left after the bills are paid, then employees at the John Lewis Partnership are genuine owners. Each year, after the company sets aside a portion of profits for reinvestment in the business, the remainder—generally between 40 and 60 percent of after-tax profit—is distributed to employees. That's the annual bonus that saw Emma off to the Canary Islands. Every employee, from shop clerk to the chairman, gets the same percentage of individual pay. As one manager told me, "In the worst year over the last 30 years, it was 8 percent, in the best year, 24 percent" of salary.

In a recent year, the annual figure was announced in March with much fanfare on the floor of the company's flagship store on Oxford Street, where a partner held up a poster bearing the number "18%," and employees clapped and cheered. That bonus amounted to about nine weeks' pay. For a person stocking shelves and earning $22,000, it was close to $4,000. For Chairman Charlie Mayfield, pay with bonus came to £950,000 (US$1.6 million). That's a handsome sum by any measure. But it's modest compared with those of S&P 500 CEOs, who with stock options took home an average of $10 million the same year.[3]

Profit sharing at the John Lewis Partnership is seen as good business practice. It forms part of what executives describe as a "virtuous circle"—profit comes back to partners, which motivates them to provide excellent customer service. It's the way that private enterprise is supposed to work: if you help create company success, you share in the financial rewards. Employee ownership at JLP does indeed contribute to notable commercial success. One study of 20-year performance among major retail competitors showed that the John Lewis Partnership ranked "high or top in profitability and productivity." It found, in addition, that "the human side of the business" was "of major importance" to that success.[4]

FIRMS AS LIVING COMMUNITIES

In addition to Living Purpose, this firm employs the second design pattern of Rooted Membership: ownership in the hands of stakeholders intimately involved with the tangible workings of the enterprise. Rooted Membership is a key aspect of bringing companies back to earth—rooting them again in the real economy. It arises from a vision of companies as living communities of human beings, not simply as shares of stock rising perpetually in financial value.

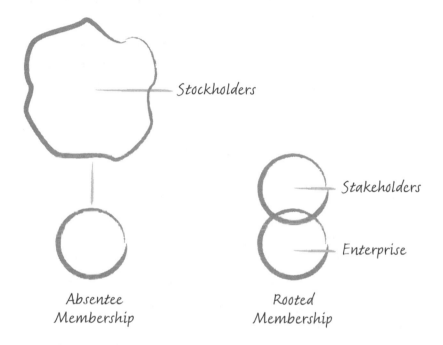

ABSENTEE VERSUS ROOTED MEMBERSHIP

There are many ways to create Rooted Membership. In credit unions and cooperative banks, membership is in the hands of *customers*, depositors. Some cooperatives root membership in the hands of *suppliers*—like Ocean Spray, a big cooperative of growers. At Hull Wind, membership is rooted in the *community*, through municipal ownership of the town's electric facility. Some generative companies, like S.C. Johnson, root membership in the hands of the *founding family*. These are all varieties of stakeholders, those with a stake in the real life of the firm. John Lewis

Partnership roots membership in the hands of *employees.* Employees are the firm. Ken Temple puts it to me just that way: "We define ourselves simply as all our employees. We see no distinction between the business and its people."

When JLP draws a boundary to define who's inside the firm, it draws that boundary around employees. Capital providers, on the other hand, are outside the perimeter of the firm. They are suppliers providing capital, not members of the firm. This arrangement at JLP corrects an oddity in our economy that we rarely notice: that in extractive enterprise, the people who go to a company every day and do its work, the employees, are considered outsiders. Those who never set foot in the place, the stockholders, are insiders.

With the Absentee Membership of publicly traded companies, the soul of the firm is outside itself, trading hands thousands of times every second in capital markets. This makes a firm, in Alexander's terms, divided against itself. It shows how the traditional view of property is potentially a deadening concept. In the classic view of property rights, the source of life and vitality is the owner. What is owned is subordinate, with no will or integrity of its own, subject entirely to the master's whim. In William Blackstone's words, the owner possesses "sole and despotic dominion" over that which is owned.

In corporate law, this tradition of thinking makes the relationship of employer to employee one of master and servant. In common law tradition, this pattern of relationships involves a one-way duty of loyalty. The employee owes a duty of loyalty to the employer. But the employer owes no loyalty to the employee. The employer can work employees harder and harder, with no obligation to share with them the fruits of their own labor. To the contrary, employers traditionally aim to pay employees as little as possible and can dismiss them at will. This master–servant relationship arises all too easily from the design of Absentee Membership and Governance by Markets. These patterns are at the root of some of the most destructive outcomes of modern capitalism.

One contemporary result is the increased speed-up in workplaces seen across Europe, Japan, the United States, and elsewhere in recent years.[5] In an interview with *Strategy+Business* magazine, Margaret Wheatley said that in recent years she'd noticed increasing levels of anxiety at formerly progressive workplaces, with everyone working harder yet seeing years of good efforts swept away. People are required to produce more with fewer resources, she said, and "new leadership is highly restrictive and controlling, using fear as a primary motivator."[6] The reason is that the forces in control are outside the life of the firm, in capital markets, which are already swollen with excess yet demand still more, every quarter.

This is a very different situation than at employee-owned South Mountain Company, where the people who experience the pressure are able to control it. Both results trace back to how the boundaries of a firm are drawn. Is there Absentee Membership—with ownership disconnected from the life enterprise? Or Rooted Membership—with ownership in living hands? Is a company seen as an inert object or a set of living relationships? Grappling with this distinction is about more than words written in a corporate charter.

Generative design begins with relationships.

It's a human process. For when we are no longer removed from the scene—no longer focused on the abstractions of capital markets or legal theories—but are instead in intimate relation with others doing the work of a single real enterprise, it's hard to avoid that most human of imperatives: fairness.

A GUIDING STAR OF FAIRNESS

When people who do the work of a company are in control of their own fate, they're more likely to be treated fairly and, as a consequence, to feel alive when they go there. I feel this at the John Lewis Partnership. In the management offices of the Peter Jones department store—back behind the men's underwear department—I sit at a long table crowded with eight or ten workers one afternoon, listening to person after person talk about their long family history of working at this company.

Janice says she's been there 28 years. "I come from a partnership family," she tells me. "My father worked here. My son works here. My sister works here. I went to my first partnership function when I was two."

Andrew's story is similar. "My sister's friend came here; then my sister came here; then I came here," he says.

An assistant registrar,[7] Bob Rosch Iles, tells the story of having to close a warehouse operation and how everyone was given the option of taking a job elsewhere at the company. Those who left received eight weeks' pay, were allowed to take an early pension, and were given help from JLP staff in drawing up a résumé. He talks about how one recovering alcoholic who'd been with JLP for 12 years was assisted in finding work with a train service. "The man was on psychotropic drugs and was quite vulnerable," Bob says. "I offered to walk him down the first day on the job but didn't need to. I called him a week later and found he was delighted he could get reduced fares on the train."

After conversations like these, I lose interest in my sniff test. I want to know more about what makes the John Lewis Partnership work, how it all began. Peter Jones was the seedbed of it, for this is the store where the company's principles of democratic ownership were first developed. Earlier in the day, I'd arrived for my interviews through the employee entrance to Peter Jones, which has a legend inscribed in stone above it: "Here is Partnership on the scale of modern industry." Something remarkable, at large scale, is indeed at work at this company. And it began small, in one human heart.

The company's mission was first articulated by its founder, John Spedan Lewis. As a company booklet explained, his "guiding star was a personal vision of 'fairness.'" Spedan, as he is commonly called, was born in 1885 to a wealthy and famously dictatorial father who ran a draper's shop in London, which he named after himself, John Lewis. He'd done so well with it that he purchased another shop, Peter Jones. Young Spedan was dismayed to learn that his family, as owners of those shops, earned more than all their workers combined. As he wrote later, it seemed to him that "the present state of affairs is a perversion of the proper workings of capitalism," and that "the dividends paid to some shareholders" for doing nothing were obscene when "workers earn hardly more than a bare living."

He determined to show that there was another way. Working for his father, he introduced new systems into the family stores—like shortened working days, additional paid holidays, and a staff committee. As his father began to show alarm at these practices, the two quarreled. The father struck a bargain with his son. Spedan could have total control of the money-losing Peter Jones if he kept his hands off the other store. That was 1914. Spedan went for it and told his staff that if the store became profitable, they'd share in the profits. Within a few years, he made good on that promise. In 1920, he introduced the firm's first profit-sharing scheme, as well as a representative staff council. After his father's death, he received total ownership of both stores. Soon afterward, he created the first constitution. Within a decade, he began turning ownership over to employees, and in 1950, he relinquished his remaining interest. For his ownership transfer, he was paid over 30 years, without interest.[8]

It wasn't only company ownership that Spedan passed to employees. Eventually the partners came to possess Leckford Abbas, an ivy-covered manor with an oak-paneled library and billiard room that had once been Spedan's country home and is today run as a hotel for partners. The partnership also now owns the entire Leckford Estate, with a dozen cabins, two golf courses, two swimming pools, tennis courts, and fly-fishing on the river Test. This is the family home where the eccentric Spedan—an avid naturalist—had once brought a mini-zoo and kept peacocks, meant to live in the garden, which often escaped into the village to cause havoc. Partners stay there now at modest rates. The place also serves as a working farm, supplying Waitrose with barley, oats, organic milk, apples, mushrooms, and free-range eggs. It is one of five holiday centers run for partners.

This is generative design in fully developed form—unfolding over nearly 100 years, working out its design in ways that keep it true to its founding ideal of fairness. There is no mistaking the fact that moral ideals are at the heart of this major corporation. In 1954, Spedan published a book, *Fairer Shares*, in which he made clear that his essential aim with the John Lewis Partnership was to create "an experiment in industrial democracy," which he believed to represent, as the subtitle said, "a possible advance in civilization."

The fairness that Spedan sought was not a flat equality of the sort that communism attempted or that I'd seen tried at a worker co-op. The Williamson Street Grocery Cooperative in Madison, Wisconsin, where I served as president of the board for many years, at one point paid everyone the same—from the general manager of that million-dollar store down to the person newly hired to stock shelves. Those of us on the board led a drive to pay the manager more, to raise that person's pay to closer to industry standards. The staff dissented vigorously, and more than a year of tumult ensued. But ultimately, the co-op did institute differential pay, raising the manager's pay substantially. As many of us insisted, it simply wasn't fair to pay everyone the same. The manager deserved more. Fairness isn't the same as equality.

"Wide differences of earnings seem necessary, if possessors of uncommon ability are to discover it in themselves and to develop and exert it as the common good requires," Spedan wrote. "But the present differences are far too great," he continued. "Our world of millionaires and slums is more and more volcanic." Yet in Spedan's mind, taxing away some profits and giving a bit to workers through food stamps or welfare was an inefficient design. Better to get wealth in the right hands in the first place, through a fair distribution of the profits that workers themselves create.[9]

Pursuing that didn't mean Spedan's family gave up its wealth. Spedan was paid for his ownership shares a sum that Ken Temple estimates would today total more than $100 million. Just as Spedan had no interest in renouncing wealth, he also was not interested in dispensing a bit with a benevolent hand. He was after *fairness on a large scale*—the scale of major industry—and in his broader vision, the scale of civilization itself. It is fairness designed into how businesses are owned and run.

BEYOND MONARCHIES OF CAPITAL

In the words of modern-day philosopher Martha Nussbaum, creating this kind of advanced social order is an issue not of *charity* but of *justice*.[10] It's about the essential moral rightness of an arrangement that honors the dignity of labor. "[T]he supreme problem," Spedan wrote, is the "prevention of a galling sense of needless inferiority of any kind" and prevention of that sense of "being exploited, victimized, for somebody else's benefit." In theory, he continued, this will be achieved in private enterprise if all the workers share "as equally as possible all the advantages of ownership, not merely profit but power, security, intellectual interest, sheer fun."[11]

Drawing social boundaries as the John Lewis Partnership does—embracing every employee as a member of the enterprise—is as revolutionary in its import as the design of political democracy. In a democracy, the people are the state, in contrast to an aristocratic world, where the king is the state (in Louis XIV's famous dictum, "*L'etat, c'est moi*").

Today, the ruling oligarch in our economy is capital, for capital is sovereign within enterprise. Only capital has the right to vote inside most publicly traded companies, and only capital has a claim on profits. Capital is master. Labor is servant. The reason is the way society chooses to draw the membership boundaries of enterprise.

Social boundaries are of our own making. Redrawing them more expansively over time is essential to the movement of social progress. In the Anglo-Saxon tradition, there was a time when only white, property-owning men were considered members of the democratic polity and eligible to vote. But over time, democratic society redrew those boundaries to include blacks and women. The building of a generative economy is the next step in that historical movement. "We can get lost talking about this abstraction, the corporation," journalist William Greider said at one gathering of Corporation 20/20. "The relationship of people to their work is one of the central next strands in the human story. It's a story of natural rights, human rights." Framed as an issue of human rights, a key issue might be stated this way:

> *Do people have a right to the*
> *fruits of their own labor?*

This is a principle articulated often in the history of democracy. Thomas Jefferson defended a right "to the acquisition of our own industry." Abraham Lincoln said, "Labor is the superior of capital, and deserves much the higher consideration." Thomas Paine said the question was the status of the common man and "whether the fruits of his labor shall be enjoyed by himself." Paine further articulated a vision of "every man a proprietor." Since in the modern world it's not practical that all people could start and own a company, the contemporary version of Paine's ideal is *every employee an owner.*[12]

We're approaching a historical inflection point in the United States where realizing this vision may be within our grasp, with the pending retirement of baby boom entrepreneurs. The moment of Founder Departure is about to occur on a massive scale. According to a Federal Reserve Survey of Consumer Finance, just 50,000 businesses changed hands in 2001 in the United States; but by 2009, that number was estimated to total 750,000. A wave of sales of closely held companies is beginning, and it is projected to go on for 20 years. These businesses account for close to half of private sector payroll, and in the last decade, they generated eight out of ten net new private sector jobs. According to a study by White Horse Advisors, only one in seven of these company founders expects to pass the business to family. An "age wave" of ownership transfer is coming.[13]

Will ownership of these enterprises flow into the hands of capital or of labor? The few or the many? With the right tax incentives and supportive social ecosystem, we could see a massive surge in employee ownership. As a company like JLP demonstrates, employee ownership can work at companies of large scale. And in both the United States and the UK, employee ownership is a model that has been shown to appeal politically to both right and left. Policies to advance employee ownership are also being adopted by governments in Cuba, South Africa, and elsewhere.[14] Employee ownership may be a model whose time has come.

Yet if it's to represent a truly generative alternative, there's more to this design than getting the membership boundaries right. Many employee-owned companies still consider it their purpose to maximize profits and give employees no say in governance. In systems terms, simply changing the players in a game doesn't change much. Take out every player on a football team and put in all new players—it's still football. As systems theory tells us:

The more potent approach is to
change the rules of the game.

That is what Spedan Lewis did. He didn't accomplish this simply by substituting one group of owners for another—taking out capital providers and putting in employees. And he didn't accomplish it simply by creating that elegant statement of purpose, about serving the happiness of employees. Living Purpose and Rooted Membership were a vital start. But something else helped create the feedback loops that brought the whole thing to life and kept it running over more than 100 years. It was Mission-Controlled Governance.

ELEVEN

MISSION-CONTROLLED GOVERNANCE

Humans at the Helm

O ne of the highlights of my visit to the John Lewis Partnership was touring its Peter Jones department store, a glass-walled shopping emporium on Sloane Square in the Chelsea neighborhood of London. I'll confess that I'm a fan of magnificent department stores: the Marshall Field's in Chicago, where my grandmother took me as a child, and whose elegant green boxes appeared under our Christmas tree every year; the old Dayton's in Minneapolis, where to stride through its aisles was to feel the riches of the world at your fingertips (yes, I know, consumerist excess and all that: more on that point in a moment). Walking into Peter Jones in London, one has that same feeling of abundance. The oval central atrium stretches eight stories to the sky, letting natural light fall on the richly colored bolts of fabric in the carpets and window coverings department, there in the center of the store.

It is through that light-filled space that I am passing, a little entourage of executives in tow (more accurately, I am in tow behind them), when we bump into a distinguished gentleman, a midlevel manager on the floor. "Oh, here's a member of the Partnership Council," one of the executives says. I'd read about the bicameral governance design of JLP, which has a traditional board of directors as well as a second employee house, the Partnership Council, directly elected by employees. Here is my unscripted chance to get a sense of how it works. That central employee council is the body on which this gentleman serves. He gives his name as Harry Goonewardene.

"How did you get on the council?" I ask him. "Did you campaign?"

"Very much so," he says. "I stood at the door and grabbed people, told them, hi, this is who I am." He carries himself as a city council member might, calmly, with an air of dignity that is striking—arresting, almost. He is impeccably dressed in a dark suit and has the dark olive skin of someone from the Middle East—from Sri Lanka, I am later told. He lacks that harried, pinched sense that one often sees among floor managers at other low-price retailers. (This is a company whose slogan is, "Never knowingly undersold," a company that competes based on price as well as quality—not a high-end, Hermès-type luxury retailer.) A meeting of the Partnership Council will be held soon, he tells me.

"What will you be discussing?" I ask.

"An adjustment to the pension scheme is coming up," he says. Every employee at JLP is eligible for the pension plan after five years. Each year, the company contributes to employee accounts a sum not far below their annual pay; employees aren't required to contribute anything. People are concerned that this probationary period means they are losing five years' worth of pension contributions and wonder if an adjustment should be made. "A committee has been looking at this, and we'll take it back to constituents and present a plan," he says. By "constituents" he means the employees he represents. (I find out later that the company did in fact approve a shift, shortening the eligibility period from five to three years.) Another issue is on the table, he says. "Charitable giving—what is its future direction?" At the next meeting, Harry tells me, "we'll actually make the decision."

By giving employee-owners a genuine voice in high-level decision-making—a voice in company governance—the John Lewis Partnership helps bring its purpose to life. It changes the rules of the game. Later in the day, Ken Temple and I walk to a nearby English pub, the Constitution, and sit and talk about it over a beer.

This trim, dapper gentleman in his 60s would strike most people as an unlikely revolutionary, but there is a fire in his heart that is unmistakable.

That was evident to me from the moment we first connected. I'd given a talk in London, years earlier, after my first book came out, and afterward Ken read it and got in touch. "Your book hit me between the eyes," he said. It had articulated the intellectual underpinnings for Spedan's approach. Immediately recognizing in one another a kinship, Ken and I began a dialogue that stretched over many years, through calls, e-mails, a trip by Ken to Boston, and ultimately my London visit.

THE MANY FACETS OF GOVERNANCE

"I view our business as part of a movement," he says to me. "We're more than just a retail organization." He'd been with the John Lewis Partnership for more than 25 years prior to his recent retirement. For a good part of that time he served as Partners' Counselor, responsible for "all of our democratic mechanisms and the behaviors that flow from being employee owned," as he put it. While most businesses have a single structure of command—with a board of directors at the top, overseeing a CEO, who oversees managers—JLP has essentially two parallel structures: that traditional commercial structure, plus a second democratic one.

Ken's job was to keep the spirit of partnership alive in the company. The essential frame of the democratic structure he oversaw was a nested series of employee-elected forums—at the department, branch, division, and company levels. These are places for employee input, information sharing, and decision making. In the linens department, employee representatives might work out things like setting goals or devising better scheduling. Each operational unit—shops, warehouses, factories—has a branch council, giving input to unit management. At the company level, the Partnership Council has oversight of pensions, charitable contributions, and the Committee for Financial Assistance—which Harry and John spoke about—as well as a voice in other policies. Chairman Charlie Mayfield appears formally before the council twice a year, where he sometimes faces tough questioning. The council has the formal power to sack him, should he fail in his duties. Imagine that: employees with the power to fire their boss.

The Partnership Council works primarily as advisor to the board of directors, which holds much of the final power. The employee council selects five out of 14 members of that board. The aim of this design, as Spedan wrote, is to have sharing of power "as far as seemed practicable … with sufficient care not to go suicidally too far."

"That formal structure needs to be there, absolutely," Ken tells me. "But the way the structure and ideals are played out in daily behavior actually makes the difference." To keep democratic values alive on a daily basis, the company has a team of 30 or so "registrars," headed by the Partners' Counselor.

"We have weird and wonderful titles," he says with a laugh. "The closest US equivalent would be director of ethics."

"Your role seems to be to safeguard the soul of the partnership," I say.

"Yes," he agrees. "The registrar staff tries to keep the partnership dimension real and in focus."

One of the tools that the company has developed to advance its mission in recent years is a partnership survey. "We have pages of financial targets, but we're getting better at setting targets around satisfaction and happiness," Ken says. To gauge progress on those goals, the survey asks employees to rate their experience along such dimensions as "I am treated fairly by my line manager" and "I understand how the forums will enable me to discuss and resolve the issues that matter to me." The aim is to make working at the company a satisfying experience.

Taken as a whole, the ownership design of the John Lewis Partnership—the mission of employee happiness, the constitution, the cascading bodies of employee representation, the bicameral legislature, the registrars—adds up to one of the most remarkable designs I've ever encountered. That it has worked across the span of many decades, on such a large scale, is testament to its effectiveness.

Is it a bit elaborate? Perhaps. Granted, this is a company with more than 76,000 employees, comparable to the population of a rather substantial town. Yet it offers far more avenues for input than a town democracy does.

It's close to the model of city/state/federal democracy: a lot to pack into one company.

Is it too self-consciously modeled on democracy? Perhaps. Spedan lived in an era when Queen Victoria sat on the throne—when monarchy was the dominant governing institution around the world. In that aristocratic age, as he reached for alternatives to the unfairness he saw at work in his dad's shops, he instinctively reached for the tools of democracy. But the fit seems to me not a perfect one. There is not a one-to-one correspondence between the kinds of social architectures suited for nations and for companies.

While cities and states provide the frame for all of life—childrearing, churchgoing, vacationing, living day to day—companies are goal-oriented entities of a largely economic sort. Importing the tools of democracy into business, whole cloth, may not be the most effective approach to dealing with the daily rigors of running a company. What Spedan devised does work. But it also might be a model that in all its detail will not be widely replicated.

Its deeper *design patterns*, on the other hand, seem to me to be of wide relevance. Living Purpose is the first of these—a purpose of serving a broad base of human needs, not simply the interests of the financial elite. The second is Rooted Membership—in this case, drawn to encompass employees as owners. The third design pattern is Mission-Controlled Governance, which in the case of JLP is embodied in the constitution, the employee-elected councils, and the registrar structure. It is the combination of these patterns that allows the John Lewis Partnership to set up feedback loops that succeed in changing the rules of the game.

SOLVING THE LEGACY PROBLEM

In the same way that membership boundaries can be drawn in various ways, Mission-Controlled Governance can also take a variety of forms. Spedan Lewis articulated its fundamental aim well: the goal is to make a focus on values "permanent, not dependent upon the inclinations of some particular individual."[1]

More than a century ago, Spedan solved the legacy problem. He kept the value of fairness alive inside a large company, long after he as founder was gone. Yet his particular design isn't the only way to solve it.

In the United States, another example of Mission-Controlled Governance is the family-controlled New York Times Company, a cultural institution with a mission of journalistic excellence. Although the majority of shares in the Times Company trade on public stock markets and can be purchased any day, by anyone, the Ochs-Sulzberger family holds super-voting shares, enabling them to control the board of directors. This single design pattern protects the Times Company from predatory takeover. The design's power can be seen, for example, in the fact that Rupert Murdoch has not been able to buy the *Times*, although his desire to do so is widely known, and Murdoch rarely fails to capture what he seeks. But the *Times* is not for sale. At any price. In the wake of the scandal at Murdoch's *News of the World*—where reporters were caught hacking into the voicemail of a murdered child and bribing police for information—one shudders to imagine what Murdoch would do, were he to acquire the *New York Times*. Our world might be a very different place.

Super-voting shares do not, in themselves, constitute Mission-Controlled Governance. Also essential is Living Purpose. In the wrong hands, super-voting shares can be a tool of mischief. Witness, for example, the fact that Murdoch himself uses super-voting shares to maintain control of his own firm. When there is Living Purpose, combined with a way to keep governing control in the hands of those concerned with mission, Mission-Controlled Governance is created.

Governance design—like JLP's democratic structure or the *New York Times*' family-controlled board—is a way to keep a generative mission alive in a world often indifferent to the notion of social mission in business. These designs might be likened to the way a room is kept warm when the outside environment is cold. Keeping the temperature from sliding toward the ambient norm takes more than walls—more than elegant purposes put down on paper or social boundaries drawn correctly. It takes the ongoing process of making sure the furnace is running and the thermostat is adjusted: the process of governance.

There are weak and strong forms of Mission-Controlled Governance. The weak version might, for example, mean having a single public interest director on a board. The strong version involves vesting literal, legal *control* of an enterprise in mission-oriented hands. The hands might be those of a family, a foundation, a trust, a nonprofit, employees, or the community.

Mission-Controlled Governance works not only at corporations. Community land trusts, for example, are traditionally governed by a three-part structure, with one-third of board seats reserved for those who live in the community land trust homes, a third for those who live in adjacent homes, and a third for public interest representatives, which might include a mayor's staff member or representatives of nonprofits.

Mission Control exists in a variety of forms, all over the world. In Latin America, one example is the VIVA Trust, which holds ownership of Grupo Nueva, a consortium headquartered in Santiago, Chile, with operations in the forestry and construction materials industries. Revenues of the company are $1 billion, and annual profits of up to $30 million flow into the charitable trust, where they're used for the mission of promoting a sustainable Latin America. VIVA stands for "vision and values." In creating the VIVA Trust in 2003, founder Stephan Schmidheiny—a Swiss billionaire who previously founded the Business Council for Sustainable Development—said his aspiration was to promote values of human dignity. The design he created, intended as a model to inspire others, is characterized by *trust control*.[2]

Another approach to Mission Control is *foundation control*—a model seen in the US company Newman's Own, as well as in many companies across northern Europe, like the Dutch firm Ikea, Bertelsmann of Germany, and Novo Nordisk of Denmark. In many of these foundation-controlled companies, one executive said privately, "There's less going on than meets the eye." Foundation control constitutes generative design only when it is accompanied by authentic Living Purpose.

If these models of large companies are in many ways inspiring, I find that they leave me with an unanswered question: what about ecological impact? More specifically, what about growth? Are these models any better than traditional companies on that point? The John Lewis Partnership, I find, is in fact vigorously focused on growth. It opened close to two dozen new shops in a recent year and has plans to open many more. Here is that issue of consumerist excess: isn't the John Lewis Partnership—by its very nature as a shopping emporium—committed to helping everyone consume as much as possible? The answer seems unavoidable: yes.

I'll add that in the years I've been watching JLP, it has stepped up its environmental commitments considerably. While its sales in a recent year increased 11 percent, its total emissions grew only 5 percent. That's progress. And the company has set a target of achieving a 15 percent *absolute* reduction in carbon dioxide emissions from operations by 2020. It also gets 97 percent of its electricity from green sources, and it is minimizing refrigeration and cooling emissions, exploring alternative fuels for transport, and managing water consumption. It has diverted 81 percent of operational waste from landfills. These are big steps in the right direction, if not yet the truly generative economy we need.[3]

I ask Ken about this at the Constitution. How can a department store chain shift into a low-consumption, no-growth economy? He doesn't have an answer. Maybe none of us do.

"I can't envisage the future world my children will live in, any more than my parents could envision talking on a cell phone," he says. Fair enough. He adds that in moving into a wholly different world, companies will need to be nimble, ready to adapt. Employee ownership would help in that, he says. I think he's right. But are there other ways in which generative governance designs might help in transitioning to a sustainable economy?

SYMBIOSIS

To explore the answer, there is another company I want to see among mission-controlled corporations. It's Novo Nordisk, the foundation-owned Danish pharmaceutical with $11 billion in revenue. When I find myself traveling to nearby Stockholm on a business trip, I decide to add a detour to Copenhagen. There I rent a Corsa Diesel and take Highway 21/23 west through the greening fields of rural Denmark—guided by my trusty Global Positioning System. (For some reason, I find Copenhagen to be short on three things: decaf coffee, soymilk, and maps of Denmark.) My destination is the small coastal town of Kalundborg. With only a few episodes of "recalculating," I find my unflappable robot companion delivering me to the door of the Kalundborg Center for Industrial Symbiosis.

Visitors from across the globe come here to study the town's model of industrial ecology, one of the most famous in the world. Industrial ecology sees industrial systems as living systems, interdependent with the natural world. In plain language, industrial symbiosis means that waste products from one company are used by another. A complex mix of these arrangements has been in place in Kalundborg for more than three decades. One of the premier players is Novo Nordisk. That it is a mission-controlled corporation seems to me not an accident.

Center director John Kruger, a blue-eyed Dane, tells me he is leading a seminar later that afternoon and invites me to follow him to the conference center. As we drive along the coast—past whitewashed cottages with terra cotta roofs—I see large green tubes running unobtrusively through the town, a foot or so aboveground, carrying steam from the local power plant. This is the "district heating" arrangement that means thousands of local homes have no need for furnaces—one element of the industrial symbiosis at work.

As John and I sit at a picnic table to talk, the aroma of another element of the scheme is in the air. Pig farms. "There are more pigs than people in Denmark," he tells me. The hundreds of thousands of tons of slurry left from Novo Nordisk's production of insulin and enzymes are not thrown out; they're treated and spread on fields as fertilizer and given to pigs for food. John tells me that the gypsum plant I passed in town—with its tall white windowless silos—is another player in the arrangement, making wallboard and other products from the fly ash waste produced by the power plant. It's all so simple and sensible, like everything should be (and so little is, in the extractive economy).

In my drive back, I pass the Novo Nordisk production facility, where 40 percent of the world's insulin is made. At a dirt road nearby, I pull over and get out at the point where three large green pipes emerge from the ground. I put my hand to each one in turn and find the central one warm to the touch—likely carrying steam from the power plant for Novo Nordisk's use. In this visit, I want to experience the company as the natural world does, so I decide to forgo the managerial entourage. I walk along the dirt path that runs for 200 yards alongside the pipes, escorted only by a black cat, which demonstrates for me how the pipes can be used as a walkway to ford the creek and clamber through a thicket of hedges into the plant. It's clean and quiet there—a small village filled with massive round metal buildings where yeast is no doubt doing its work making insulin.

This is a company tangibly conscious of its humanitarian and ecological footprint, and its foundation ownership supports both of those aims. It uses the Mission Control tool of super-voting shares, held by the Novo Nordisk Foundation, to give that nonprofit control of this publicly traded company. Its mission is to defeat diabetes, and it has a stated philosophy of balancing financial, social, and environmental considerations. Its reputation among corporate social responsibility experts tells me that aim is real. In a recent period when the company saw 13 percent sales growth, for example, it reduced CO_2 emissions by an impressive 35 percent.[4]

The symbiotic arrangements at Kalundborg came together gradually, over many years—arising from the stable human relations that are possible only when ownership is also stable. When companies merge or change hands—or live beneath the relentless eye of hedge funds and day traders intent only on the moment—the pressure on management often drives out all considerations beyond immediate financial performance. Novo Nordisk's Mission-Controlled Governance allows it the luxury of managing for the long term, for a Living Purpose. Mission Control allows capital to trade freely, in public markets, even as it ensures that that mission is not for sale.

When my visit to Denmark is at an end and my business in Sweden complete, I spend a final afternoon on a boat tour of the harbors around Stockholm—a city built on an archipelago of some 30,000 islands. Settling comfortably in the boat, I push the button for the canned tour in English. As we pass a row of magnificent seaside residences, the voice intones, "With the rising seas from global warming, all of Stockholm's waterfront buildings may have to be abandoned." How different the European sensibility is from the American one: so much more frank and open about the fact that the economy of the future will be unimaginably different from the economy of today.

The new era we're entering is one where the realities of the natural world are likely to displace the fantasies of infinite financial growth, around which our existing economy is self-organized. What models of ownership will be suited for that emerging world is a question likely to loom large, one day, in the public consciousness. The models I visit—mission controlled and employee owned—aren't the complete answer. But they hold hints, glimpses, and elements of what we'll need. And there's yet another key element that I need to understand—in many ways the most important: capital. How can finance begin to come back to earth? What can the role of finance be in a generative economy?

....

TWELVE

STAKEHOLDER
FINANCE

Capital as Friend

In our talk at the Constitution, Ken Temple said something about the John Lewis Partnership that I found later in my notes. "We believe labor should employ capital, rather than capital employ labor," he said. I recognized that formulation. It was also found in the writings of David Ellerman, an economist formerly with the World Bank, who was an early participant in Corporation 20/20.

After I return from London, I send an e-mail to David and find that he's soon coming to Boston. I ask him to meet me for lunch. We sit down together at Mr. Bartley's Gourmet Burgers on Massachusetts Avenue near Harvard Square, where David orders the Ted Kennedy, "a plump, liberal amount of burger" with fries, while I settle for the chicken wrap. With his white hair and long beard, David might easily be cast in the role of wizard or guru. He's an articulate proponent of employee ownership and a critic of the absentee ownership that characterizes most corporations today. As we sit and talk about the financial crisis and its aftermath, he begins explaining why he thinks the key culprit is absentee decision making.

"The first principle is self-governance," he says. "Markets only work when you couple decision making with consequences. Bearing responsibility for one's actions is the whole basis of our legal system." When you commit a crime—even when you are hired to do it—you are legally responsible. You bear the consequences. But this timeless principle is violated in the design of absentee-owned, limited liability corporations, he says.

189

When a company uses absentee ownership and absentee decision making—with boards representing shareholders who never set foot in the place—that design allows costs and consequences to be put onto others. Future generations may bear the cost of bad stewardship of the environment, David says. Employees may bear the cost of increasing productivity demands, decoupled from rising wages. Capital, meanwhile, enjoys the gains from production processes in which it plays little or no part. Actions and consequences are decoupled. Indeed, the whole aim of extractive ownership is to accomplish that decoupling, allowing capital to extract as much as possible (*maximize gains*) while bearing none of the negative consequences (*minimize risk*).

"If you bear the costs and get the rewards of your activity, you have a responsible relationship to your work," David says. "If someone else bears the costs, you have an irresponsible relationship."

REMOTENESS VS. CONNECTION

Economist John Maynard Keynes made a similar observation. "Experience is accumulating," he wrote, "that remoteness between ownership and operation is an evil in the relations among men, likely or certain in the long run to set up strains and enmities which will bring to naught the financial calculation."[1]

Remoteness arises subtly, and for seemingly good reasons. When a company sells shares or a government issues bonds, investors trade their money for a document giving them title to a future flow of earnings. This is productive investment in the real economy. But when a secondary market arises in the financial economy, things change. Investors sell their pieces of paper to other investors, shuffling ownership. Over time, making money through this trading often becomes the goal. Today, well over 95 percent of what goes by the name investing is really secondary market activity. Investing comes to resemble gambling, subject to the fears and fantasies of the casino. "When the capital development of a country becomes a by-product of the activities of a casino," Keynes famously wrote, "the job is likely to be ill-done."[2]

The holders of paper investments become more and more remote from real enterprises. As this happens across borders, it's worse still. In times of stress, it becomes intolerable, Keynes said. "I am irresponsible toward what I own, and those who operate what I own are irresponsible toward me," he wrote.[3]

Systems thinking has a name for this kind of arrangement. It's called *suboptimization*: allowing a subsystem to benefit, to the detriment of the whole.

When the goals of a subsystem dominate and the larger system suffers, that's suboptimization.[4] It's the systems term for the 1 percent problem. When the 1 percent wealthiest own an estimated 40 percent of the globe's wealth, as a United Nations study found, the stage is set for this problem to become global in scope.[5] When their wealth is largely financialized, sliding around liquidly in capital markets, and when those markets are organized for investor convenience and profit, the fate of the world essentially becomes captive to capital markets.

Financial assets, as we saw, originate as the liquefied value of the real world (houses, businesses, various flows of cash). Lots of folks hold dribs and drabs of that wealth. But the big guys are the 1 percent wealthiest. The value of the real world, to a large extent, is in their hands. But "hands," these days, basically means algorithms on autopilot. How it all impacts real life—creating jobs, destroying jobs, renewing the environment, damaging the environment—isn't in the algorithm.

Yet here's the really odd part. This suboptimal arrangement doesn't even make wealthy people truly happy. Tim Kasser, a psychologist who studies well-being, says that when people *organize their lives* around the pursuit of wealth, they actually undermine their well-being. People with strong materialistic values experience more anxiety and depression, greater alcohol and drug use, and problems with intimacy. Their increasing wealth not only fails to satisfy them but also distracts from the things that would satisfy. Kasser finds that our genuine needs are for security, efficacy, connectedness, autonomy, and authenticity. Yet the single-minded pursuit of wealth and status leads away from these. Instead of feeling empathy with others, people feel competitive. Instead of feeling free, they feel pressured and anxious. The end result is lower vitality and life satisfaction.[6]

Happiness, on the other hand—as Christopher Alexander observes—comes in those moments when we feel most alive. A critical piece of that is being true to ourselves and in control of our own fate. In Kasser's terms, it's about authenticity and autonomy. In David Ellerman's terms—and in terms of enterprise design—it's about self-governance. In an interdependent world, there's also the need for connectedness.

In generative design, connectedness and autonomy work together freely to create a whole that feels alive. Instead of 1 percent extracting most of the wealth, the 100 percent becomes fully alive. The quality without a name—that sense of wholeness and authenticity—tends to appear, Alexander says, "not when an isolated pattern lives, but when an entire system of patterns, interdependent at many levels, is all stable and alive." A town becomes alive when every pattern in it is alive—"when it allows each person in it, and each plant and animal, and every stream and bridge, and wall and roof, and every human group and every road, to become alive in its own terms." When that happens, he continues, "the whole town"—or enterprise, or world—"reaches that state that individual people sometimes reach at their best and happiest moments, when they are most free."[7]

FROM MASTER TO FRIEND

The notions of suboptimization versus wholeness, 1 percent versus 100 percent, and connection versus remoteness are useful in approaching the issue of finance. They help bring the question of capital design into focus. To phrase the question in a human way, in terms of relationships:

> *How can capital become a friend to enterprise*
> *rather than a remote master?*

One way to consider this, David Ellerman says, is through the question of who hires whom. In the dominant ownership design, capital hires labor. Capital is the corporation, the insider, and labor is the outsider hired to do work. In an employee-owned firm, that's turned around. Employees are the insiders, and they hire capital. When employees bring capital into the firm, they bring it in as their friend, not their master.

This is the formulation that Ken Temple was referring to, when he said the John Lewis Partnership believes labor should employ capital. It's an arrangement that's real at JLP, where employee-owners bring in capital primarily through debt. A loan does not make the capital provider into an owner. Instead, that party is a supplier, conceptually outside the daily working of the enterprise, supplying something it needs. It's no different from the way a department store might buy clothing or sporting goods from the suppliers making those items.

In recent times, JLP is making capital its friend via its John Lewis Partnership bond, available only to customers and staff members (not available through brokers). Over five years, the bond pays 4.5 percent annually, with an extra 2 percent in store vouchers. At the end of five years, the investment is returned in full.[8] This is a paradigmatic design for Stakeholder Finance. It's an approach to capital design that is personal and direct, in contrast to the anonymous and overcomplicated designs of Wall Street.

What JLP does *not* do is issue common stock, also called *equity*. This is the arrangement that creates that ownerlike relationship between investors and publicly traded companies. Equity investing means that an investor receives a variable return instead of the fixed return from debt. Return on equity comes in two forms: *dividends* (a slice of profits paid out directly to investors) and *capital gains* (the rising price of the company itself, reflected in the rising price of its stock). Because equity investors do well only when the company does well, they are in a position like that of owners.

By declining to issue equity to investors, the John Lewis Partnership is essentially refusing to liquidate the value of the firm. The billions of dollars it is worth remain frozen. The company retains strictly a *use value*: its value as a place to work and to shop. Its financial value—that invisible life along-side its material existence—never appears. This is so not only because of the nonissuance of equity but also (and closely related) because the company has a policy that *it will never be sold*.

In 1999, Ken told me, there was public speculation in a newspaper article about how much the partnership might be worth if it were sold. "It was very harmful at the time," he said, because it created talk among partners about how much financial wealth each would hypothetically be able to pocket. The estimate was about £100,000 apiece (US$156,000). "For someone working in a shop, that's untold wealth," he said. But a sale will never happen at JLP, because no partner has any individual shares in the company; a trust holds all the shares. And the trust arrangements prohibit the sale of any of its equity. "It's a tight design so we can be invested for long-term outcomes," Ken said.

This is the final element, then, that completes the ownership design of JLP: its capital design. Stakeholder Finance joins with Living Purpose, Rooted Membership, and Mission-Controlled Governance to create an enduring, successful generative design at large scale.

We might call the JLP approach to capital the *equity lockup*. The firm's financial value is locked up in perpetuity, never to be liquidated and sold. There's more than one way to accomplish an equity lockup. I've seen it take a slightly different form at the Massachusetts firm Equal Exchange, a fair trade coffee and chocolate company that is also employee owned. Its governing documents stipulate that if the firm is ever sold, net proceeds must be donated to charity. That's another path to preventing the sale of a firm. Or, to turn this formulation around:

It's a path to ensuring that an enterprise remains a living community—that it's never reduced to simply a piece of property.

All companies potentially have that dual identity—as living system and as property. Because property is often a deadening concept, viewing a company as nothing more than dollars and cents in investor pockets, protecting mission generally means *protecting a company's living essence from the demands of capital.*

But companies need not go to zero liquidity to accomplish this. We might think of mission designs for capital as lying along a continuum. At one end is zero liquidity, the equity lockup. At the other end is full liquidity, as when shares trade in public stock markets, yet mission is still protected. That's the capital design at Novo Nordisk. At that publicly traded pharmaceutical, Mission-Controlled Governance keeps control of the board in mission-oriented hands, via super-voting shares held by the foundation.

Equity lockup   *Mission-Controlled Governance*

Zero liquidity   *Full liquidity*

PROTECTING MISSION ACROSS THE LIQUIDITY CONTINUUM

Questions of full liquidity or zero liquidity are technical matters, details of ownership engineering. What's really at issue is the deeper question of how to balance that dual identity of living system and property. While the John Lewis Partnership's capital design ensures that the company is *only* a living system, many firms can't go that far. Equity capital may be required.

In those situations, another way to make capital a friend is to create living relationships with local investors, socially responsible investors, or others with a stake in a company's mission. This can be done with debt, as JLP does, or with equity.

THE OPPOSITE OF ABSENTEE

One of the best examples of *stakeholder equity* is found at Minwind, the wind development firm in southern Minnesota, which I decide it is time to visit. I set out one day for the drive there under a sky of robin's-egg blue, taking Highway 169 south out of Minneapolis, with rows of corn fanning away on my right and left like tall fields of corduroy. My destination is Luverne, population 4,745, where I sit down with Minwind CEO Mark Willers.

Mark is a farmer, and the series of wind developments he's helped to create are mostly on farmers' land—sleek towers standing in cornfields and soybean fields that I drive out to see. When most farmers put wind turbines on their land, they lease wind rights to absentee developers. This might yield them a small fraction of the revenue, generally $4,000 to $12,000 a year. That's the familiar path of rural poverty.

Minwind took another approach. Mark and other farmers decided they wanted to own the wind developments themselves. To raise the $4 million needed to put up the initial four turbines, they sold shares locally for $5,000 apiece. "And 66 investors snapped up all the shares in 12 days," Mark tells me. These were among the first farmer-owned turbines in the nation. Minwind soon built more. Today there are some 350 owners in Minwind developments. The company created a requirement that no one can own more than 15 percent of any development. All shareholders must be Minnesota residents. And 85 percent of investors must be from rural communities.[9]

Now when one of these wind farms generates hundreds of thousands of dollars in revenue, all of it flows through local communities, to be used to pay wages, expenses, and returns to local investors. The wealth stays local, by design. Mark points to a GAO study that found when wind developments are locally owned, they generate three to five times the economic benefit of absentee-owned projects.[10]

In Minwind's equity design, we see the opposite of the Absentee Membership and Governance by Markets used in extractive design. Here, those in control are not employees but farmers and local community members. Through the combination of Rooted Membership and Stakeholder Finance, Minwind's design creates benefits both for communities and for the biosphere.

As we move into an era of ecological limits, "we face some tough choices ahead," Mark says to me. "Really on a grand scale, we now have to limit things. We'll have limited amounts of water. Do you want water to grow broccoli or to cool a coal plant? We've never had to make that choice before.

"When I look at an acre of land, I could put corn on it, wheat on it, solar panels on it, or wind turbines on it. I can grow soybeans for fuel," he says. "The businessman tells me, 'I don't care about any of that; the only thing I want is a buck tomorrow.' We're talking about something far different." Minwind is about keeping control of economic choices in the hands of those close to the land.

"What form of energy and what form of food do we want?" Mark says. "People need to ask, do they want broccoli, cows, solar, water—which is it you want? Then I'll tell you how it'll all turn out."

Rerooting capital and ownership in human hands is far more than a technical issue. It's about the kind of world we want to live in, and who gets to decide: the algorithms of the 1 percent or real people who care about the earth? But this isn't about pointing fingers at anyone. The 1 percent are potential friends in the work of generative design. In fact, they're often leaders. If places like Minwind and the John Lewis Partnership make capital a friend through generative design at the enterprise level, investors are playing a generative role on the other side of the equation, the capital side.

INVESTORS STANDING WITH THE EARTH

One of the most transformative movements of investors is Slow Money, the brainchild of Woody Tasch, a former venture capitalist who has helped launch a network of more than two dozen local investor groups across the United States (and one in Switzerland). Their aim is to "bring money back down to earth," as Slow Money Principle 1 states. Intended as a companion to the Slow Food movement, Slow Money is about direct investments into the farmers and businesses that make healthy food possible, at relatively low rates of return. In St. Louis, a $6,000 loan was made to an urban farm. In Portland, Oregon, a Slow Money member loaned $40,000 for a new farm incubator on 80 acres of agricultural land. In North Carolina, baker Lynette Driver borrowed $2,000 to buy baking equipment.[11]

If this stuff sounds like small potatoes (one Slow Money group is called the No Small Potatoes Investment Club), it isn't. It may represent the seeds of the future. Industrial finance is dying, according to Woody. "The deadly dull, making-a-killing-minded, buy-low/sell-high mentality of the 20th century fiduciary is dying. … Robber-baron invented Wealth Now/Philanthropy Later is dying. Something more integral is trying to be born, and we are among its midwives," he wrote.[12]

What may be dying, in particular, is investing based on multiples of earnings. One of the rare people willing to stand up and talk about this is Leslie Christian, president of Portfolio 21 Investments—the person who devised the ownership model that inspired the B Corporation guys. Leslie used to be in the business of managing risk the old way, in her days long ago at the hedge management unit of Salomon Brothers. These days, she focuses on ecological risk. As we confront ecological limits, there's a chance that we could face "an extended period of material economic contraction," she wrote in a blog post. "To be blunt, this means no growth. This is the risk that no one talks about." To ask Leslie more about this, I catch up with her by phone.

"We cannot assume growth as we have known it will go on forever," she says. "It's so obvious. And yet in the financial world, this hinges on heresy. When you talk about no growth or the end of growth to financial people, they laugh at you. They say you're naïve, that you just don't understand. They often default to human ingenuity, saying, we've gotten ourselves out of a lot of messes, we can do this.

"But the truth is, there will be limits to financial growth," she continues. "I don't know how it will manifest. It could be a social uprising. It could be another financial crisis and massive default, where governments hit limits on how much they can prop up lenders. New capital requirements are already slowing things down.

"There are a lot of points at which limits will be reached," she says. "It's going to crumble. That will result in lots of disruption. The crumbling will be very painful. That's why we need to be designing all these models of alternatives. People need something to turn to.

"One possible change coming," she says, "is a sudden or gradual shift in the P/E ratio—the multiple of company earnings that investors are willing to pay today because they expect earnings to continue and to grow in the future. Let's say we're now at an average P/E of 15. What if it goes to 10? That's a 35 percent drop. If it goes down to a five-to-one ratio, that's a two-thirds drop. Then the Dow would be down to 3,000 or 4,000 [compared with 12,000 to 13,000, which is where it stood in early 2012]. I cannot rule that out as a distinct possibility. But what's the timing? It could be 50 years from now or one day from now.

"But still," she continues, "I can't dismiss public stock markets. I want to be invested in companies that will be here in the future, providing beneficial goods and services." Her bet is on "selective growth"—growth in certain sectors that serve real human needs. And things could play out many different ways. "There may be a return to a situation where investors are seeking current dividends rather than future capital gains," she says. "I think that would be really beneficial."

As I begin trying to make sense of it all with my own tiny retirement portfolio, I sit down with my adviser, Donna Clifford, a member of the Progressive Asset Management network of socially responsible investment advisers. In a lovely bit of serendipity, we meet at the Equal Exchange Café next to North Station, as we talk about the possibility of my investing in Equal Exchange itself. The deal, it turns out, is the kind of thing Leslie talked about: no capital gains, only dividends. It feels similar to the kind of locavore deal that Mark Willers put together at Minwind, since Equal Exchange is local, about a half-hour from my house.

This worker-owned, fair trade coffee company is selling equity shares in the form of *preferred stock*—shares with lower voting rights than traditional common stock, paying an annual dividend of around 5 percent (not guaranteed, but historically the dividend averaged 5 percent over 20 years). The stock itself will not appreciate in value. I put in $10,000 and agree informally to a term of three years. After three years, if all goes well, I'll get my $10,000 back. Plus the annual dividend.

I sign up. I write out a check to "Equal Exchange" and mail it to them. Imagine that. No impenetrable complex of intermediaries. About ten days later, I get an envelope in the mail from them. This trade is moving not at the speed of light but at the speed of life. My stock certificate is enclosed. Here I am, capital, being employed by labor. They in turn are working on behalf of small coffee growers in the developing world. "We are currently writing checks for coffee harvests in Colombia and Peru, so your dollars will be in the hands of small farmers in a matter of weeks," the enclosed letter says. Dealing with these people fairly is the Living Purpose of this fair trade firm. Its policy is to pay steady, good prices for coffee beans—even if market prices tank.

Donna finds another similar deal, a wind bond being issued by about a dozen municipal lighting plants in Massachusetts, borrowing $65 million from state residents like me to fund wind towers. There are lots of other investments she and I agree are a good fit for me, like Portfolio 21 (Leslie's fund), a Pax World bond fund, New Alternatives Fund, Parnassus Equity Income, plus other bond and mutual funds, all of it socially screened. Yes, I am investing in (gasp) the stock market.

Donna and I agree that we'll try to shift 25 percent of my portfolio into impact investments, also called *community investments*—those direct investments that make a positive impact on the world, like the Equal Exchange and wind bond deals. Those deals can be hard to find. "They're what more and more of my clients are asking for," Donna says. "It's part of the work that's left to be done." She adds that in two major recent crises—2001 to 2002 and 2008—"community investments were the only categories where some people made money." Someday, I think, I might try to go 100 percent community investing. Couldn't be much riskier than what the Dow's been doing.

My journeys are nearly complete. I have a sense of what makes a company a living company and how various firms have solved the legacy problem. It has something to do with law but is really more about aliveness, about institutionalized patterns of fairness, about relationships where all parties can take care of themselves and work together for the good of the whole at the same time. Yet some of the best companies I've seen, like JLP and Minwind, are anomalies, single instances of designs that work but haven't yet been replicated widely. This is the final piece I want to explore: networks, those living patterns that reach out beyond single companies to create whole systems of aliveness. It's clear to me what the best example of that is. It's the worldwide network of cooperatives.

....

THIRTEEN

ETHICAL

NETWORKS

Reinforcing Shared Values

I
t is the day before Thanksgiving when I set out from Madison for the hour-and-a-half drive to the tiny town of La Farge, on a winding route that takes me deep into the rural rolling hills of Wisconsin, through corn-fields and river bottomlands that are serene, uncrowded, and good for the soul. I lived in Madison in my early 30s, when I was launching *Business Ethics* magazine, and I used to take off for those hills on stressful after-noons when I needed to clear my head, to unloose the tight bands from the demands of business and remember who I was and what my life was about. It's a land conducive to expansive dreams of possibility and creativ-ity, the land that spawned the genius of Frank Lloyd Wright, who designed the majestic home and studio called Taliesin—in Welsh the word means "shining brow"—which resides as the brow of a cliff not far away, outside of Spring Green. That was where my car would point on those meandering afternoons of decades ago, when I would wander the grounds of Taliesin, which was at that time virtually abandoned, so that I could breathe in its ordinariness and its majesty.

In spiritual symmetry, the hill country of Wisconsin is also the land that spawned Organic Valley, the farmer-owned dairy with more than $700 mil-lion in revenue, which I am on my way to see this day.[1] I have an interview with CEO George Siemon. When I pull up in front of the company head-quarters, I find that at the center of the complex stands a shiny metal build-ing—cherry red—surrounded by cornfields and shaped like an outsized barn: a deceptively ordinary building that turns out to be LEED-certified. George himself is likewise deceptively ordinary, though he stewards one of the four largest organic brands in the nation. With his shoulder-length blond hair, new blue jeans, and cotton zip-up sweater, he looks every bit the farmer that he is. He talks about the 2,500 hens he used to keep when he had his own farm down the road. And during our interview in his office, he slips off his Dockers and sits with his feet bare under the table.

Organic Valley is owned today by close to 1,700 organic family farms. Not many years ago, it was owned by 900 family farms. To keep up with mushrooming consumer demand, the company reaches out to help farming families through the rigorous, three-year process of going organic. Each farm, as it's added to the fold of organic certification, represents additional acres cleared of chemicals, additional watersheds washing clean of Roundup and Lasso. It represents the return of life to the soil, greater nutrition in the bodies of customers, and the advent of financial health for formerly stricken farm families. This company is growing rapidly, but it's generative growth, leaving the world not diminished but enhanced.

For its organic milk, the company pays a price that historically has been typically 60 percent higher than the commodity price that farmers receive for nonorganic milk. That's at the heart of it all. When former Texas agriculture commissioner Jim Hightower completed a study of the family farm crisis in America some time ago, he observed, "When all is said and done, it came down to one word. Price." The overwhelming consensus among farmers was that most other concerns—such as overproduction, soil and water conservation, lack of credit, young farmers' leaving the farm, and the industry's high costs—could be managed if farmers got a fair price for their products.

Paying a fair price for farmers' products is the Living Purpose of this company. The reality of that was demonstrated a number of years back, when the nationwide average price paid for milk was falling to $11, but Organic Valley that year increased its pay price from $17 to $22. Company profits that year were 1 percent—half those of two years prior. That was a deliberate decision made by the board of directors. Farmers not only compose the Rooted Membership of this company, but they're also responsible for its Mission-Controlled Governance, via a board made up of farmers elected directly by farmer-owners. That board decided to accept lower profits in order to increase the price paid to their fellow farmers.

At the traditional agribusiness corporation, farmers are at the bottom of the supply chain. They sell product into a Commodity Network, where one gallon of milk is no different from the next. And for this commodity, the company pays as little as it can. Those are the rules of the game. Maximizing profits is the goal. Yet here is a successful company that puts the last first and the first last. It decreases profits so that it can pay farmers more.

MAXIMIZING MISSION

Wanting to talk with George about it all, I've asked for an hour of his time. He's read my materials on the Web beforehand and greets me as a co-conspirator and friend, offering to extend our talk over lunch. My partner joins us as we drive to the only place nearby, Rockton Bar, 16 miles down the road, where 17 deer antlers line one wall, eight mounted deer heads hang on the wall opposite, and a wood stove crackles in the corner. At tables around us, a crowd of hunters in blaze orange drink Coors Light and Mountain Dew, cracking open peanuts and dropping the shells on the floor. As we lunch on deep fried cheese curds and beef chili, the bill for three comes to $16.

"We're not trying to maximize share price but maximize mission," George tells me. "Most CEOs wake up in the morning and look at their stock value and sweat bullets about how to raise it. When you take away that whole aspect, you now have a clearer focus," he says. With no emphasis on stock value, there is no need to maximize the earnings that are the foundation of that value. Organic Valley tries to manage profits rather than maximize them. It aims for 2.2 percent annual profit, within the normal range for its industry. "We don't have any need for profits much over 2 percent," George tells me. "We'd just pay taxes on it. We'd rather give it to the farmers."

Organic Valley has often received buyout offers from major corporations, he says. But he and his board aren't interested. "There's no exit strategy in sight. Farmers are into the long term." One result of this refusal to monetize the value of the firm is that George will never pocket the tens of millions from stock options that he might have arranged for himself if earlier on he'd decided to make this a publicly traded company. He doesn't seem to mind. He apparently prefers things as they are, having work he feels passionate about, a community where he feels at home, and plenty of personal income.

George's reluctance to put himself far above everybody else is central to what makes Organic Valley what it is. From the beginning, he's been part of a community of farmers who banded together to market their milk collectively in an effort to save their family farms.

Their interest is in staying on the farm. In helping them to do this, the company also aims to nurture local communities, creates healthy products for customers, contributes to environmental sustainability, pays a healthy wage to employees, and offers an attractive return to investors. "We're a farmer cooperative that serves a whole community of stakeholders," George tells me.

As founders of the company, they drew the social boundaries of the firm in ways appropriate to their mission, creating a cooperative owned by the suppliers who create its milk, cheese, eggs, meat, and other products. Different kinds of cooperatives draw their member boundaries in different ways. Farm co-ops like Organic Valley often encompass producers. Housing co-ops involve the people who live there. Consumer co-ops are about shoppers, while worker co-ops are composed of employees. All involve Rooted Membership. That's fundamental to the cooperative model. A cooperative, by definition, is a private business that is owned by the people who use its products or services and is controlled democratically by them.

Organic Valley is owned by people intimately connected to the life of the company—people like David and Susan Hardy, who regularly go into New York City to talk about farming and butter making to kids in elementary school, who may never have been to a farm and don't know where milk comes from. Other owners are people like the Meyer family in Hardwick, Vermont, where sons Taylor and Nick run the farm and asked for donations from neighbors to help in the transition to organic farming, honoring their most generous donors by naming milk stalls after them and adding little blue nameplates to each stall.

Governance at Organic Valley—as at all cooperatives—is also in the hands of those dedicated to Living Purpose. Co-ops are governed democratically by their members. Yet in a design similar to that of the John Lewis Partnership,[2] Organic Valley employs not only a traditional board of directors but also a separate network of advisory farmer councils. These councils are the executive committees of the producer pools through which distribution is organized. They provide a place where farmers can talk together about issues they care about, like the quality of milk being sold or standards for pasturing cows. These committees also provide critical input to the board and management team on topics such as supply management, pay price, and pool policies. They serve as the communication link between the members they represent and the board. And they're the seedbed for the future leadership of the cooperative.

Producers are organized into regional pools as a way to get fresh milk and other products to market efficiently, without having to truck them long distances. For a customer like me, it means that when I buy Organic Valley milk in Boston, I can be sure that I'm buying New England milk. When customers in Seattle buy Organic Valley milk, they're buying milk produced in the Pacific Northwest. This is a design that makes Organic Valley *nationally local.* Customers can find its products across the nation yet can trust that production is mostly local.

In an intriguing way, this design also embodies the new notion of the economic person that theologian John Cobb and economist Herman Daly talked about, the idea of person-in-community. In the old notion of *Homo economicus,* all of us are lone individuals out to maximize our own income. But person-in-community sees his or her own well-being as integrally related to the well-being of others. We see this at work in the case of Organic Valley, where its farmer-members enjoy the strength of a national brand—the strength of being in community—but they have the dignity and independence of privately owning their family farms.

Organic Valley also uses the approach of Stakeholder Finance. Like Equal Exchange, it sells preferred stock. This makes the financial statements strong, because preferred shares represent long-term investments that appear on the balance sheet as equity. Yet the co-op views it as debt. Investors get a fixed return, 6 percent annually, and have limited voting rights. From 2004 to 2010, Organic Valley raised more than $40 million this way from outside investors. "We raised a phenomenal amount of money within 60 miles of here," George says. The company had its first annual investors' reception for preferred shareholders at the Kickapoo County Fair in 2006. It's since grown to attract more than 500 shareholders every year.

These investors are "a new group of friends," he says. "That's what they are, they're friends." This isn't Casino Finance, with distant, speculative relationships to the company based solely on numbers, but Stakeholder Finance, with intimate relationships based in community. Not incidentally, Organic Valley's issuance of preferred shares has limits. I tried to invest in the company myself but found that its offering had closed. Having raised the money it needed, it was no longer accepting new funds. At least for the time being. (I was told that the cooperative may decide to offer the stock again in the future.) It struck me how different this approach was from that of the investment banks that kept bundling and selling mortgage derivatives, long after the process made any sense.

Holding all these design patterns together—Stakeholder Finance, Mission-Controlled Governance, Rooted Membership, Living Purpose— is a fifth design pattern. It's outside this company, found in the Ethical Networks that reach out to the social and ecological communities of which this firm is a part. One network holds organic standards that originated in the work of people close to the soil and later were formalized in federal law. There is the network of consumers who want organic products, which allows this firm to charge more for its products and thus to pay more to farmers. And there is the network of investors and investing advisers, like the network that Donna is part of, where people seek to partner with companies they believe in.

Perhaps most important, there is the global network of cooperatives— a network that's found in many nations of the world and that reaches back in time to the Rochdale Pioneers, who created the model in the 1800s. In terms of excellence in generative ownership design, the cooperative form is the most highly developed in remaining focused on serving the common good. A key reason is that all cooperatives operate inside an explicitly ethical frame. It is articulated in a formal set of ethical principles, the Rochdale Principles. These include open membership, democratic member control, cooperation among cooperatives, and concern for community. Because of these principles, the way they're embodied in the law of many states and nations, and the way they're celebrated by cooperatives, the cooperative form becomes elevated beyond a technical, legal ownership design. It becomes an ethical design—a set of patterns holding explicit moral standards. Cooperatives themselves become an Ethical Network.

An Ethical Network is the pattern that microfinance lacks and the reason why some of these companies began to lose their way. The original microfinance pioneer, Grameen Bank, does operate in a deliberately ethical way. But its standards have yet to be codified, industrywide. The same might be said of employee ownership. Many employee-owned firms are deeply committed to fairness, as the John Lewis Partnership is. But many give no voice to employees in governance. Such matters are left to individual company choice rather than being codified in standards.

BEING OF BENEFIT TO LIFE

Holding up cooperatives as emblematic of excellence in generative design doesn't mean that all companies should be cooperatives. The design has its drawbacks—raising capital from outside investors can be difficult, for example. But it does mean that other generative ownership models might benefit from creating more explicitly ethical frameworks. We can think of these as ethical design standards. Developing such standards for microfinance, employee ownership, social enterprise, CDFIs, and other models may be an important future step in the progression of generative design.

Because of the many supportive networks that surround it, Organic Valley is not out there alone. It's able to work with a full-fledged design—cooperative design—and introduce its own elements of excellence on top of it (such as the farmer councils and preferred shares). The combination makes Organic Valley a model of generative excellence, from top to bottom. Being of benefit to life is why the company exists. This living aim is woven into its purpose, ownership, governance, and capital design. It's also in the way the firm is consciously networked into the communities around it. This is a profit-making company, but it isn't profit maximizing. It offers a healthy return to capital, but its primary focus is *living returns*.

Organic Valley is a living system, with a life like that of a forest or a stream, where what benefits one species tends naturally to benefit other species. Because of its paradigmatic generative design, this living enterprise naturally generates the conditions for life—benefiting the web of life with which it is interdependent. Like an oak tree harboring birds, knitting together the soil, giving off oxygen, feeding insects, and sheltering travelers, this enterprise is a wellspring of benefits. Farmers benefit from healthy income. Employees benefit from stable jobs and rewarding work. Customers benefit from chemical-free food. Investors benefit from dependable rates of return. The biosphere benefits from the restoration of soil and watersheds. Farming communities benefit from the return of vitality that flows from farmers' prosperity.

Yes, I know, saying all these things makes me sound like a commercial for Organic Valley. It's hard to wax poetic when it comes to business—hard to talk about things like "revolution" (the word has been so thoroughly co-opted by advertisers). And it's true—talking about business and investing isn't what most of us think about when we think about social revolution. But this may be it: ownership and financial design as the foundation of a generative economy. This may be the unlikely thing we've been searching for—found in a place where we never even dreamed of looking. The compass point we need, to find our way through the colossal messes that our civilization is making.

As I sat there in the bar with George, with the deer antlers on the wall, the whole notion of property as dominion—the idea of turning every molecule of the earth into financial capital, using that capital to create more capital, trying to amass limitless amounts so as to exalt the self over all others—it all began to seem so archaic. Absurd, really. A kind of remnant from an earlier age, past its time. Sitting there with the peanut shells on the floor, I could feel what it is that might come next. On a large scale, it won't come quickly or easily. But on the other hand, it's already here, rising invisibly all around us, the generative economy.

NEXT

I t's a long way from the New York Stock Exchange to the rolling hills of Wisconsin, many miles from that Greco-Roman edifice to the cherry red, LEED-certified headquarters of Organic Valley—itself down the road apiece from George Siemon's old farm. It's a return journey, I think. It takes us back to where we began—back to when economies existed to meet human needs, not to ratchet up earnings per share, quarter after quarter. Back to a place where there's dirt under our feet. Water tables. Biotoxins accumulating (or not accumulating) in the flesh of toddlers. The place where we live. Planet Earth.

At the start of these journeys, the source of our troubles seemed to be the stock exchange—the ancestral home of the founders of the industrial order, the robber barons. If any of us ever manage to get inside the New York Stock Exchange, we'll see that it's now just a backdrop for CNBC. A ghost town. The real action has moved elsewhere, everywhere: hedge funds, investment banking firms, our own 401(k) plans, the pension plans of fire-fighters like Michael Haroldson, the endowments of colleges and founda-tions, the balance sheets of the troubled banks and nations of Europe.

The problem's not on Wall Street but in us. For the last half-century we've been living in the midst of an economic explosion, assuming that it will go on forever. It won't. We live in the real world, not the world of stock markets and collaterized debt obligations and balance sheets. We need to live more consciously in this finite world. When there's less growth, how we divvy things up becomes more critical. If financial income keeps trying to grow more than the incomes of everyone else, it becomes more extrac-tive. The wealthy become wealthier by extracting more from the rest of us.

The problem is that even as our world changes rapidly, in our minds we're still trying to play the economic game by the rules that the robber barons left us. The rules that say financial capital is sacred beyond all else.

The rules that say capital must expand quarter by quarter, forever. The rules that say those who own the most property have the right to rule.

If those rules are in our ideas, they're also—and more rigidly—in the ownership and financial designs of corporations and capital markets. They're embedded in the structures of Financial Purpose, Absentee Membership, Governance by Markets, Casino Finance, and Commodity Networks.

There are some today who are unintimidated by the ritual incantations of P/E ratios and return on equity and shareholder primacy. There are a few—actually, quite a few—standing up and suggesting that perhaps the measure of our lives is not how much we accumulate for ourselves but how much we feel alive and enliven those around us. Maybe the measure of our success is not how extractive we are but how generative.

The ownership revolution begins in the human heart. It begins when we allow ourselves to hope that a different kind of economy just might be possible. The ownership revolution becomes a force when we allow ourselves to imagine that generative designs might one day become not merely a sideshow but a beacon. A collective ideal.

Set aside for a moment the task of trying to imagine the entire world embodying a generative economy; the real world always departs from our ideals. The reality of democracy is far from ideal—but still the democratic values of liberty, justice, and equality remain our ideals. Where are the corollary ideals in the world of the economy? The regulatory approach of stopping this or preventing that is not about ideals. That's why few people burn with a zeal for regulation. We need regulation; we will always need it, and more of it. But it's time to dream a deeper dream, the dream of an economy that is built around ideals like fairness, community, and sustainability—an economy that in *its normal functioning* tends to create fair and just outcomes, benefits the many rather than the few, and enables an enduring human presence on a flourishing earth.

That world is possible. This is the heresy that the keepers of the temple do not wish us to utter: *there is an alternative.*

When we begin to share a common vision, that vision can spread if it finds fertile soil in the human heart. It takes root in the things we care about, in what we value. When our values shift—as they are beginning to today, with ecological and financial crises looming larger—then the ground of social legitimacy shifts. This makes change possible on a broader scale. As the tumultuous 20th century taught us, and the more recent Arab Spring showed yet again, even the most dictatorial regime proves weak in the face of a people enlivened by ideals. We become enlivened when our hearts are touched by something real, something we long for, collectively—something we naturally value in our heart of hearts.

As values and legitimacy shift, the ground of the social order begins to shift. It has done so before and can do so again. Social legitimacy shifted beneath the monarchy. Beneath slavery. Beneath racism and sexism. On a less grand scale, we've seen the ground of legitimacy shift beneath the perceived necessity of eating meat and the attractiveness of smoking cigarettes. We've seen it shift toward recycling, choosing organic food, buying local. Things that begin on the fringe move toward the mainstream. What at one time is accepted as normal comes to be perceived as unseemly, distasteful.

Can we imagine the ground of social legitimacy shifting beneath the capitalist value system that sees financial capital as the goal above goals, the pinnacle? Can we imagine people saying, "Enough financial wealth—I choose life"?

Many of the people I visited in this book have already made that shift. Happily. Like the organizations they lead, they're not interested in maximizing their financial wealth. They know it's possible to have plenty and recognize that enough is enough. There are other things they value more highly, like being happy, living authentically, feeling alive. Living well in community. Leaving the world a better place.

If we can imagine such values spreading in the culture—if we can imagine massive wealth being seen not as the ultimate prize but as vaguely distasteful, and if we can imagine people realizing that great wealth is in reality a kind of relentless, extractive demand laid on the shoulders of those least able to withstand it—then change is likely to come.

Once values and legitimacy are there, we can build the social architecture. It may be that we do both at once: we build the values and legitimacy by building the architecture. These things are a matter of strategy, policy, ideas. Ownership designs.

TWO RESPONSES TO A HURRICANE

A few thoughts about strategy. Let's start with the fact that there are two ways to respond to a hurricane. First, you pull people out of the water, get them off rooftops, and provide them with food and shelter and blankets. But if that's all you do, you doom the world to an endless string of hurricanes, increasing in frequency and severity. The second response to a hurricane is to tackle the challenge of global warming. That's a longer-term response that leads far afield from blankets. It leads to putting a price on carbon, driving and flying less, weatherizing homes, and living in smaller homes—as well as all the other byways and alleyways that our culture has yet to fully explore. Ultimately, responding to a hurricane means changing our civilization, root and branch.

It's the same with a financial hurricane. The first response may be to shore up the banks, strengthen regulation of finance, tighten expenditures among governments facing debt overload, help people facing foreclosure and unemployment. But if that's all we do, we're dooming the world to an endless string of financial crises, increasing in frequency and severity. We need to begin focusing on a longer-term response in addition to immediate responses. That means confronting the uncomfortable fact that our economy is built to manufacture so-called wealth, which in reality means an endlessly growing house of financial claims. We need to build a new economy designed to sustain life.

This longer-term strategy includes creating deliberate ways to advance the ownership revolution, ramping up the nascent, emergent movement we've seen thus far. This is potentially among the most transformative strategies we can pursue, because ownership is about who decides everything else in an economy.

Ultimately, we will need to change the operating system at the heart of major corporations. But if we begin there, we will fail. The place to begin is with what's doable, what's enlivening—*and* what points toward bigger wins in the future. The place to begin is with advancing generative alternatives.

At the policy level, this may mean, for example, taking steps to advance employee ownership and the growth of cooperatives. It might mean working not just for solar power but for distributed ownership of solar power, not just for wind but for community wind. It may mean supporting community development financial institutions and community development corporations in a much bigger way.

We might take a lesson from the Maine lobster industry and tackle the issue of corporate power by trying to make certain areas of the economy off-limits. We might draw a bright line prohibiting extractive ownership models from operating in certain sectors, like education and health care. We might decide that these are areas where only generative models should operate. We need to begin making the case that it's OK to make a profit, but *maximizing* profit is a dangerous game. It's not a game that can be played everywhere.

When the next financial crisis hits, we might take a generative approach, shifting assets to cooperative banks and credit unions. The United States could create more state banks, and other nations might emulate the Bank of India. The next time a major corporation needs a government bailout, we should require it to recharter as a generative company, writing into its articles that a majority of board seats are reserved for public interest directors and employees. Instead of trying to abolish the Federal Reserve, as some at Occupy Wall Street suggested, we might propose that it be turned into a generative institution, with seats for folks besides the banks.

But we don't need to wait for federal policymakers in Washington or European Union leaders in Brussels to lead the way. At the individual level, we might consider moving our money to the community and cooperative banking sectors. We can shift our assets to responsible investing. Join or start a Slow Money group. Buy and invest locally. Join a food co-op. Find community loan funds and invest as much as we can.

We might consider generative alternatives for retirement. Instead of pretending that each family will have enough financial assets to live comfortably to the end of life—a model that's failing a lot of us—we might explore cohousing. Instead of doing reverse mortgages as a way to get money out of our houses, maybe we create ways to sell our land to community land trusts, allowing us to continue living in our homes, even as we create new affordable housing for future generations.

Ultimately, advancing generative alternatives is about creating the designs into which the future can flow. Today's major corporations may seem eternal. But as economist Joseph Schumpeter observed, creative destruction is ever present in capitalism. In industrialized nations, an estimated 15 percent of jobs are destroyed every year, and new jobs replace them. It's the same with companies.[1] Hypothetically, an entirely new economy can come into existence every seven years. Think of the transformation of the recording industry from vinyl to CDs to digital. Think of the death of many newspapers and the growth of the Internet. Think of declining oil reserves and what that will mean for auto and oil companies, and for the growth of wind and solar power. In the not-so-long run, trying to remake the operating systems of the major companies of today may be less important than getting the next economy into the right kinds of ownership. We might aim for 20 percent of the economy to be generative within ten years, 30 percent a decade later, and so on. One day, a shift in the zeitgeist—perhaps a citizen uprising—could make generative design the new norm.

Perhaps most important, instead of seeing all these things as random and disconnected, we need to recognize that they form a coherent whole. They are part of a single movement for a generative economy. It is when we embrace a common vision and a common language that our separate efforts become one movement. And that movement gains momentum.

RESPONDING, NOT CONTROLLING

The thoughts offered here are nothing like a blueprint for the redesign of capitalism. They're gestures, idea starters. Transforming the social architecture of the economy is as large a task as tackling global warming. It will take many minds.

In talking of strategy, it's important not to delude ourselves into think-ing this is a process over which we have control. Old ways of organizing our world are breaking down. This is not something we can stop. But it is something to which we can respond. Our greatest challenge lies in the realm of imagination and ideas. Capitalism has been such a totalizing force that it has left little room—politically, economically, philosophically— where alternatives could take shape.

Our task is to reimagine our economy. Our challenge is to dream deeply enough, all the way down to the root social architecture with which civilized life began, when humans stepped out of the life of hunting-gathering and took up the settled life of agriculture. That root economic architecture is ownership—the source of untold blessings and untold mis-chief over thousands of years, today potentially the source of renewal and rebirth.

Many unexpected events might intervene to move change along. On the positive side, there could be galvanizing media events, similar to the role that Al Gore's film, *An Inconvenient Truth*, played in shifting attitudes toward climate change. One possible galvanizing event with generative design, for example, is the United Nations' declaration of 2012 as the Year of the Cooperative. Other forces include the ownership movements of every kind taking shape across the globe. Unions and community founda-tions are working with employee ownership groups to spread the model of the Evergreen Cooperative Laundry to other cities. Social enterprise initia-tives are taking root at places like Harvard, Yale, and Oxford, with funding from people like Jeff Skoll, former president of eBay. A movement for the solidarity economy is occurring in Quebec and Latin America. And many groups and nations around the world are working to advance employee ownership.

On the negative side, there could be new financial crises, spikes in the price of oil, a massive season of hurricanes, new citizen revolts. On many fronts, things are likely to be messy, and get messier. How it all might come together to create deep change is impossible to say. But what else besides massive disruption could change the operating system of capitalism?

We might recall a prediction made a half-century ago by economist Robert Heilbroner. "Capitalism will inevitably change," he wrote, "and in the longer run will gradually give way to a very different kind of social order."[2] The deep transformation of the capitalist order may not be an idle pipe dream. It may be something closer to an inevitability.

That's not to say we'll come through it unscathed. Things may get harder than we think we can bear. But we will come through. That's something I said to Leslie Christian in our phone conversation about limits to financial growth.

"It's going to be OK," I said. "This is not something I think. It's something I know. Even if I can't say exactly how I know it."

"You need to write that," she said. "People need to hear it. *I* need to hear it."

I take confidence, in part, from systems thinking, which teaches us that crisis is a natural part of how systems evolve. Living systems have the ability to make sudden, creative leaps into novelty, reorganizing themselves into something wholly new. They do this when they're undergoing intolerable stress. At critical points of instability, some new way of organizing things emerges.

This may be what generative ownership design is: the something new emerging—the thing we need, at the very moment we need it.

There's something else I take comfort in, and that's the resilience of life. My sister Valerie Kelly, now a hydrologist with the US Geological Survey, had the good fortune of visiting Mount St. Helens as part of her graduate studies, following the massive volcanic eruption there in 1980. The place initially looked like a wasteland. Rock and mud covered it thickly for 20 square miles, with trees flattened like matchsticks and forests seared by heat up to 17 miles away. In this moonscape, it seemed nothing could have survived. Yet over time ecologists found that some animals had survived, finding refuge under overhangs and in burrows beneath the snow.

"Scientists expected the vegetation to fill in slowly from the outside," Valerie told me. "But instead they found microzones protected from the blast, which extended out to meet one another."

Mount St. Helens proved a story not only of devastation but also of unexpectedly rapid renewal. It transformed scientific thinking. According to pre-blast ecological theory, the land should have been rendered virtually sterile. Instead, there were species of toads, frogs, and salamanders, some of them previously endangered, that took up a robust new life there before their predators recovered. More than 120 new lakes and ponds were created by the blast, and somehow water-loving creatures crossed miles of near-desert to populate them. The blast allowed a rapid adaptive response known as *ecological release.* Three decades later, there's far more variety and exuberance than before the eruption.[3]

As I listened to Valerie and read other scientists who spoke of *refugia,* of those forms of refuge found in crisis, I found myself thinking of the community land trust, the metaphoric house still standing after the subprime mortgage blast. I thought of the cooperative banks, community banks, and credit unions that remained healthy while Northern Rock and Lehman Brothers melted down. I thought of that lone Bank of North Dakota, which other states rushed to emulate. I thought of the community investments that made money during two financial meltdowns.

Where the next disruptions will come from, or when they will come, we don't know. But perhaps we can find refuge by organizing ourselves around serving the needs of life. This may be how—even as things break down—we carry on the generations, one after the other, in unbroken flow. The way we've organized life on earth will not continue. But we will.

From the multiplying crises we face, a new worldview is already emerging, along with a new set of values, like sustainability, community, sufficiency, and fairness. These are new forms for the age-old pursuit of happiness. When these values are embodied in institutional form, in various kinds of generative ownership design, they will become enduring. When enough of the microzones of generative design extend out to meet one another, they might create, ultimately, not only a new economy but also a new social order—possibly an age of inclusion, with more variety and exuberance than the industrial age. It may be that what we're moving toward is an age defined not by the nature of our machines (however green they become) but by the nature of our connections—an era when we may find dominion's end.

NOTES

Prologue

1. Gar Alperovitz, Thad Williamson, and Ted Howard, "The Cleveland Model," *Nation*, March 1, 2010, www.thenation.com/article/cleveland-model.

2. David MacLeod, "Blowing in the wind," *Alternatives Journal*, Winter 2004, http://findarticles.com/p/articles/mi_hb6685/is_1_30/ai_n29093635/.

3. Conventional homeowners were ten times more likely to be in foreclosure than CLT homeowners at the end of 2010 (4.63 percent in the conventional market versus 0.46 percent among CLT homeowners). Emily Thaden, "Stable Home Ownership in a Turbulent Economy," the Housing Fund and Vanderbilt University, www.lincolninst.edu/pubs/1936_Stable-Home-Ownership-in-a-Turbulent-Economy.

4. B Lab, "B Corp Legislation," www.bcorporation.net/publicpolicy.

5. Matthew Brown, Associated Press, "Climate Activists Target States With Lawsuits," May 4, 2011, http://abcnews.go.com/Business/wireStory?id=13524147.

6. Medard Gabel and Henry Bruner, *Global Inc.: An Atlas of the Multinational Corporation* (New York: New Press, 2003), 2–8, 31. The overwhelming majority of those companies are publicly traded.

7. Jeffrey Birnbaum, "The Road to Riches Is Called K Street," *Washington Post*, June 22, 2005.

8. Corporation 20/20, www.Corporation2020.org.

9. See Marjorie Kelly and Shanna Ratner, *Keeping Wealth Local: Shared Ownership and Wealth Control for Rural Communities*, Tellus Institute and Yellow Wood Associates, November 2009, supported by the Ford Foundation's Wealth Creation in Rural Communities—Building Sustainable Livelihoods Initiative, www.yellowwood.org/Keeping%20Wealth%20Local.pdf. For more on this project, see www.CreatingRuralWealth.org.

10. John Tozzi, "America's Most Promising Social Entrepreneurs 2011," *Business Week*, June 22, 2011, www.businessweek.com/smallbiz/content/jun2011/sb20110621_158462.htm.

11. Social Investment Forum Foundation 2010 study, Center for Social Philanthropy, http://socialphilanthropy.org/knowledge.php. The US government operates a grant-making CDFI Fund; read more at www.cdfifund.gov/who_we_are/about_us.asp.

12. "Catch shares: New hope for fisheries," Environmental Defense Fund, www.edf.org/oceans/catch-shares.

13. "Conserving Land, Water, and a Way of Life," Nature Conservancy, www.nature.org/aboutus/privatelandsconservation/conservationeasements/index.htm.

14. Community Interest Companies, www.bis.gov.uk/cicregulator/.

15. Americans for Community Development, http://americansforcommunity development.org/.

16. "Bank of North Dakota," New Rules Project, www.newrules.org/banking/ rules/bank-north-dakota. Gar Alperovitz, "Worker-Owners of America, Unite!" *New York Times*, December 15, 2011.

17. "Chantie de l'economie sociale" (Quebec), http://fiducieduchantier.qc.ca/ ?module=document&uid=56.

18. Mission-driven family businesses are catalogued in *Managing for the Long Run: Lessons in Competitive Advantage from Great Family Businesses*, by Danny Miller and Isabelle Le Breton-Miller (Boston: Harvard Business School Publishing, 2005). The term "mission-controlled corporation" first appeared in Marjorie Kelly, "Not Just for Profit," *Strategy+Business*, Spring 2009, www .strategy-business.com/media/file/enews-02-26-09.pdf.

19. Marjorie Kelly, "Not Just for Profit," *Strategy+Business*, Spring 2009, www .strategy-business.com/media/file/enews-02-26-09.pdf.

20. "Ostrom Wins Nobel Prize in Economics," Indiana University, http:// elinorostrom.indiana.edu/.

21. One of the earliest people to use the term "living economy" was Paul Ekins, who wrote *The Living Economy: A New Economics in the Making* (London: Routledge & Kegan Paul, 1986).

22. The phrases "living wealth" and "phantom wealth" were first used by David Korten.

23. United Nations International Year of Cooperatives, http://social.un.org/ coopsyear/.

24. Community Wealth, www.community-wealth.org/strategies/panel/coops/ index.html. Stacy Mitchell, "Credit Unions Hang Tough, See Surge in Deposits," NewRules.org, July 5, 2011. "Safe Havens: Credit Unions Earn Some Interest," *Wall Street Journal*, March 15, 2009, http://online.wsj.com/article/ SB123708535764231521.html.

25. Johnston Birchall, *Rediscovering the Cooperative Advantage* (Geneva: International Labor Organization, 2003), 48–51; cited in Johnston Birchall and Lou Hammond Ketilson, *Resilience of the Cooperative Business Model in Times of Crisis* (Geneva: ILO, 2009), 7.

26. "Fortress World" is one among a group of possible future scenarios created in a Tellus Institute modeling exercise. Another scenario is the "Great Transition" to a just and sustainable world. See Paul Raskin et al., *Great Transition: The Promise and Lure of the Times Ahead* (Boston: Stockholm Environment Institute, 2002), http://tellus.org/documents/Great_Transition.pdf.

27. Marjorie Kelly, "Redesigning private ownership to create a truly generative economy," *Memo to the Left* (London: Policy Network, 2011), www.policy-network.net/publications_detail.aspx?ID=4002.

28. Margaret Wheatley and Deborah Frieze, "Using Emergence to Take Social Innovation to Scale," Berkana Institute, http://margaretwheatley.com/articles/ using-emergence.pdf.

29. Christopher Alexander, *The Timeless Way of Building* (New York: Oxford University Press, 1979), 267.

30. "Physical and social technologies" is the terminology of evolutionary economist Richard Nelson. See his 2003 paper, "Physical and Social Technologies and Their Evolution," Columbia University, working paper, available from the author, cited in Eric D. Beinhocker, *The Origin of Wealth* (Boston: Harvard Business School Press, 2007), 15.

Chapter 1: Debt, Inc.

1. Alexandra Andrews, ProPublica, "Freddie Mac loan contractor, Ocwen Financial, has spotty record," *Palm Beach Post*, March 29, 2009, www.palm beachpost.com/opinion/content/business/epaper/2009/03/29/sunbiz_ocwen_0329.html. Knight Ridder/Tribune Business News, "Florida-based firm Ocwen Financial Solutions to hire 5,000 in India," December 9, 2004.

2. Peter S. Goodman, "Late-Fee Profits May Trump Plan to Modify Loans," *New York Times*, July 30, 2009.

3. *New York Times*, Business, "Ocwen Financial Corporation, Company Information," http://topics.nytimes.com/topics/news/business/companies/ocwen-financial-corporation/index.html (accessed July 30, 2009). In the 52-week period leading up to July 30, 2009, the stock climbed 139.97 percent.

4. Donella H. Meadows, *Thinking in Systems: A Primer*, ed. Diana Wright (White River Junction, VT: Chelsea Green Publishing, 2008), 80. Fritjof Capra, *The Hidden Connections: A Science for Sustainable Living* (New York: Anchor Books/Random House, 2002), xviii.

5. Meadows, *Thinking in Systems*, 81.

6. In systems thinking, the term "archetypes" generally refers to particular patterns of feedback loops. See, for example, "Appendix 2: System Archetypes" in Peter Senge, *The Fifth Discipline* (New York: Currency Doubleday, 1990, 378–90). I use the term here in a related but broader sense, to refer to two schools of design for ownership: extractive design is characterized by the reinforcing feedback loops of maximizing profits; generative design is characterized by the balancing feedback loops of Rooted Membership, Living Purpose, and other patterns.

7. Meadows, *Thinking in Systems*, 5.

Chapter 2: The Community Bank

1. The Haroldsons dealt with Community First Bank Loan Services, the mortgage-origination division of Community First Bank, headquartered in Baltimore County, Maryland.

2. AllMortgageDetail.com, www.AllMortgageDetail.com.

3. The Haroldsons dealt with Community First Bank Loan Services, the mortgage-origination division of Community First Bank in Baltimore, Maryland. In late 2009, it reported 11 locations in seven states. In late 2011, the FDIC reported that one branch remained, in Maryland. In late 2009, the bank reported assets of $70 million. According to the FDIC, its total assets as of

June 30, 2010, were $58 million, and a year later they had declined to under $50 million. www2.fdic.gov/IDASP/main_bankfind.asp.

4. CDFI Fund, www.cdfifund.gov/what_we_do/programs_id.asp?programID= 9#certified.

5. Jim Wise, "Prudent lender prevails amid crisis," *Durham News*, August 16, 2008. Robert Kropp, "CDFIs Offer Responsible Alternative to Predatory Lending," SocialFunds, September 26, 2008, www.socialfunds.com.

6. Self-Help, www.self-help.org.

7. "Newsweek's Daniel Gross Calls Subprime Loans 'Risks Worth Taking,'" MicroCapital.org, December 5, 2008, www.microcapital.org/news-wire-united-states-newsweeks-daniel-gross-calls-subprime-loans-risks-worth-taking/#more-2793.

8. For first quarter 2010, the annualized net charge-off rate for the CDFI industry was 1.23 percent, compared with 2.84 percent for all FDIC-insured banking institutions. "Opportunity Finance Network Market Conditions Report, First Quarter 2010," Opportunity Finance Network, www.opportunityfinance.net/store/downloads/CDFI_Market_Conditions_Q110.pdf.

9. There are various kinds of CDFIs, including banks, credit unions, loan funds, and venture capital funds. The membership of Opportunity Finance Network includes all kinds of CDFIs, but the vast majority are community development loan funds; thus their survey largely covers loan fund performance. Making a cross-sectoral comparison—looking at the performance of these loan funds (which have no disclosure requirements) versus the performance of banks—is not a strict apples-to-apples comparison. Thus the figures offered here should be considered suggestive rather than definitive.

10. Connie Bruck, "Angelo's Ashes," *New Yorker*, June 29, 2009.

11. "The CDFI Banking Sector: 2009 Annual Report on Financial and Social Performance," National Community Investment Fund, Chicago, Illinois, www.ncif.org/images/uploads/20100519_2009_NCIFAnnual_Report_FINAL.pdf.

12. Saurabh Nairan, e-mail message to author, July 17, 2010.

13. Mark Maremont, "U.S. Moves to Bail Out Credit Union Network," *New York Times*, January 29, 2009. Ralph Nader, "How Credit Unions Survived the Crash," *CounterPunch*, February 23, 2009, http://counterpunch.org/nader02232009.html.

14. David Segal, "We're Dull, Small Banks Say, and Have Profit to Show for It," *New York Times*, May 12, 2009. "Small Banks' Failure Rate Grows, Straining FDIC," *Wall Street Journal*, October 11, 2009. FDIC study about small banks remaining best capitalized reported by Zachery Kouwe in "Small Banks Move In As Giants Falter," *New York Times*, November 2, 2009.

15. Eric Bellman, "State Bank of India—Has Cash, Will Lend," *Wall Street Journal*, March 30, 2009, C1.

16. *The Ecology of Finance: An Alternative White Paper on Banking and Financial Sector Reform* (London: New Economics Foundation, November 2009).

17. Statement by ICBA President Jean-Louis Bancel, International Co-operative Banking Association, www.icba.coop/news/more-than-ever-appropriate-and-relevant-icba-chairman-bancel-on-coops-and-the-crisis.html.

18. "Globalisation and Banking Regulation: Challenges and Impacts for Co-operative Banks," speech by Bancel to Organization for Economic Development and Cooperation, March 17, 2010, www.icba.coop/images/stories/pdf/mondialisation%20et%20regulation%20bancaire%20colloque%20ocde%20march%202010%20english.pdf.

19. Ibid.

20. Herman E. Daly and John B. Cobb Jr., *For the Common Good: Redirecting the Economy Toward Community, the Environment, and a Sustainable Future* (Boston: Beacon Press, 1989).

21. Interview with the author, 2009.

22. Bill Howard explained that Beverly Cooperative Bank had a few years earlier converted to holding company ownership, which meant that technically it was no longer owned by depositors. But it still had a mutual bank charter. Its mission was still to serve depositors' interests, and it had no shareholders whose demands it had to satisfy. Depositors also retained rights in liquidation, a traditional ownership right.

23. The website BankInvestor.com (www.bankinvestor.com/) tracks the conversion of mutual banks into publicly traded companies. In September 2009 there were 788 mutual banks; 316 mutual banks went public between 1996 and 2008.

24. Beverly Cooperative Bank had a Community Reinvestment Act rating of satisfactory in November 2011, www.ffiec.gov/craratings/default.aspx.

25. Meadows, *Thinking in Systems*, 25–34.

26. Dalton Conley, "Safe at Home," *New York Times*, August 3, 2009. Adam Serwer, "Banks as Heroes," *American Prospect*, August 10, 2009, www.prospect.org/cs/articles?article=banks_as_heroes.

27. See Move Your Money Project, http://moveyourmoneyproject.org.

Chapter 3: Wall Street

1. In late 2011, the New York Stock Exchange was on the verge of being sold again to Deutsche Boerse, until European regulators killed the deal in February 2012.

2. Eric J. Weiner, *What Goes Up: The Uncensored History of Modern Wall Street* (New York: Back Bay Books, 2005).

3. Hernando de Soto, *The Mystery of Capital: Why Capitalism Triumphs in the West and Fails Everywhere Else* (New York: Basic Books, 2000), 6–8.

4. Homer, *Hymn to Hermes*.

5. Joel Covity, "Myth and Money," in James Hillman et al., *Soul and Money* (Dallas, TX: Spring Publications, 1982).

6. In 2007, JPMorgan Chase made a net income of 21.5 percent; in 2006, net income was 23.5 percent, according to Morningstar, http://quote.morning-star.com/Stock/s.aspx?t=JPM&culture=en-US&region=USA&r=600634&by refresh=yes.

7. Between 2000 and 2009, the P/E ratio of JPMorgan Chase varied between 10 and 45. In 2007, it averaged 10. On January 4, 2010, its P/E ratio was 21, according to Morningstar.

8. Samuelson findings cited by John C. Edmunds, "Securities: The New World Wealth Machine," *Foreign Policy* (Fall 1996), 126.

9. The 10-year P/E ratio of the S&P 500 was 20.3 at the end of 2009, up from 13.3 in March 2009. The average for the last 130 years was 16.4, according to Yale economist Robert J. Shiller. Vikas Bajaj, "Heart-Stopping Fall, Breathtaking Rally," *New York Times*, December 31, 2009.

10. Lawrence E. Mitchell, *The Speculation Economy: How Finance Triumphed Over Industry* (San Francisco: Berrett-Koehler Publishers, 2007), 1–7.

11. Liz Moyer and Emily Lambert, "Wall Street's New Masters," *Forbes*, September 21, 2009, 41. Market share of daily trading going through the New York Stock Exchange ultimately declined; Graham Bowley, "Stock Exchange Shrinks as Rivals Take Over Trades," *New York Times*, October 15, 2009.

12. Moyer and Lambert, "Wall Street's New Masters," 44.

13. Michael Mackenzie, "SEC Runs Eye Over High-Speed Trading," *Financial Times*, July 9, 2009.

14. The Tabb Group estimated that high-frequency trading accounted for 73 percent of US daily equity volume in 2009; Michael Mackenzie, "SEC Runs Eye Over High-Speed Trading," *Financial Times*, July 29, 2009. Also interview with John Katovich, former attorney with Nasdaq.

15. The study was by Mercer and IRRC Institute, cited by Jason Zweig, "Buy-and-hold hasn't looked too good lately, but churn-and-burn is no better," *Wall Street Journal*, February 13, 2010.

16. Rainer Maria Rilke, *Duino Elegies*, second elegy. From *Duino Elegies and the Sonnets to Orpheus*, translated by A. Poulin Jr. (Boston: Houghton Mifflin Co., 1977), 17.

17. Robert G. Wilmers, "Small Banks, Big Banks, Giant Differences," Bloomberg.com, June 13, 2011, www.bloomberg.com/news/2011-06-13/small-banks-big-banks-giant-differences-robert-g-wilmers.html.

Chapter 4: Overload

1. Richard D. Freedman and Jill Vohr, "Goldman Sachs/Lehman Brothers," Case Series in Finance and Economics, New York University Salomon Center, 1991 (revised 1999).

2. Michael Lewis, *The Big Short: Inside the Doomsday Machine* (New York: W.W. Norton & Co., 2010), 257–64.

3. Fernand Braudel, *Civilization and Capitalism, 15th–18th Century, vol. 1, The Structures of Everyday Life* (Berkeley, CA: University of California Press, 1992), 23–24; vol. 3, *The Wheels of Commerce*, 22–23.

4. The notion of real wealth in the real economy, or true wealth, has been articulated by theorists such as David Korten and Juliet Schor.

5. Charles R. Morris, *The Trillion Dollar Meltdown: Easy Money, High Rollers, and the Great Credit Crash* (New York: PublicAffairs/Perseus Books Group, 2008), 134. An International Monetary Fund analysis found global financial assets 3.7 times as high as global GDP at the end of 2005. By 2007, the number had no doubt "ratcheted up much higher still," he wrote.

6. Kevin Phillips, *American Theocracy: The Peril and Politics of Radical Religion, Oil, and Borrowed Money in the 21st Century* (New York: Viking Penguin, 2006), 268. John Bellamy Foster, "The Financialization of Capitalism," *Monthly Review* 58, no. 11 (April 2007), 1–12, http://monthlyreview.org/2007/04/01/the-financialization-of-capitalism.

7. Phillips, *American Theocracy*, 265–68.

8. Nouriel Roubini, *Foreign Policy*, early 2009, quoted in the *New Yorker*, June 29, 2009, 54.

9. In the dot-com crash, the Nasdaq composite declined 78 percent, from a high of 5,047 in 2000 to 1,114 in 2002. On September 29, 2010, it stood at 2,369. "Historical Prices," Nasdaq, www.nasdaq.com/quotes/historical-quotes.aspx.

10. Phyllis S. Pierce, ed., *The Dow Jones Averages, 1885–1995* (Chicago: Irwin Professional Publishing, 1996). The Dow Jones ended 2010 at 11,577.

11. Ben Levisohn in "The Decline of the P/E Ratio," *Wall Street Journal*, August 30, 2010. The average P/E ratio approached 30 in several peaks in the late 1990s and early 2000s. By end of August 2010, it was below 15. Source of data: Standard & Poor's.

12. James Gleick, *Chaos: Making a New Science* (New York: Viking, 1987), 23–24.

13. Ibid.

14. Meadows, *Thinking in Systems*, 90–92, 190–91.

15. Richard Riordan, Alexander Rubalcava, "How Pensions Can Get Out of the Red," *New York Times*, September 16, 2010, www.nytimes.com/2010/09/16/opinion/16riordan.html. "Investor, heal thyself," *Economist*, September 16, 2010, www.economist.com/node/17046748.

16. Phillips, *American Theocracy*, 288–97.

17. Robert Freeman, "Why Obama's Economic Plan Will Not Work—And a Better Plan," *Common Dreams*, January 17, 2010, www.commondreams.org/view/2010/01/17.

18. Phillips, *American Theocracy*, 328.

19. Charles R. Morris, *The Trillion Dollar Meltdown: Easy Money, High Rollers, and the Great Credit Crash* (New York: Public Affairs/Perseus Books Group, 2008), 134. The figure of ten times GDP represents the *notional value* of derivatives, which refers to the value of the underlying contracts if they were to be exercised in full. When I hold an option to sell $1,000 worth of Google in November, the notional value of that derivative is $1,000.

20. Floyd Norris, "Naked Truth on Default Swaps," *New York Times*, May 20, 2010, www.nytimes.com/2010/05/21/business/economy/21norris.html.

21. Quoted in Louise Story and Edmund Andrews, "Life After Lehman Brothers," *New York Times*, September 16, 2008, www.nytimes.com/2008/09/16/business/16lehman.html?scp=1&sq="Life%20After%20Lehman%20Brothers"&st=cse.

Chapter 5: Collapse

1. Morris, *The Trillion Dollar Meltdown*, 70. Testimony by Julia Gordon, Center for Responsible Lending, before the US House of Representatives' Committee on Financial Services Subcommittee on Financial Institutions and Consumer Credit, March 11, 2009.

2. Morris, *The Trillion-Dollar Meltdown*, 146–47.

3. "The Rich and the Rest," *Economist*, January 20, 2011, www.economist.com/node/17959590.

4 . Robert Buchele et al., "Show Me the Money: Does Shared Capitalism Share the Wealth?" in *Shared Capitalism at Work: Employee Ownership, Profit and Gain Sharing, and Broad-Based Stock Options*, ed. Douglas L. Kruse, Richard B. Freeman, and Joseph R. Blasi (Chicago: University of Chicago Press, 2010), 351.

5. Leslie Parrish, "Overdraft Explosion," report from Center for Responsible Lending, October 6, 2009, www.responsiblelending.org/overdraft-loans/research-analysis/crl-overdraft-explosion.pdf.

6. Jessica Fargen, "Spike in Hub Burglaries," *Boston Herald*, March 14, 2011.

7. According to the US Bureau of Labor Statistics, in February 2010, "underemployment" stood at 16.8 percent.

8. Bob Herbert, "An Uneasy Feeling," *New York Times*, January 5, 2010, www.nytimes.com/2010/01/05/opinion/05herbert.html.

9. Robert Reich, *Aftershock: The Next Economy and America's Future* (New York: Alfred A. Knopf, 2010), 19.

10. Lawrence Mishel and Heidi Shierholz, "The sad but true story of wages in America," Economic Policy Institute, March 15, 2011, www.epi.org/publication/the_sad_but_true_story_of_wages_in_america/.

11. Reich, *Aftershock*, 3–4, 7–8.

12. Andrew Sum and Joseph McLaughlin of Northeastern University's Center for Labor Market Studies looked at the second quarter of 2009 and the first quarter of 2010, finding that pretax corporate profits rose $388 billion while wages increased $68 billion. Harold Meyerson, "Business Is Booming," *American Prospect*, March 2011, 14.

13. C. S. Holling, Lance H. Gunderson, and Donald Ludwig, "In Quest of a Theory of Adaptive Change," in *Panarchy: Understanding Transformations in Human and Natural Systems*, eds. Lance H. Gunderson and C. S. Holling (Washington, DC: Island Press, 2002), 3–22. Fikret Berkes, "Understanding uncertainty and reducing vulnerability: Lessons from resilience thinking," *Natural Hazards* 41 (2007), 283–95.

14. Herman Daly, *Beyond Growth* (Boston: Beacon Press, 1996), 37.

Chapter 6: Waking Up

1. Kelly and Ratner, *Keeping Wealth Local.*

2. Luis Ubiñas, president of the Ford Foundation, "At Global Climate Change Talks, an Answer Grows Right Outside," *Huffington Post,* November 29, 2010, www.huffingtonpost.com/luis-ubi/at-global-climate-change-_b_788256 .html. Elisabeth Malkin, "Growing a Forest, and Harvesting Jobs," *New York Times,* November 22, 2010, www.nytimes.com/2010/11/23/world/ americas/23mexico.html.

3. The Nature Conservancy, "Conserving Easements: Conserving Land, Water and a Way of Life," www.nature.org/aboutus/privatelandsconservation/ conservationeasements/conserving_a_way_of_life.pdf.

4. "Catch shares: New hope for fisheries," www.edf.org/page.cfm?tagID=69. "How catch shares work: A promising solution," www.edf.org/oceans/ how-catch-shares-work-promising-solution.

5. Kelly and Ratner, *Keeping Wealth Local,* 15–16.

6. Paul Gipe, Wind-Works.org, www.wind-works.org. Bertrand d'Armagnac, "Lesson in wind power," *Guardian Weekly* (UK), August 13, 2010, 31. "Cooperatives—a local and democratic ownership to wind turbines," Danish Wind Turbine Owners' Association, www.dkvind.dk/eng/faq/cooperatives .pdf.

7. Others in the United States working for community wind include Lisa Daniels of Windustry, www.windustry.org; and David Morris of the New Rules Project at the Institute for Local Self-Reliance, www.newrules.org/.

8. In 2007, Dominion spent $5.8 billion buying back its own stock. www.dom .com/investors/annual2010/domannual.pdf.

9. Stock buybacks are paper maneuvers that remove shares from circulation, so as to increase the value of remaining shares. I'll return to this transaction in the next chapter.

10. Jim Motavalli, "Hull Wind: A Renewable Energy 'Cash Cow,'" *E* magazine, February 28, 2005, www.emagazine.com/archive/2345. Also see Hull Wind, "History of Hull's wind project," www.hullwind.org/history.php.

11. He was quoting loosely from Aldo Leopold's *A Sand County Almanac:* "A thing is right when it tends to preserve the integrity, stability, and beauty of the biotic community. It is wrong when it tends otherwise." Aldo Leopold, *A Sand County Almanac* (New York: Oxford University Press, 1966).

12. Fritjof Capra, *The Web of Life: A New Scientific Understanding of Living Systems* (New York: Anchor Books/Doubleday, 1996), 5.

13. Ervin Laszlo, *The Systems View of the World: A Holistic Vision for Our Time* (Cresskill, NJ: Hampton Press, 1996), 61–63.

14. Capra, *The Web of Life,* 6.

15. Ibid.

16. "Sole and despotic dominion" from William Blackstone's *Commentaries on the Laws of England.* See chapter 3 of Kelly, *The Divine Right of Capital: Dethroning the Corporate Aristocracy* (Berrett-Koehler Publishers, 2001).

17. Quoted in Fritjof Capra, *The Hidden Connections: A Science for Sustainable Living* (New York: Anchor Books/Random House, 2002), 5–7.

18. American Farmland Trust, www.farmland.org.

Chapter 7: The Island

1. LEED standards are a set of design criteria for environmentally responsible buildings. Platinum is the highest level of excellence.

2. John Abrams, *Companies We Keep: Employee Ownership and the Business of Community and Place* (White River Junction, VT: Chelsea Green Publishing Co., 2008); revised edition of *The Company We Keep*, 2005. Quotations from both editions.

3. Thomas Princen, *The Logic of Sufficiency* (Cambridge, MA: MIT Press, 2005), 6.

4. Fritjof Capra remark in class he and I cotaught at Schumacher College in England, July 2004, "Business and Sustainability: From Complexity to Responsibility."

5. Angus Maddison, *The World Economy: A Millennial Perspective* (Paris: Organization for Economic Co-operation and Development [OECD], 2001); Maddison, *The World Economy: Historical Statistics* (Paris: Development Centre of the OECD, 2003); Maddison, *Contours of the World Economy, 1–2030 AD* (New York: Oxford University Press, 2007), 379. Output is real (inflation-adjusted) gross domestic product, measured in purchasing-power-parity-adjusted 1990 dollars.

6. John Stutz, *The Tellus Scenarios in Historical Perspective* (Boston: Tellus Institute, 2007).

7. Maddison figures reworked by Andrew Mold, head of finance, development unit, OECD, "What Will the World Look Like in 2030? Maddison's Forecasts Revisited," October 24, 2010, www.voxeu.org/index.php?q=node/5708. Mold revised downward the growth estimates for rich countries in the aftermath of the financial crisis, and revised estimates for Asia, Latin America, and Africa as well. Calculations by Kelly performed with assistance of John Stutz.

8. Island Cohousing, Guiding Principles, http://islandcohousing.org/about#tabs-panels-tabs-About-2.

9. Jewish National Fund, "Our History," www.jnf.org/about-jnf/history/.

10. Robert Swann et al., *The Community Land Trust: A Guide to a New Model for Land Tenure in America* (Cambridge, MA: Center for Community Economic Development, 1972), xiii, http://neweconomicsinstitute.org/publications/essays/swann/robert/the-community-land-trust-a-guide-to-a-new-model-for-land-tenure-in-america.

11. Karl Polanyi, *The Great Transformation: The Political and Economic Origins of Our Time* (Boston: Beacon Press, 1960; originally published 1944).

12. Capra, *The Web of Life*, 31–33.

Chapter 8: Bringing Forth a World

1. Author communications via e-mail and telephone with Hugh Cowperthwaite of Coastal Enterprises, Inc. Also www.ceimaine.org/Fisheries.

2. Coastal Enterprises, Inc., "Fishtag Program," www.ceimaine.org/Resources/ Documents/FISHTAG.pdf.

3. Coastal Enterprises, Inc., www.ceimaine.org/.

4. Ted Ames, interview with the author at Bowdoin College, March 30, 2011.

5. James Acheson, *Capturing the Commons: Devising Institutions to Manage the Maine Lobster Industry* (Lebanon, NH: University Press of New England, 2003), 8. Acheson also wrote *The Lobster Gangs of Maine* (Hanover, NH: University Press of New England, 1988).

6. Garrett Hardin, "The Tragedy of the Commons," *Science* 162 (1968), 1243–48, www.sciencemag.org/site/feature/misc/webfeat/sotp/commons.xhtml.

7. Elinor Ostrom, *Governing the Commons: The Evolution of Institutions for Collective Action* (New York: Cambridge University Press, 1990), 14; Ostrom, "Beyond Markets and States," Nobel Prize lecture, December 9, 2009.

8. For this notion of an "ecosystem" of supportive institutions, I am indebted to Heerad Sabeti. See the paper "The Emerging Fourth Sector," Fourth Sector, www.FourthSector.net/learn/fourth-sector/.

9. Acheson, *Capturing the Commons*, 105.

10. Ibid., 119.

11. Ibid., 105.

12. Ibid., 24.

13. Ibid., 41, 221, 224.

14. Fritjof Capra, *The Hidden Connections: A Science for Sustainable Living* (New York: Anchor Books/Random House, 2002), 14.

15. Marjorie Kelly, "Not Just for Profit," *Strategy+Business*, issue 54 (Spring 2009), 48–57.

16. Margaret Wheatley and Deborah Frieze, "Lifecycle of Emergence: Using Emergence to Take Social Innovation to Scale," Berkana Institute, 2006, www .berkana.org/articles/lifecycle.htm.

17. Amy R. Poteete, Marco A. Janssen, Elinor Ostrom, *Working Together: Collective Action, the Commons, and Multiple Methods in Practice* (Princeton, NJ: Princeton University Press, 2010), 48.

18. Muhammad Yunus, "Sacrificing Microcredit for Megaprofits," *New York Times*, January 14, 2011, www.nytimes.com/2011/01/15/opinion/15yunus .html.

19. Community Wealth, Democracy Collaborative, www.community-wealth.org/ strategies/panel/coops/index.html.

20. John Restakis, *Humanizing the Economy: Co-operatives in the Age of Capital* (Gabriola Island, BC, Canada: New Society Publishers, 2010).

21. United Nations, International Year of Cooperatives 2012, http://social.un.org/coopsyear/. Some data from International Labour Organization Fact Sheet *Cooperatives and Rural Employment*, and from International Co-operative Alliance, www.ica.coop.

22. European Federation of Share Ownership, *Economic Survey of Employee Ownership in European Countries in 2010*, May 4, 2011, www.efesonline.org/Annual%20Economic%20Survey/2010/Presentation.htm.

23. Corey Rosen, National Center for Employee Ownership, letter to editor in *Wall Street Journal*, September 11–12, 2010.

24. Erik Olsen, University of Missouri–Kansas City, "Majority Employee Owned Enterprises in the U.S.: A Profile," draft paper, February 22, 2011.

25. Capra, *The Hidden Connections*, 33–54.

26. Penobscot East Research Center, www.penobscoteast.org/research_ted_ames .asp (accessed July 13, 2011).

27. Ted Ames, "Multispecies Coastal Shelf Recovery Plan: A Collaborative, Ecosystem-Based Approach," *Marine and Coastal Fisheries: Dynamics, Management, and Ecosystem Science* 2 (2010), 217–31, www.penobscoteast .org/documents/C09-052.1GOMplan_000.pdf.

Part III: Creating Living Companies

1. With deep gratitude to architect Christopher Alexander for his root insights about design and pattern language in *The Timeless Way of Building*, from which I paraphrase.

Chapter 9: Living Purpose

1. Christopher Alexander, *The Timeless Way of Building* (New York: Oxford University Press, 1979), ix–x.

2. Ibid., 25–27.

3. Ibid., 38–39.

4. Meadows, *Thinking in Systems*, 1–15, 188.

5. Alexander, *The Timeless Way of Building*, 51, 36.

6. Lynn Stout, *The Shareholder Value Myth: How Putting Shareholders First Harms Investors, Corporations, and the Public* (San Francisco: Berrett-Koehler Publishers, 2012). Quotations from draft manuscript.

7. B Lab, www.bcorporation.net/.

8. Upstream 21, "How We're Different," www.upstream21.com/?page_id=64.

9. Fourth Sector, "For-Benefit Corporations," www.fourthsector.net/learn/for-benefit-corporations.

10. B Lab, "Benefit Corp Legislation," www.bcorporation.net/publicpolicy.

11. *Business Ethics* hosted a meeting on "The Legacy Problem" in October 2003. The Summer 2003 issue of *Business Ethics* carried a special section on "The Legacy Problem."

12. *Spheres of Influence*, 2007 Seventh Generation Corporate Consciousness Report, www.seventhgeneration.com/files/assets/pdf/2007_SevGen_Corporate-Consciousness.pdf.

13. B Lab, "About Seventh Generation," www.bcorporation.net/seventhgeneration.

14. *Inc.* magazine created a list of the "100 Fastest Growing Companies in America," and I met a CEO once who made that list and attended the gathering of winning CEOs. He told me, "I've never been in a room of 100 more miserable people in my life."

15. Telephone and e-mail conversations with Jeffrey Hollender. Also Marc Gunther, "Seventh Generation sweeps out its founder," November 1, 2010, www.marcgunther.com/2010/11/01/seventh-generation-sweeps-out-its-founder/.

16. Jen Boynton, "Jeffrey Hollender Shares Four Reasons He Got Fired from Seventh Generation," TriplePundit, June 9, 2011, www.triplepundit.com/2011/06/jeffrey-hollender-seventh-generation-fired/.

17. This evolutionary approach is happening with employee stock ownership plans (ESOPs), for which Congress initially set the bar deliberately low, with no requirement for employee voice in governance; but there is now a movement to see that step as a best practice. As Chris Mackin of Ownership Associates told me, had ESOPs started with more rigorous standards, there would be far fewer ESOPs today. Governance standards may be part of what's next for benefit corporations. With B Corporation legislation, some states already require a public interest director on the board.

18. Meadows, *Thinking in Systems*, 76.

19. B Lab, "Why B Corps Matter," www.bcorporation.net/why.

20. Alexander, *The Timeless Way of Building*, 246.

Chapter 10: Rooted Membership

1. John Lewis Partnership, "Financials," www.johnlewispartnership.co.uk/financials.html. Fortune 500 list of America's Largest Corporations in 2011 by revenue.

2. Alexander, *The Timeless Way of Building*, 288–92.

3. "John Lewis Chief Hits the Pay Jackpot," This is Money, April 21, 2011, www.thisismoney.co.uk/money/markets/article-1720836/John-Lewis-chief-hits-the-pay-jackpot.html. AFL-CIO Executive PayWatch, 2011, www.aflcio.org/corporatewatch/paywatch/.

4. Study data covered the period 1970–1989, comparing JLP with firms like Sainsbury, Tesco, and Marks and Spencer. Keith Bradley and Simon Taylor, *Business Performance in the Retail Sector: The Experience of the John Lewis Partnership* (Oxford: Clarendon Press, 1992).

5. Francis Green, *Demanding Work—The Paradox of Job Quality in the Affluent Economy* (Princeton, NJ: Princeton University Press, 2007).

6. Art Kleiner, "The Thought Leader Interview: Meg Wheatley," *Strategy+Business*, issue 65 (Winter 2011), 80–90.

7. "Registrars" at JLP aim to keep its democratic spirit in focus; more on this management structure is found in chapter 11.

8. John Lewis Partnership, "Our history," www.johnlewispartnership.co.uk/about/our-history/our-history-text-version.html. Also interviews with Ken Temple from JLP by the author.

9. John Spedan Lewis, *Fairer Shares: A Possible Advance in Civilization and Perhaps the Only Alternative to Communism* (London: Staples Press Limited, 1954), 1–5.

10. Martha Nussbaum, *Frontiers of Justice: Disability, Nationality, Species Membership* (Cambridge, MA: Belknap Press of Harvard University Press, 2006), 9–95.

11. Lewis, *Fairer Shares*, 12–13.

12. Quotations from Marjorie Kelly, *The Divine Right of Capital: Dethroning the Corporate Aristocracy* (San Francisco: Berrett-Koehler Publishers, 2001), 110.

13. Barbara Taylor, "Are Baby-Boomers Ready to Exit Their Businesses?" *New York Times*, February 10, 2011. White Horse Advisors, Exit Planning Research & Resource Center, "2008 Survey of Closely Held Business Owners," http://exitplanningresearch.com/.

14. Loren Rodgers, "The Employee Ownership Update," National Center for Employee Ownership (NCEO), May 16, 2011, www.nceo.org/main/column.php/id/393.

Chapter 11: Mission-Controlled Governance

1. Lewis, *Fairer Shares*, 10.

2. VIVA Trust, www.vivatrust.com/creation/. Tatiana Serafin, "The Bill Gates of Switzerland," *Forbes*, September 16, 2009.

3. *John Lewis Partnership Corporate Social Responsibility Report 2011*, www.johnlewispartnership.co.uk/csr/our-progress-and-reports/csr-reports/latest-reports.html.

4. *Novo Nordisk Annual Report 2010*, "Environmental," http://annualreport2010.novonordisk.com/environmental/environmental.aspx.

Chapter 12: Stakeholder Finance

1. John Maynard Keynes, "National Self-Sufficiency," *Yale Review* 22, no. 4 (June 1933), 755–69.

2. Quoted in Nicholas Shaxson, *Treasure Islands: Uncovering the Damage of Offshore Banking and Tax Havens* (New York: Vintage, 2011), 53.

3. John Maynard Keynes, *The General Theory of Employment, Interest and Money* (New York: Harcourt, Brace & World, 1965).

4. Meadows, *Thinking in Systems*, 85.

5. Study by the World Institute for Development Economics Research of the United Nations, reported by James Randerson, "World's Richest 1% Own 40% of All Wealth, UN Report Discovers," *Guardian*, December 6, 2006, www.guardian.co.uk/money/2006/dec/06/business.internationalnews.

6. Tim Kasser, *The High Price of Materialism* (Cambridge, MA: MIT Press, 2002).

7. Alexander, *The Timeless Way of Building*, 136.

8. Simon Lambert, "John Lewis 6.5% bond: Should you invest?" March 7, 2011, www.thisismoney.co.uk/money/investing/article-1714414/John-Lewis-65-bond-should-you-invest.html.

9. Kelly and Ratner, *Keeping Wealth Local*, 8–9.

10. Government Accountability Office 2004 study, *Wind Power's Contribution to Electric Power Generation and Impact on Farms and Rural Communities*, cited by Lisa Daniels of Windustry, www.windustry.org/.

11. Slow Money, "Local Groups," www.slowmoney.org/local-groups.

12. Slow Money, www.slowmoney.org.

Chapter 13: Ethical Networks

1. "Take Stock," CROPP Cooperative newsletter, first quarter 2011, www.organic valley.coop/fileadmin/pdf/TAKE_STOCK_Q1-11.pdf.

2. JLP is not legally chartered as a cooperative. Some employee-owned firms are cooperatives; others are not.

Epilogue: Next

1. Pierre Cahuc and André Zylberberg, *The Natural Survival of Work: Job Creation and Job Destruction in a Growing Economy* (Cambridge, MA: MIT Press, 2006).

2. Robert Heilbroner, *The Limits of American Capitalism* (New York: Harper & Row, 1965).

3. Charles Goodrich et al., eds., *In the Blast Zone: Catastrophe and Renewal on Mount St. Helens* (Corvallis: Oregon State University Press, 2008). Richard Lovett, "Mount St. Helens, Revisited," *Science* 288 (June 2, 2000), 1578–79.

ACKNOWLEDGMENTS

All the folks who participated in Corporation 20/20 over the years are first on my list for deepest thanks. This is your book as much as mine, and I wish I'd been able to fit more of you into the narrative. You're all here in spirit. It wouldn't have been written without you.

I also owe special thanks to the people of the Tellus Institute, especially John Stutz, who generously funded some of the very earliest of this thinking, which appeared as a paper I wrote for the Toda Institute. For Allen White, my longtime partner in corporate design and the director of Corporation 20/20, no thanks are enough. I simply would not be doing this work if not for him. Nor would I be doing it without Paul Raskin and Rich Rosen, who, with John Stutz, influenced my thinking with their research and vision of a Great Transition to a new social order. I'm also grateful to Paul for the lessons he's imparted about systems thinking. I am thankful to be the colleague of all these men.

All the people I interview in this book are owed an enormous debt of gratitude for their time and wisdom. Leslie Christian and John Katovich are particularly dear friends and partners in the area of enterprise design, as well as in my life. Many thanks to Orion Kriegman for sharing his story and journeying with me. I am especially and very personally grateful to "Helen and Michael Haroldson," for so graciously opening their home to me and sharing their story. My hope is that they are able to resolve their situation into stability and ease.

I am indebted to those who generously agreed to read versions of this book and offer feedback, including Karen Kahn, Carrie Rich, Robert Ellman, Kristen Moussalli, Jill Swenson, Neva Goodwin, David Korten, Valerie Kelly, Ben Linder, and Alex Lamb. Alex also suggested the title for the book: hats off (I owe you a bottle of champagne). Many, many thanks to Robert Ellman for help in finding the Haroldsons and allowing that journey to come to a close. Ben Linder gave a particularly close reading and helped reshape a number of key design points, including the definition of Ethical Networks.

I am exceedingly thankful for Gar Alperovitz's longtime work and thought leadership in promoting the importance of ownership; I consider him one of the key advocates and theorists of this field. I'm grateful to Fritjof Capra, from whom I learned a good deal about systems thinking. It was from Mike Thomas that I first heard the phrase "social architecture." Heerad Sabeti has done more than I can say to deepen and broaden my thinking, and the thinking of all of us, on issues and language of social enterprise design and the benefit corporation. He is a true pioneer. Other thought leaders in ownership design to whom I am grateful are Mary Ann Beyster, Susan MacCormac, Kent Greenfield, and Todd Johnson.

My work with the Ford Foundation, while separate from this book, informed my research in valuable ways. I am grateful to Wayne Fawbush and Frank DeGiovanni for their leadership of the Wealth Creation in Rural Communities—Building Sustainable Livelihoods Initiative, and to Shanna Ratner of Yellow Wood Associates for encouraging me to pursue research into ownership in rural areas.

Agent Scott Edelstein was enormously helpful in getting this book off the ground, in many many ways. Johanna Vondeling gave me brilliant early guidance in shaping this book as a work of nonfiction narrative; it is her book, in more ways than anyone can know. Steve Piersanti and the other staff of Berrett-Koehler are, as always, a delight to work with. The production team of editor Elissa Rabellino, designer Laura Lind, and coordinators Linda Jupiter and Dianne Platner gave this book a final editorial and graphic polish and elegance for which I am enormously thankful. I am proud to be a stakeholder in Berrett-Koehler, the most generative publisher I know.

Finally, and most important, I am grateful to my wife, Shelley Alpern, for her insight, support, and patience as I gave over my life (and my weekends) to this book for several years. She listened to more conversations about ownership design than any human being should ever have to endure (and did so with graciousness, if not entirely without complaint). It is Shelley more than anyone else who, in many, many ways, made this book possible.

INDEX

Abrams, Chris, 118, 130
Abrams, John, 117–21, 123, 126–27, 130
Abromowitz, David, 3
Absentee Membership: of extractive owner-
  ship, 14, 18, 138, 210; and master-servant
  relationship, 168; and responsibility,
  189–90; Rooted Membership compared
  to, 167–69, 195–96
Acheson, James, 133, 136, 137, 138
Addison, Medrick, 1
Adelphia, 6, 121
Aegis Asset-Backed Securities Trust, 69–70
Aegis Mortgage Company, 23–24, 45, 69,
  79–80, 89, 96, 152
Africa, 128, 134
Alaska, 106
Alden, Robin, 135
Alexander, Christopher, 14, 149–54, 161,
  164–65, 168, 192, 230n1
Ameriquest Mortgage, 23, 34, 57
Ames, Ted, 134–36, 138, 144–45
Arab Spring, 211
archetypes: of generative ownership, 38–40;
  as patterns of organization, 28, 221n6
Arendt, Hannah, 11
Argentina, 12–13
Arizona, 106
Asia, 134
assets: of credit unions, 12; and derivatives,
  77–81; financial economy as collection
  of, 68, 79; liquidating, 90–91; and magic
  of the multiple, 53; and middle-class
  base, 90; phantom assets, 67–70, 97;
  real wealth transformed into financial
  wealth, 74, 191
Australia, 106
Aveda, 157

baby boom entrepreneurs, 174
balancing feedback loops, 43, 44
Bancel, Jean-Louis, 37
Bangladesh, 139
bank franchises, 32–33
Bank of America, 63, 73
Bank of North Dakota, 9, 217
Bazzy, Derrill, 120
belonging, sense of, 114

benefit corporations (B Corporations),
  ownership design of, 3–4, 155–56, 157,
  158–59, 160, 198, 231n17
Ben & Jerry's, 157
Bertelsmann, 9, 183
Beverly Cooperative Bank, 40–41, 42, 45, 58,
  152, 153, 223n22
Big Short, The (Lewis), 65–66
Bisson, Keith, 132
B Lab, 4, 156
Blackstone, William, 114, 168
Boston Options Exchange, 76–77
Boston Stock Exchange, 75–76
Braudel, Fernand, 67
Brazil, 143
Brown, Malcolm, 110–11
building societies, 36, 38, 41, 53
Business Council for Sustainable
  Development, 183
Business Ethics, 6, 7, 17, 42, 117, 154, 157,
  165, 201

California, 134, 156
CalPERS, 73
Canada, 106, 109
capital: capital infusion, 159, 160; changes in,
  215–16; and derivatives, 80; and excess
  financial extraction, 50; formation of,
  50–51, 63; and magic of the multiple,
  53–57; and master-servant relationship,
  192–95; myths upholding rights of, 15;
  as pattern of ownership, 14, 147, 187,
  209–10; property as, 49–50, 129; and
  responsibility, 189–91; sovereignty of,
  173; and Wall Street, 49–52, 193. *See also*
  Casino Finance; Stakeholder Finance
capital gains, 193, 199
capitalism: communism versus, 139; and
  community, 128–29; and corporation
  design, 5, 7; creative destruction in, 214;
  and financial economy, 68; and master-
  servant relationship, 168; and ownership
  design, 12, 115; paradigm shift in, 113–
  14. *See also* industrial-age capitalism
capital markets: and corporations, 15; design
  of, 102, 114, 210; and growth, 122, 123;
  and suboptimization, 191
Capra, Fritjof, 113, 124, 129, 130, 139, 143,
  228n4

ABOUT THE AUTHOR

Marjorie Kelly is a fellow with the Tellus Institute, a 35-year-old nonprofit research and consulting organization in Boston. She is also director of ownership strategy with Cutting Edge Capital consulting group. She is author of *The Divine Right of Capital* (Berrett-Koehler Publishers, 2001), named one of *Library Journal's* 10 Best Business Books of 2001. For 20 years, Marjorie was president of *Business Ethics* magazine, which she cofounded. She also cofounded Corporation  20/20, an initiative to envision and advocate enterprise designs that integrate social, environmental, and financial aims. Marjorie advises private firms and is a consultant on projects such as the Wealth Creation in Rural Communities initiative of the Ford Foundation, for which she authored the report *Keeping Wealth Local*, exploring alternative ownership designs used in rural areas. Marjorie has done unique research on what she calls the "mission-controlled corporation," such as the foundation-owned Novo Nordisk of Denmark and the family-controlled New York Times, which are publicly traded but have a strong social mission that is protected through dual-class share structures.

She has served on advisory boards for the Center for Corporate Governance and Accountability at George Washington University Law School and the *Newsweek* listing of the Greenest Big Companies in America, among many others. She speaks often on corporate responsibility and building a new economy, and her writings have appeared in publications such as *Harvard Business Review, New England Law Review, Strategy and Business, Chief Executive,* the *Boston Globe, Yes! Magazine, Utne Reader,* and the *San Francisco Chronicle.* See www.MarjorieKelly.com.

Also by Marjorie Kelly

The Divine Right of Capital
Dethroning the Corporate Aristocracy

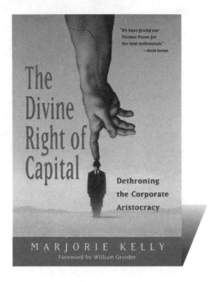

Excesses arise inevitably from a system that measures success only as a rising share price. There is outrage today about the illegitimacy of CEO gains. But nowhere will you find outrage about the illegitimacy of shareholder gains, for that is the sun around which the system revolves. To question this is to question the divine right of capital.

This is not the story of a few bad-apple CEOs but of an economic system designed to do what it did: to enrich a few—a corporate aristocracy—at the expense of the many. This book questions the idea that achieving a 15 percent return for a billionaire is more important than paying employees a living wage or protecting a community's water. *The Divine Right of Capital* shows how to fundamentally redesign the system—using the founding ideals of America.

$19.95, paperback, 288 pages, ISBN 978-1-57675-237-1
PDF ebook, ISBN 978-1-60994-194-9

Berrett–Koehler Publishers, Inc.
www.bkconnection.com   800.929.2929

Berrett–Koehler
Publishers

Berrett-Koehler is an independent publisher dedicated to an ambitious mission: *Creating a World That Works for All*.

We believe that to truly create a better world, action is needed at all levels—individual, organizational, and societal. At the individual level, our publications help people align their lives with their values and with their aspirations for a better world. At the organizational level, our publications promote progressive leadership and management practices, socially responsible approaches to business, and humane and effective organizations. At the societal level, our publications advance social and economic justice, shared prosperity, sustainability, and new solutions to national and global issues.

A major theme of our publications is "Opening Up New Space." Berrett-Koehler titles challenge conventional thinking, introduce new ideas, and foster positive change. Their common quest is changing the underlying beliefs, mindsets, institutions, and structures that keep generating the same cycles of problems, no matter who our leaders are or what improvement programs we adopt.

We strive to practice what we preach—to operate our publishing company in line with the ideas in our books. At the core of our approach is stewardship, which we define as a deep sense of responsibility to administer the company for the benefit of all of our "stakeholder" groups: authors, customers, employees, investors, service providers, and the communities and environment around us.

We are grateful to the thousands of readers, authors, and other friends of the company who consider themselves to be part of the "BK Community." We hope that you, too, will join us in our mission.

A BK Currents Book

This book is part of our BK Currents series. BK Currents books advance social and economic justice by exploring the critical intersections between business and society. Offering a unique combination of thoughtful analysis and progressive alternatives, BK Currents books promote positive change at the national and global levels. To find out more, visit **www.bkconnection.com**.

Berrett–Koehler
Publishers

A community dedicated to creating
a world that works for all

Visit Our Website: www.bkconnection.com

Read book excerpts, see author videos and Internet movies, read our authors' blogs, join discussion groups, download book apps, find out about the BK Affiliate Network, browse subject-area libraries of books, get special discounts, and more!

Subscribe to Our Free E-Newsletter, the *BK Communiqué*

Be the first to hear about new publications, special discount offers, exclusive articles, news about bestsellers, and more! Get on the list for our free e-newsletter by going to **www.bkconnection.com**.

Get Quantity Discounts

Berrett-Koehler books are available at quantity discounts for orders of ten or more copies. Please call us toll-free at (800) 929-2929 or email us at **bkp .orders@aidcvt.com**.

Join the BK Community

BKcommunity.com is a virtual meeting place where people from around the world can engage with kindred spirits to create a world that works for all. **BKcommunity.com** members may create their own profiles, blog, start and participate in forums and discussion groups, post photos and videos, answer surveys, announce and register for upcoming events, and chat with others online in real time. Please join the conversation!